THE EVERYTHING Horse Book

Dear Reader,

I don't remember a time when I wasn't "horse crazy." My friends and I "played horses," pretending we were in horse shows or running free as wild horses. But every time I asked my parents for a horse, the answer was always the same: "When you grow up and get a job, you can buy one for yourself." My family always indulged my obsession with gifts of horse statues (of which I now have an enormous collection), horse jewelry, and horse books, but alas, never a real horse.

When I was thirty years old and out on my own I bought my first horse, a dead-broke, trustworthy Morgan mare named Dolly. I learned to ride on her and various other school horses, taking up saddle seat equitation before moving on to hunt seat.

My real yearning, however, was to learn dressage, having grown up with Walt Disney's *The Miracle of the White Stallions*, the story of General Patton's rescue of the Lipizzaner stallions in Vienna during World War II. Before I reached junior high school, I already knew what "piaffe" and "passage" were. Unfortunately, there weren't any dressage instructors in my neck of the woods, at least not until about a decade or so after I started riding.

That's when I met Holly Veloso and Judy Westenhoefer, who taught me the classical principles of horsemanship. Although dressage isn't the only style of riding to choose from, I'm now convinced it's the best place to begin. Once you learn the basic principles of dressage, you can apply them to any horse and any riding discipline and realize improvement in yourself as well as in the horse.

I wish you all the best in your equine endeavors. Above all, stay safe, enjoy your horse, and may your trails and those of your equine companions be lined with good footing and capped with cloudless blue skies.

Sincerely,

Karen Leigh Davis

Welcome to the EVERYTHING Series!

These handy, accessible books give you all you need to tackle a difficult project, gain a new hobby, comprehend a fascinating topic, prepare for an exam, or even brush up on something you learned back in school but have since forgotten.

You can choose to read an *Everything*® book from cover to cover or just pick out the information you want from our three useful boxes: e-questions, e-facts, e-ssentials. We give you everything you need to know on the subject, but throw in a lot of fun stuff along the way, too.

We now have more than 400 *Everything*® books in print, spanning such wide-ranging categories as weddings, pregnancy, cooking, music instruction, foreign language, crafts, pets, New Age, and so much more. When you're done reading them all, you can finally say you know *Everything*®!

QUESTIONS?
Answers to
common questions

FACTS
Important snippets
of information

ALERTS!
Urgent
warnings

ESSENTIALS
Quick
handy tips

PUBLISHER Karen Cooper

DIRECTOR OF ACQUISITIONS AND INNOVATION Paula Munier

MANAGING EDITOR, EVERYTHING SERIES Lisa Laing

COPY CHIEF Casey Ebert

ACQUISITIONS EDITOR Katie McDonough

DEVELOPMENT EDITOR Elizabeth Kassab

EDITORIAL ASSISTANT Hillary Thompson

INTERIOR ILLUSTRATOR Barry Littmann

Visit the entire Everything® series at *www.everything.com*

THE EVERYTHING® HORSE BOOK

2nd Edition

Buying, riding, and caring
for your equine companion

Karen Leigh Davis

Avon, Massachusetts

I dedicate this book to the horses I've known and loved. If this book helps even one person to treat even one horse with the respect and care all horses deserve, it will be worth all the hours it took to write it.

An Everything® Series Book.
Everything® and everything.com® are registered trademarks of F+W Publications, Inc.

Published by Adams Media, an F+W Publications Company
57 Littlefield Street, Avon, MA 02322 U.S.A.
www.adamsmedia.com

ISBN 10: 1-59869-859-1
ISBN: 13: 978-1-59869-859-6

Printed in the United States of America.

J I H G F E D C B A

Library of Congress Cataloging-in-Publication Data
available from the publisher.

Photographs © American Spirit Images and Fotosearch.

This publication is designed to provide accurate and authoritative information with regard to the subject matter covered. It is sold with the understanding that the publisher is not engaged in rendering legal, accounting, or other professional advice. If legal advice or other expert assistance is required, the services of a competent professional person should be sought.

—From a *Declaration of Principles* jointly adopted by a Committee of the American Bar Association and a Committee of Publishers and Associations

Many of the designations used by manufacturers and sellers to distinguish their products are claimed as trademarks. Where those designations appear in this book and Adams Media was aware of a trademark claim, the designations have been printed with initial capital letters.

This book is available at quantity discounts for bulk purchases.
For information, please call 1-800-289-0963.

Contents

Acknowledgments

Thanks to:

Cheryl Kimball, who authored the first edition of this book and whose original words I have retained in many sections of this book;

Grace Freedson, my agent, for securing for me the opportunity to write the second edition of this book;

Katie McDonough, project editor for Adams Media, for her expert guidance throughout this project;

Everyone else at Adams Media who touched this project—I know how hard they work to make good books;

Holly Veloso and Judy Westenhoefer, my riding instructors, for helping me realize my riding dreams;

My horses, my teachers, for the pleasure, companionship, and exhilarating rides they've willingly offered me throughout the years.

Top Ten Reasons to Ride a Horse

1. Riding horses is good exercise and lots of fun.

2. Learning to ride instills confidence and self-esteem in kids and adults alike.

3. Taking care of a horse teaches kids valuable lessons about ownership, responsibility, and respect for another creature's well-being.

4. Learning to ride teaches you how to face and deal with your own fears and self-doubts.

5. Being around horses helps you stay in touch with and appreciate the natural world.

6. Riding gives you an opportunity to enjoy the outdoors and view vistas from trails and meadows like no other sport can.

7. Sharing an interest in horse-related activities enables family members to spend quality time with one another.

8. Riding horses is good exercise and lots of fun.

9. Learning to communicate with an animal that doesn't speak our language is an immensely satisfying and fulfilling achievement.

10. Gaining a horse's trust, getting to know him as an individual, and learning to enjoy his companionship are growth experiences that will change you forever.

Introduction

▶ TRUE HORSEMANSHIP IS an almost spiritual quest to the person who pursues it seriously. As you ride on the trail to enlightenment, you'll discover things about yourself you don't admire much, such as triggers for fear, anger, and frustration. If you keep going, you'll also discover moments and emotions you can't experience many other ways, including the deep and enduring satisfaction and sense of fulfillment that comes from being able to communicate with another species.

After you come to know horses well, your world—and your perspective of it—changes forever. You find that they have unique personalities of their own, as well as needs and feelings similar to ours. The task of caring for a horse is at once a rewarding and daunting task, especially to someone new to horses. Horses are not objects to be treated however you wish and then disposed of when you tire of them. They are sentient, thinking beings that deserve to be treated the way we would want to be treated if we stood in their horseshoes.

There's an endless amount be to be learned. You can pick up knowledge through books, but the most valuable wisdom will come from your interactions with the horses themselves. With a horse or two around the house, you will never be bored again. You also won't have to visit the gym as much because riding and caring for horses will keep you in shape.

In the true tradition of the Everything® series, this book aims to give you enough information and resources to direct you down the path toward the knowledge of what it means to be a true horseman. Above all, this book aims to help you enjoy your horse. So when you can't be in the barn, enjoy this book, read it and others like it, and learn all you can about horses.

CHAPTER 1

History of the Horse

Humans and horses have a long, interrelated history, yet no one is truly certain when and where horses were first domesticated and ridden. We do know, however, that the first horses had toes, not hooves, and looked nothing like the horses of today. This chapter highlights the current facts known about the early ancestors of the modern-day horse and its evolution. It also covers the ways in which the horse helped advance human civilization, from conquering foreign lands in battle to plowing and settling new frontiers.

The Ancient Horse

Fossils of *Eohippus,* as the first horses have been called, showed the mammal to be an herbivore smaller than a dog. *Eohippus* lived primarily in North America but vanished from the continent entirely around 8,000 years ago for reasons that remain a mystery. Horses did not return to North America until the fifteenth century A.D.

QUESTION?

What is an herbivore?
An herbivore is an animal that eats plant life exclusively. As grazing animals, horses are herbivores. This distinction makes the horse a prey animal. Animals that hunt and eat horses are considered predators. Being an animal of prey contributes greatly to the horse's overall behavior and endows it with the natural speed and athleticism necessary to flee from danger.

Changing habitat from swamplands to dry savannahs caused the horse to evolve from a creature with multiple toes to one with a single toe, which later became a hoof and which is better adapted to roaming dry ground. We can thank the Pliocene epoch for *Pliohippus*, the first single-toed horse. *Pliohippus* serves as a prototype for our own *Equus*, the modern horse. According to *The Kingdom of the Horse*, by Elwyn Hartley Edwards, *Pliohippus* had a ligament-sprung hoof and longer legs with flexing ligaments, which gave way to a running action similar to that of the modern horse.

FACT

Partway up the horse's leg, past the knee on the inside, is what seems to be a callused piece of skin, usually around the size of two quarters. Called the chestnut, this is said to be what remains of the first of three toes the horse lost during its evolution. The two other toe vestiges can be found as a hard nodule behind the fetlock.

The evolution from *Pliohippus* to our modern *Equus* took another 5 million years or so to accomplish. Due to changes in climate and landmass during that time, the early horse found its way from North America to South America and spread across Asia, Europe, and Africa.

Age of Domestication

Humans probably first valued the horse as a source of a food long before they were ridden. The period from 4000 to 3000 B.C. is considered the true age of the domestication of the horse. Domestication is believed to have first taken place on the steppes north of the Black Sea. Evidence of mounted warriors found in China supports the theory that horses were extensively ridden for the first time around 4000 B.C.

Early Interactions

The horse was thought to be first harnessed in the Near East around 2000 B.C. Evidence of man's early interactions with the horse comes mostly in the form of tapestries, relief pottery, and other works of art depicting battle scenes and exemplifying the human reverence for the horse's beauty.

According to Xenophon (430–355 B.C.), a Greek soldier and historian who advocated humane horsemanship in the earliest known book on the subject, *On Horsemanship*: "If one induces the horse to assume that carriage which it would adopt of its own accord when displaying its beauty, then, one directs the horse to appear joyous and magnificent, proud and remarkable for having been ridden."

Until 1500 B.C., horses were typically too revered to do lowly agricultural work. Initially, they were hitched up with oxen yokes, but the design cut off the horse's wind. A padded collar was designed to better suit the horse. Metal snaffle bits were perfected to take the place of nose rings, which were used to control the animal. In China, horses were used to pull chariots by this time.

The first records of systematic training, conditioning, and caretaking of horses date back to around 1350 B.C. They were written by a man named

Kikkuli. Kikkuli was a Mittani, an Aryan group with cultural ties to India. Tablets that have been found show Kikkuli's instructions to the Hittite rulers prescribing care of harness racing horses. The Hittites, although they clearly gained their equestrian knowledge from other peoples, were credited with the development of the Arabian horse and were noted for their highly mobile equestrian troops.

FACT

In 1994, Dr. David Anthony and Dorcas Brown founded the Institute for Ancient Equestrian Studies in the Department of Anthropology at Hartwick College in Oneonta, New York. The institute, which is dedicated to archaeological research concerning the origins of horseback riding and the impact of riding on human society, is affiliated with the Institute for the History and Archaeology of the Volga in Samara, Russia. Both institutes can be found online at *http://users.hartwick.edu/~iaes*.

By well into the last centuries B.C., horseback riding not only had been mastered but had become common. Scythian warriors, who had the first recorded geldings (castrated stallions) and whose wealth was measured in horses, were skilled in the art of battle on horseback. Since they believed that their wealth followed them to the afterworld, many artifacts were found in their burial grounds. Sometimes hundreds of horses were found buried with them.

A Significant Recent Equine Discovery

In 1879 Marcelino de Sautuola, a Spanish engineer who was also a serious amateur archaeologist, was exploring a cave with his daughter in the mountains of France when his five-year-old daughter noticed on the cave ceiling drawings that included horses. Studies of these drawings in the now-famous Altamira cave have determined that they are from a period between 30,000 and 10,000 years ago. Such discoveries help us better understand the shared history of horses and humans.

Finding Przewalskii's Horse

Przewalskii's horse was discovered in the remote regions of Mongolia around 1879 by the Russian explorer Nikolai Mikhailovich Przewalskii.

It is believed to be the closest ancestor to the ancient horse in existence. Described as being around twelve hands, with a stocky body and short legs, it is currently believed to be extinct in the wild and to exist only in captivity, although it remains a truly wild horse that has never been thoroughly domesticated.

Horses in North America

One of the great mysteries of the horse is its disappearance about 8,000 years ago from the North American continent, this despite the fact that *Eohippus* evolved here over a period of millions of years. Fossil evidence tells us that early horses definitely resided in North America and then vanished for reasons we can only speculate about.

The Great Disappearing Act

Apparently, the horse somehow migrated south to South America and west across the land bridge, probably across what is now the Bering Strait into Asia. Further climate and geographical changes during the ice age possibly pushed them farther into the Middle East and Africa. Some speculate that those that remained behind in North America may have succumbed to a fatal disease.

Many Thanks, Spanish Conquistadors!

The horse was being ridden and domesticated and becoming a crucial member of civilization in other parts of the world long before it reappeared in North America. Spanish explorers and the missions that followed are generally credited with this reappearance. They brought large numbers of livestock, including horses, to the New World for their settlements. Ponce de Leon is thought to be responsible for bringing Andalusian-bred stock into what is now Florida.

By the seventeenth century, Native American tribes along the Mexican border began to use horses, as did American settlers in the West. In addition, the Native Americans used horses to barter with other tribes, which allowed the horse to move across the rest of the western United States.

Wild Horses of the West

It's easy to imagine how some of these horses either escaped captivity or were turned loose, thus marking the beginning of the wild (or, more accurately, feral) horse bands in the American West. Today, the Bureau of Land Management (BLM) is the U.S. government institution responsible for the care and management of the wild equine herds still in existence in the United States.

In the 1950s, Velma B. Johnston became concerned about the manner in which wild horses were being harvested for commercial reasons. Her campaign was loud and her audience receptive, leading to the passing in 1959 of Public Law 86-234, which controlled the way wild horses and burros were hunted. But it wasn't until 1971 that Public Law 92-195, the Wild Free-Roaming Horse and Burro Act, was passed. It provided for the management, protection, and control of the wild horse and the burro populations. Numerous amendments have passed since. Management of the wild horses, commonly referred to as mustangs, has included regular removal and dispersal, partly through private adoption.

ALERT!

Mustangs have been wild all their lives. Their first interaction with humans is often when they are rounded up, branded, castrated, and vaccinated—making their impressions of humans rather unfavorable. Only people who are experienced at handling difficult horses or who have access to experienced help should attempt to adopt them.

For information about adopting a mustang, contact the Bureau of Land Management, National Wild Horse and Burro Program at its website, *www. wildhorseandburro.blm.gov.*

Cowboys, Horses, and the Settling of America

Prior to the advent of the horseless carriage, horses were everywhere. Especially essential in the settling of the American West, they were used for mounted transportation, hauling carriages and stagecoaches, moving cattle, and inevitably for entertainment in the form of racing and rodeos. Rodeos provided an avenue for cowboys to show off the roping and roundup skills they used every day. Such competitions continue to celebrate the heritage of the American West today.

The Pony Express

The Pony Express was a short-lived and much romanticized part of American history. St. Joseph, Missouri, was the site of the eastern edge of the Pony Express route, and Sacramento, California, was the western destination. Up until that point, most mail was sent around South America to California by steamship, which took a month. The intent was to shorten the time for mail to cross the country until the railroad was complete. William Russell, William Waddell, and Alexander Majors thought of the idea of offering ten-day delivery via a horse-and-rider relay. Each rider would cover seventy-five to 100 miles, and each horse would be expected to cover less than fifteen miles. The Pony Express company bought 400 horses to stock the route through Kansas, Nebraska, Colorado, Wyoming, Utah, Nevada, and on into California.

As an innovative idea, the Pony Express was a great success. However, as a business, it was a failure; it lasted only nineteen months, and its owners lost $500,000. If you want to learn more about this fascinating venture, check out the Pony Express Museum in Saint Joseph, Missouri, or visit its website at *www.ponyexpress.org*.

Recent History of Horses in the United States

Western movies romanticized the cowboy and his relationship with the horse to such an extent that the ideas viewers took home in their minds may have contributed to the horse's continued popularity long after automobiles and mechanized farm machinery replaced it as a beast of burden. Unfortunately, these movies also perpetuated many misconceptions about horses and riding in general, leading some to believe that hopping on a horse and galloping across an open field is easy and all there is to riding. Of course, nothing could be further from the truth.

Perhaps the most significant development to take shape in the latter half of the twentieth century was the horse's elevation in status from work animal to animal companion. Although still considered property by law, many people today tend to view their horses more as beloved pets than as mere livestock. Some prized show horses live lavishly pampered lives and are valued into the thousands of dollars because of their talent and the quality of training invested in them.

The Horse's Influence on American Civilization

Who knows what the world would be like today were it not for the existence and domestication of the horse? Man invaded and conquered foreign lands from the back of his warhorse and built civilizations with his workhorse hitched to a plow or wagon. Our partner for centuries, perhaps no other animal has served man in so many diverse ways, nor suffered so dearly for it.

Horses as Transportation

Before the invention of the automobile, the horse served as man's primary means of transportation in many parts of the world. The horse can cover a lot more ground in a day's travel than a person can on foot. It can also haul heavy loads, transporting goods along with people in stagecoaches, wagons, and trolleys. Horses carried homesteaders and their belongings in covered wagons into the wild American West and helped expand and transform a few struggling colonies into a great nation.

Horses and Agriculture

The development of harnesses and agricultural equipment made using horses to operate farming equipment a viable option. This enabled people to plow and till the land and grow crops on a larger scale than they had before. In time, evolving agricultural practices changed the landscape, as settlers felled trees, hitched horses to the heavy trunks, and cleared the woods to allow for bigger fields and farms.

American settlers desired horses that were multifunctional. They wanted horses they could ride, plow fields with, and hitch to a carriage for a drive to church on Sunday. One of the first American breeds, the Morgan horse, is noted for its versatility and easily filled this bill. Other American breeds such as the Saddlebred and the Tennessee Walker developed from plantation horses, bred for their easy gaits. A man could sit comfortably and ride them over miles and miles of farmland without tiring.

The Warhorse

Ancient civilizations utilized the horse in battle to carry soldiers and pull chariots, making armies mobile in some of the harshest climates in the world. The ancient Persians went so far as to develop an armored cavalry, a mounted army on horseback, that required heavily muscled horses capable of bearing more weight. Perhaps the most recognized armored soldiers that carried on this tactic are the knights of the Middle Ages. Aside from combat and transport, horses served in other war-related capacities as well, including reconnaissance and supply transport.

The Lipizzan Legacy

Warhorses required a great deal of training to face weaponry noise and the confusion of battle without panic. They also needed to be easily controlled with limited use of the reins, freeing the rider's hands to wield a spear or saber. The discipline of dressage developed from the need to train horses to be exquisitely responsive to the rider's leg and weight aids, to move with balance and agility, and to remain calm and obedient, even under pressure. Dressage is a centuries-old, tried-and-true means of gymnastically conditioning a horse to a high degree of athleticism so that it moves with as much ease and grace while carrying a rider as it does while running free.

The haute école movements of classical dressage, which originated from maneuvers needed on the battlefield, are preserved and performed today in their purest tradition by the famous Lipizzaner stallions at the Spanish Riding School in Vienna, Austria. The highly stylized leaps, or airs above the ground, performed by the most gifted stallions are also believed by some to have their roots in war maneuvers deployed in battle. However, these movements were later refined and demonstrated primarily in exhibitions.

The Horse in Modern Warfare

The horse's partnership with man in battle is evident in many public plazas around the world, where mounted equestrian statues commemorate this or that moment of glory in history. People tend to think of such colossal statues as representing ancient battles, but noteworthy human-equine partnerships existed as recently as the Civil War era and both World Wars.

Robert E. Lee's horse, Traveller, and General Stonewall Jackson's horse, Little Sorrel, are nearly as well known as their owners. The stuffed remains of Little Sorrel were on display at the Virginia Military Institute's Museum in Lexington until the horse was finally laid to rest in 1997 on the campus parade grounds more than a century after his death. The horse was buried with military honors near Jackson's monument.

Horses have been heavily used in modern warfare on other occasions as well. The Boer War in South Africa (1899–1902) produced a huge demand for horses, mules, and donkeys. Thousands of wild horses in America were captured and shipped overseas, and more than 500,000 died during the course of the war. Horses were also in great demand during World War I. Records show that hundreds of thousands were abandoned in the deserts.

The riderless horse is one of the oldest and most poignant equestrian military traditions still in existence in the United States. Led behind a caisson and wearing an empty saddle with riding boots reversed in the stirrups, the riderless horse represents the fallen warrior hero who will never ride again. Perhaps the most famous riderless horse of modern times was Black Jack, who took part in numerous state funerals at Arlington National Cemetery, including that of President John F. Kennedy.

CHAPTER 2

Horse Breeds

Members of a breed share a similar ancestry and bloodlines, which make their physical characteristics and behavioral traits more predictable. For example, Thoroughbreds are bred to run fast. Clydesdales, the famous Budweiser beer horses, are draft animals bred to be big and strong enough to pull heavy loads. Purebreds are registered with an association that represents and promotes their breed. They are often purchased and bred based on their pedigrees, the papers that historically document their bloodlines. Unregistered horses that have no documented parentage are referred to as "grade" horses.

Different Breeds for Different Uses

Certain breeds are better suited for certain uses than others. For example, you wouldn't enter a Shetland Pony in the Kentucky Derby with much hope of winning. Horse lovers typically favor a particular breed or two, usually due to the breed's physical appearance or the kind of horse-related activity or sport the person wants to undertake.

When deciding what breed to buy, consider what you want to do with the horse. If you're interested in dressage, consider one of several warmblood sport horse breeds that excel in this discipline, such as the Hanoverian or the Holsteiner. If you're interested in Western riding events, such as roping, cutting, or barrel racing, then an American Quarter Horse is probably more your speed. If you're looking for a mount for a child, size matters, so investigate the various pony breeds.

Some Popular Light Horse Breeds

Breeds used mostly for riding under saddle are known as light horses, as opposed to heavy workhorses, which are called draft horses. The next few sections highlight the more common light horse breeds.

QUESTION?

What is a hand?
In tack room terms, a hand is the unit used to measure horse height. One hand equals four inches. Fractions of a hand are expressed in inches. Thus, a horse that is sixty-two inches tall is said to stand at 15.2 hands (fifteen hands, two inches). Horse height is measured from the ground to the highest point of the horse's withers.

Thoroughbred

Nonhorse people are most familiar with this breed because of its predominance on the racetrack. Thoroughbred ancestry, as well as that of many other breeds, can be traced back to the Arabian horse. The Thoroughbred's tall, lean conformation, good lung capacity, and competitive spirit make it a perfect racing candidate. In fact, this breed is capable of a single stride of over twenty feet and speeds of up to forty miles per hour. Thoroughbreds start their race training young, typically working mounted in their yearling year and then on to professional racing as two-year-olds. Unfortunately, this is also why many of them break down at so early an age, because their bones haven't finished growing.

The overall build and structure of the horse is known as its conformation. Few horses, if any, have perfect conformation. What is considered good conformation depends a great deal on what you plan to do with the horse.

By the time they are five years old, many Thoroughbreds are retired from racing—an age when most saddle horses are just starting their riding careers in earnest. The best of the best retired Thoroughbreds are used for breeding, and the rest are often sold at reasonable prices to equestrians looking for dressage, three-day event, or jumping prospects. A significant number are destroyed at a young age or sold to slaughter due to racetrack injuries that make them unfit for any other purpose.

Purchasing a retired racehorse requires considerable knowledge and horse savvy. Lameness is a pervasive issue, although it may not necessarily inhibit the animal's suitability as a pleasure mount. Retired racehorses must be retrained to ride safely, as about the only thing they've been taught to do is to break clean from the starting gate and run fast to the finish line.

American Quarter Horse

The American Quarter Horse, native to the United States, is thought of as the "cowboy's horse," used for western rodeo-type events, roping, reining, and barrel racing. However, Quarter Horses also race. In fact, the colonists bred them for short-distance racing. The breed's propensity as sprinters—the "quarter" in their name allegedly comes from their quarter-mile racing prowess—is tested at tracks around the country.

Many celebrities have "secret" horse lives. Actor Patrick Swayze and his wife ride and raise Arabian horses on their farm outside Los Angeles. Ballplayer Nolan Ryan, golfer Hal Sutton, newscaster Tom Brokaw, actor William Shatner, former second lady Marilyn Quayle, and actresses Andie MacDowell and Bo Derek, among many others, also ride.

Arabian

Because of its stunning beauty, the Arabian is perhaps one of the most photographed of all breeds. The breed originated in the desert regions of Arabia, and its well-deserved reputation for endurance makes it the horse of choice for the long-distance riding circuit.

President Ulysses S. Grant was responsible for bringing the Arabian horse to the United States. In 1873, he was given two stallions as a gift by the Sultan Abdul Hamid II of Turkey while on a trip to the Middle East. Grant gave one of the stallions to Randolph Huntington, who imported two mares and two stallions from England in 1888, thereby creating the first Arabian breeding program in the United States.

Some Arabians have one fewer vertebrae in their lumbar spine than other horses. A shorter back, however, does not impair their ability to carry a rider. They are known to be late developers and are said to not be fully grown until they are around seven or eight years old.

Morgan

As the tale goes, a Vermont gentleman named Justin Morgan brought us this compact breed of horse. His foundation stallion, originally named Figure, proved himself to be extraordinarily strong, fast, and versatile. He later shared his owner's name, known simply as "the Morgan." When he was used at stud, he passed on his physical characteristics to all of his offspring. The demand for his stud service and the resulting offspring were so great that the army ultimately bought him.

Morgan horses have pronounced gaits characteristic of a "carriage" breed. They serve well in harness and are often taught to pull a wagon or cart. Because of their flashy gaits, they are most often ridden and shown as park horses in saddle seat equitation classes. They are very sturdy horses, usually small and with a tendency to have hardy feet, which is always a plus.

FACT

The story of Figure and the Morgan horse is told in a famous children's book, *Justin Morgan Had a Horse*, written by Marguerite Henry. The book details the adventures of Figure and the boy Morgan asks to help train him.

Standardbred

The Standardbred horse is another racing breed, although it is driven in harness instead of ridden by a jockey. Standardbreds race at the trot or pace instead of a gallop. The "pace" is a unique gait in which the front and back leg on the same side move in unison rather than the typical trot movement of alternating pairs—right front, left rear or left front, right rear. Standardbreds have an average height of fifteen hands, which usually makes them shorter than their flat-racing counterpart, the Thoroughbred.

Saddlebreds and Gaited Horses

Some horses can do more than just walk, trot, canter, and gallop. Gaited horses, as they're called, possess additional natural gaits. Because the gaits differ from breed to breed, they also have various names, such as rack, slow gait, stepping pace, running walk, single foot, and fox-trot. In some breeds, the gaits are enhanced through training to make them flashier and higher stepping in the show ring. In others, they are enjoyed more for the comfort they offer in long-distance riding. Older riders, especially those prone to sore backs, seem to enjoy the smooth, pleasurable rides gaited horses deliver on long trails.

American Saddlebred

The horse of choice during the Civil War, the Saddlebred, was ridden by a lineup of famous generals including Robert E. Lee (riding the famous Traveller), Ulysses S. Grant (Cincinnati), and William T. Sherman (Lexington). However, the Saddlebreds in those days were somewhat different from the flashy animals we see in show rings today.

The breed was first established in the Narragansett Bay area of Rhode Island from a mix of Scottish Galloways and Irish hobby horses. Until the

Thoroughbred became firmly embedded in the lineage, they were referred to as Narragansett pacers.

Saddlebreds are favored as riding horses for their easy gaits, stamina, size, and refined pedigree contributed by the Thoroughbred stock. The American Saddle Horse Association was founded in Louisville, Kentucky, in 1891, and today Saddlebreds still populate Kentucky's Shelby County, referred to as the Saddle Horse Capitol of the World. The American Saddlebred Museum is located on the grounds of the Kentucky Horse Park in Lexington, Kentucky.

FACT

Located on 1,030 acres in Lexington, Kentucky, the Kentucky Horse Park is an educational theme park devoted to the horse. Visitors can take a leisurely guided trail ride or carriage ride through the park grounds. There are also educational programs and special events throughout the year. For information, visit the website at *www.kyhorsepark.com*.

National Show Horse

This breed, established in the 1980s, is a cross between the American Saddlebred and the Arabian horse. Like their Saddlebred ancestors, these horses can perform the rack and the slow gait. Both are four-beat gaits, with the rack being merely a faster, flashier version of the slow gait.

Tennessee Walker

Founded in Tennessee, the Tennessee Walker is a mixture of Standardbred, Thoroughbred, Morgan, and American Saddlebred. The breed ranges in size from 14.3 to 17 hands, weighing around 900 to 1,200 pounds. It is found in all colors and is famous for its running walk, a smooth, inherited gait unique to the breed.

Missouri Fox-Trotter

This breed originated in the Ozark Mountains in the nineteenth century. Its four-beat fox-trot gait is comfortable over long distances and at good speed. The fox-trot is often described as a cross between the walk and the trot because the front legs appear to be walking while the hind legs are trotting. Fox-trotters can be of any color and range from fifteen to seventeen hands.

Paso Fino

Brought to North and South America by the Spanish conquistadors in the sixteenth century, the Paso Fino breed developed in Puerto Rico. Paso Finos have truly distinct gaits—the *fino*, *corto*, and *largo*—which are natural to the breed. They tend to be on the small side, ranging from 14.2 to 15 hands.

Peruvian Paso

Peruvian Pasos and Paso Finos share a common heritage, but their breeding environment took them in different directions. Peruvian Pasos were bred in the harsh conditions of the mountainous regions of Peru and are known for great stamina and gaits that are both comfortable for the rider and not tiring to the horse. This breed does not trot or gallop, but instead performs its natural four-beat lateral gaits, the *fino*, *corto*, and *largo*.

Rocky Mountain Horse

Founded in the Appalachia region of Kentucky, these medium-sized naturally gaited horses are exceptionally sure-footed and were used to traverse rugged mountain trails. Their breed association was established in 1986.

Less Common Breeds

Breed popularity waxes and wanes with time. New breeds arise from crossbreeding or genetic mutations. Some breeds enjoy greater popularity in one country than another. There are literally hundreds of breeds in existence around the world, so it's impossible to list them all here. However, here are some less common but noteworthy ones.

Andalusian

This was a significant Spanish breed in Europe from the twelfth to the seventeenth centuries and was the basis for many modern breeds, including the Lipizzaner and even the Appaloosa. They are typically gray and of average height, around 15.2 hands, and compactly built. The breed is used today primarily in exhibition riding and dressage and is the horse of choice for Spanish bullfighting.

Bashkir Curly

According to the registry for this breed, it has been in North America since the early 1800s. They are generally medium sized, but they can be pony sized or draft sized as well. Their coat is curly, as their name implies, and the curls get long in winter. The mane tends to split down the middle. They are said to be nonallergenic, which makes them attractive to people with allergies to horses. They are used in all riding disciplines.

Cleveland Bay

Thought to have evolved in the seventeenth century, Cleveland Bays peaked in popularity in the late 1800s in Britain, where they originally developed; they are now considered a rare breed, with less than 500 pure-bred horses worldwide.

They were imported to the United States in the early 1800s, and Buffalo Bill Cody was said to have used them in his Wild West show. Cleveland Bays are, as their name implies, bay in color. They stand sixteen to seventeen hands, and were often used as carriage horses because of their uniform characteristics. Purebred and part-bred (often crossed with Thorough-breds) Cleveland Bays make excellent mounts in all equine disciplines.

Norwegian Fjord

The Norwegian Fjord horse is one of the world's oldest breeds. The original Fjords are thought to have migrated to Norway more than 4,000 years ago. The present-day Fjord is believed to be descended from Przewalskii's horse and retains many of the same characteristics. The Fjord has distinct coloring, usually dun with black zebra stripes on its legs and a dorsal stripe that runs from its forelock, through the mane, down the back, and through the tail. It is relatively small in height, averaging 13.2 to 14.2 hands, and weighs in at around 900 to 1,200 pounds.

Fresian

Used in war during the Middle Ages, this breed has also been used as a draft and carriage horse. In fact, they were said to have influenced both the Clydesdale and Shire draft breeds. Fresians are black beauties with long feathered fetlocks, making them a very impressive animal. In recent years, they have become increasingly popular in the United States as dressage mounts and exhibition horses.

Hackney

One of the oldest British breeds (dating back to the eleventh century), Hackneys are a mix of Thoroughbred and Arabian. Because of their animated gaits, they are used mostly as carriage horses.

Haflinger

These horses are golden chestnut in color with a long, white mane and tail. They were used heavily as pack horses during World War II but now are popular in all types of riding.

Lipizzaner

This breed was founded in 1580 in Austria by Archduke Charles II. The stallions were originally from Spain. Foals are born black but whiten with age. The occasional rare bay Lipizzaner is considered good luck. The horses are typically small, compact, and muscular. They are best known for the choreographed quadrilles and airs above the ground (spectacular controlled leaps) they perform routinely at the Spanish Riding School in Vienna.

Miniature Horses

According to the World Class Miniature Horse Registry (WCMHR), miniature horses were thought to have been bred in Europe as pets for the children of royalty. Under 36.5 inches tall, these little horses are exactly like big horses, only reduced in size. The WCMHR website (*www.wcmhr.com*) speculates that miniatures were first used in the United States in coal mining; their sturdiness allowed them to pull many times their own weight. This horse is suitable for riding for children under forty pounds. Despite their cute, huggable size, miniatures still need to be trained, fed, and cared for in the same manner as any other horse or pony.

ALERT!

Horseshoes are considered lucky only if the open end faces up. According to folklore, all the luck runs out of a downward-facing horseshoe. Interestingly, until 1999, the horseshoe engraved on the Kentucky Derby trophy faced down. In 1999, the horseshoe was turned up for a special 125th anniversary edition of the trophy.

Warmbloods

The term *warmblood* does not refer to a specific breed but rather is a name for several breeds that are a cross between a cold-blooded draft horse and a hot-blooded light horse (typically Thoroughbred or Arabian). Not to be confused with anything remotely reptilian, in the horse world the terms *warmblood*, *cold-blood*, and *hot-blood* refer solely to temperament. Warmbloods were developed in Europe but are now popular in the United States as sport horses, used extensively in dressage and show jumping. A few warmblood breed names are Dutch Warmblood, Danish Warmblood, Trakehner, Hanoverian, and Holsteiner.

Draft Breeds

These giants of the horse world, bred for their size and strength, carried knights in heavy armor during the Middle Ages. Later, they plowed fields and hauled heavy carriages. Most of the breeds are named for their region of origin.

Belgian

The most common style of Belgian horse in the United States is the modern style, which is longer-legged than the old style. Belgians are used extensively among loggers and farmers. They average sixteen to seventeen hands, range from 1,400 to 1,800 pounds, and can be sorrel, roan, or chestnut in color.

Clydesdale

These big brown horses with flaxen manes and tails and fluffy fetlocks are best known as the Budweiser horses. The Clydesdale breed originated in Clyde Valley, Lancashire, Scotland, and were imported to the United States prior to the Civil War. Anheuser-Busch now owns the largest herd of Clydesdales in the world. Its breeding farms are located in St. Louis at Grant Farm—a wildlife preserve on land once farmed by Ulysses S. Grant—and near Los Angeles. The horses that haul the hitch are all geldings, stand at least eighteen hands, and are bay in color with a white blaze down their faces.

FACT

Ten horses travel with the Budweiser hitch. Eight pull the wagon, and two serve as backups. The pair closest to the wagon are known as the wheelhorses. The next pair are the body. The third pair are the swing horses, and the front pair are appropriately called the leaders. Visit the Budweiser Clydesdale website at *www.abclydesdales.com*.

Percheron

Gray or black in color, these heavy draft horses run an average of sixteen hands. The breed originated in France, about fifty miles southwest of Paris.

Pony Breeds

When it comes to horses and ponies, size makes all the difference. Generally speaking, ponies stand no higher than 14.2 hands. Anything taller than 14.2 is considered a horse.

Connemara

This pony is considered Ireland's only native horse breed. It is the largest of the pony breeds, averaging 14 to 14.2 hands.

Fell Pony

Originating along the England/Scotland border, the Fell (mountain) pony is flashy, with feathered legs and lots of mane and tail, probably acquired from its early Fresian influence. They are under fourteen hands, but they are strong enough to carry an adult rider and are used extensively under harness.

Chincoteague Ponies

The Chincoteague and Assateague Islands sit on the mid-Atlantic coast, along the Delmarva Peninsula, where Virginia, Maryland, and Delaware meet along the ocean. If you visit this lovely part of the country, you will see small groups of wild ponies wandering Assateague Island. Although no one really knows how they came to live there, one version is that in the mid-1600s a Spanish galleon wrecked offshore, and the ponies on board swam to safety and have roamed the island ever since.

The ponies graze on marshland grasses and browse on shrubs. The Chincoteague Volunteer Fire Department manages the herd and provides them with supplemental hay during harsh months as well as veterinary care when needed. The department has held an annual carnival since 1925, which includes the now well-known swimming of the ponies. At slack tide, the ponies are herded from their home on Assateague Island to Chincoteague Island, where around forty colts and fillies are auctioned off to help control herd population and inbreeding and to raise funds to care for the pony herds.

Icelandic

The product of a cross between Germanic and Celtic horses brought to Iceland by settlers in 874 A.D., Icelandic horses are small, quick, hardy, and strong. These horses are late to mature and typically are not ridden until they are five years old, but they commonly live a long life. They come in every typical coat color and are best known for their unusual gaits, including the tolt (a four-beat running walk) and the flying pace. Riders describe both of these gaits by saying it feels like you are floating over the ground.

Shetland

This breed from the Shetland Islands is probably what most of us imagine when we think of a pony. The height limit on the popular Shetland is forty-six inches. They tend to be hardy and have good feet, and they are easy keepers.

Welsh Pony

Welsh ponies hail from the United Kingdom and include several variations, the best known being the Welsh Mountain Pony and the Welsh Cob. They are popular mounts for young riders, used in all riding disciplines.

Mixes and Other Equines

When horses are crossed with other breeds and even other species, they produce offspring that have traits from both parents. These unique hybrids can be intentionally bred for specific purposes. A book about horses would be remiss not to discuss these as well as the other members of the equine family.

Mixed Breeds

Some breeds are commonly crossed. Although you can never know for sure until the foal drops to the ground, these crosses have consistently good enough results to have warranted giving them a name and often their own registry.

- **Anglo-Arabian:** This horse is a Thoroughbred and an Arabian.
- **Araapaloosa:** The Araapaloosa is a cross between an Arabian and an Appaloosa.
- **Morab:** This mixed breed is a cross between a Morgan and an Arabian.
- **Moresian:** The Moresian is an often stunning mix of Morgan and Fresian.
- **Quarab:** Results of the Quarter Horse/Arabian cross are usually petite, with either a Quarter Horse–type body or a tall and lanky more Arabian-type conformation.

The Long-Eared Equines

Asses come in a variety of sizes and colors, with donkeys being the smaller versions and the Mammoth Jack being the largest. The male ass is called a jack, and the female is called a jennet. The terms *donkey* and *burro* are interchangeable and refer to essentially the same animal, although the wild types are generally distinguished as burros, and the domestic varieties are donkeys. Most donkeys are dun-colored with a dark stripe running down their back and across their shoulders.

Mules are hybrid animals, the result of breeding a male ass to a female horse. The offspring of a female ass and male horse is called a hinny. Because of this crossbreeding between two species, they are nearly always sterile, yet they possess normal sexual instincts. Mules make exceptionally sturdy, sure-footed work animals. Because of their crossing with the horse, they come in all horse colors and can even have spots like the Appaloosa.

Zebra

Zebras are perhaps one of the best known of all wild African animals, easily recognized by their distinctive black and white stripes. The stripe patterns on each individual zebra are as unique as fingerprints, with no two ever exactly alike. The stripes act as camouflage that helps hide the zebra in tall grass. Likes horses, zebras live in herds, and the collective stripes of several herd members grazing together are believed to make it more confusing for predators such as lions to single out an individual zebra to attack.

There are several species and subspecies of zebras, with variations in size and striping being the major differences. Unlike the horse, zebras have never been truly domesticated, although many are kept in captivity today, and some have even been tamed enough to ride or pull carriages. Their unpredictable and often disagreeable nature makes them unsuitable for novices to ride or handle.

Zebroids are hybrid animals created by crossing a zebra with a horse or ass. These breedings have resulted in some interesting-looking animals, such as the Zorse, which looks like a horse with bold zebra striping on the legs, lower body, and neck.

CHAPTER 3

Horse Colors

The color of a horse has little to do with its soundness or performance capabilities. In the wild, natural selection saw to it that most horses were brown or some variation thereof. This allowed the horses to better blend in with their surroundings and escape the notice of predators. That's why we have more blacks, bays, and chestnuts. However, some people want a horse of a different color, and selective breeding has become big business and produced some flashy-colored horses, especially in the United States.

The Basic Colors

The names of horse colors may vary from region to region, which creates a great deal of confusion for the novice equestrian who's still trying to figure out the equine terminology. There are color breed registries in which horses of a specific color, such as a palomino, can be registered. To make matters even more confusing, some breeds not technically considered as a color breed are nonetheless very color specific. Friesians, for instance, are always black.

The following are the basic coat colors of the horse:

- Bay
- Black
- Brown
- Chestnut
- Gray

The Bays

Bay is the most common horse color and usually the most favored among sport and performance horses. The body is some shade of brown or reddish brown with black points, meaning that the mane, tail, and legs up to the knee area are black. Bays are easy to distinguish from chestnuts because the distinctive black points are always present. Bay is actually a genetically modified form of the color black. Bay occurs in many horse breeds, but only one breed so far—the Cleveland Bay—has been named for this specific color.

The Blacks and Browns

True blacks are uncommon, although they are not rare. Most horses that look black are actually dark brown. A true black cannot have any red or brown hairs mixed in the coat, not even on the muzzle. Black tends to fade when exposed to sunlight, so black show horses are generally kept stabled or blanketed to prevent a sun-bleached coat.

A brown horse, on the other hand, is brown all over, on its body, mane, and tail. Some browns are so dark that they are often mistaken for black; however, you can tell the difference by inspecting for brown hairs on the flanks and around the muzzle and eyes. Even a sun-bleached black will still have black hairs in these areas. A really dark brown horse that looks black or that has black hairs mixed in with the brown is sometimes called seal brown or, depending on the region, black and tan.

The Chestnuts

Chestnuts are a reddish color all over, including the mane and tail. Many chestnut horses have lovely white markings on the face and legs, or they may simply be red all over. They never have black points, like the bays.

Chestnut shades range from dark liver chestnut to the lighter sorrel. The liver chestnut is a deep brown color that can be found all over throughout the mane and tail or just the coat. To some, "sorrel" is just another name for a chestnut horse. Others make the distinction that the sorrel is a lighter shade of chestnut on the body and legs with a lighter or flaxen-colored mane and tail.

The Grays and Whites

Most white horses are correctly called "grays" in the horse world. The shades of gray range from almost pure white, such as the lovely Lipizzaner, to a deep blue-gray base coat with dappling. Gray horses are born dark and gradually whiten with each shedding as they get older. The degree to which the coat whitens depends upon the genetics. A gray horse that has whitened all the way can be distinguished from a true white horse by its dark skin underneath, most noticeable around the muzzle and eyes.

QUESTION?

What is a dappled gray?
Dappling is a color pattern common in gray horses. It refers to the mottled gray or lighter rings of spotting or blotches that occur over a darker background coat color. A "flea-bitten" gray is a similar color pattern, except in reverse and with smaller, colored spots—the base color speckles or flecks the gray coat.

True white is a rare color in the horse world and requires some special genetics. True white horses inherit a gene called "dominant white." Not surprisingly, they are called "dominant white horses." They are not albinos, as some mistakenly believe. Foals that inherit albinism rarely survive. Dominant whites have pink skin and colored eyes, usually blue or brown. Unlike grays, they are born white and stay that way. Interestingly, a horse can inherit only one dominant white gene and survive. Double dominant white genes are lethal.

Not So Common Colors

Most horses of a different color are genetic variations of one of the basic colors. For example, the palomino is genetically a faded chestnut horse with a white mane and tail. A single "cream gene" dilutes or lightens the chestnut coat into a creamy pale golden color. Some color breeds have been developed by selectively breeding horses of a different color to each other to increase the chances that a foal of the desired color would result.

Roans

Roans are often confused with grays, but the color pattern at work is quite different. A roan horse has white hairs mixed in with its body color, giving the coat a ticked appearance. A chestnut color mixed with white hairs is called a red or strawberry roan, and a black coat mixed with white hairs is a blue roan. Roans are born with their color and do not lighten with age as grays do. Roans also tend to have a significantly darker or solid-colored head, which does not lighten with age. The rabicano is a lovely variation that has only partial roan coloring on its body, usually the belly, flanks, legs, and tail area. Unlike the true roan, the rabicano's head is not darker.

Duns

The dun gene can lighten or "dilute" the appearance of any black, bay, or chestnut coat. The classic dun has a tan or sandy-colored coat with darker points and primitive markings. Primitive markings include a dark dorsal stripe down the center of the back and occasionally faint, horizontal zebra striping on the legs or a stripe across the shoulder blades. These markings are called "primitive" because they are reminiscent of the horse's early forebears and can still be seen in the wild Przewalskii's horses today. A chestnut coat with these dun factors is referred to as red dun. A black coat diluted by the dun gene is called a grulla (pronounced "grew-yah") or a blue dun.

Grulla is a strikingly beautiful but uncommon faded black, sometimes described as slate gray, smoky blue, mouse gray, or even silver blue. Grullas also sport primitive markings, leg striping, black points, and a dark-colored head. This rarest of all horse colors can actually range from light blue gray to brown shades.

Buckskins are frequently confused with duns, and with good reason. A buckskin may or may not be a dun, depending on the genetics at work. Typically, a buckskin is a faded bay, with a coat genetically diluted by a single "cream gene" to resemble the cream or golden color of the palomino. The buckskin retains the black points characteristic of a bay instead of the classic white or flaxen mane and tail of the golden palomino. Duns are more tan or sandy-colored than cream, and they always have the dorsal striping. Not all buckskins have a dorsal stripe, but some do. Those that carry the dun gene in addition to the cream gene will possess primitive markings, along with a cream-colored or pale golden coat, and they are generally called buckskin duns.

Cremellos and Perlinos

Cremellos may look like white horses with pink skin and blue eyes, but they are really faded chestnuts, such as the palomino. Palominos have a single cream gene that dilutes the chestnut base coat, whereas cremellos have two genes that make them even lighter in color. The double cream genes at work dilute their coat color to a cream or tan so light that it often appears nearly white. Manes and tails are white, too. Cremellos are not albinos, although they are sometimes referred to as pseudo-albinos because of their pink skin and striking blue eyes.

Perlinos are similar to cremellos, but they are faded bays, not faded chestnuts. Some people describe perlinos as "double buckskins" because they have two cream genes at work rather than one fading out the bay base color. This gives them a lighter coat, similar to the cremello's. However, their mane, tail, and points are darker than the rest of the body. They are not black like the buckskin's; they are usually reddish, orange, or rust-colored. Like cremellos, perlinos have pink skin and blue eyes.

Champagnes

Champagne is one of the newer colors on the block. Some horses with unique traits that were previously described as or registered as palominos, duns, or buckskins are now classified as champagnes. As with the palomino and the buckskin, a dilution gene is the reason for the unique color, but it's different than the cream gene. The champagne gene lightens skin, eye, and hair color. Champagnes have pink skin freckled with gray pigment. Their coat has a glowing metallic sheen that comes in shades described as amber, classic (brownish-gray), gold, sable, or ivory. Although foals are born with blue eyes, the color changes in time. The adult's eye color remains unusually light, ranging from green to the more common amber or light brown.

Color Breeds

Horses that are recognizable because of their color are generally referred to as color breeds. Some are not "true" horse breeds in the sense that their offspring do not always inherit the desired coloring. In addition, the physical characteristics don't necessarily matter as much as the color. For these horses, special color registries exist in which they can be registered for show and breeding purposes, as long as they possess the desired color characteristics.

The Palomino

Although it is recognized as a breed in the United States, some people would argue that the palomino is a horse color and not a horse breed in the strictest sense because it does not breed true. That is, palomino matings will produce palomino foals only about half the time. In addition, the palomino color can occur in almost any breed, so you may see palomino Arabians, Quarter Horses, and Saddlebreds.

The Palomino Horse Breeders of America registry describes the ideal coat color of the palomino to be "approximately the color of a United States gold coin." It also includes requirements for skin color, which must be "dark colored without pink spots wherever it shows . . . except for skin on the face, which may be pink where it is the continuation of a white marking." Further requirements are that both eyes must be the same color. The registry does allow the horse to have white legs and face markings.

Although it is a color breed, the registry also has conformation requirements: The palomino "must show refinement of head, bone, and general structure . . . and be suitable for carrying Western or English equipment. The horse must be between 14 and 17 hands when fully matured and show no pony or draft horse characteristics."

The Appaloosa

Almost 20,000 years ago, the spotted Appaloosa horse was depicted in cave drawings in what is now France. The Spanish brought this breed to North America, where the horse spread through the Native American populations in the Northwest, especially with the Nez Perce and Palouse tribes in Washington, Oregon, and Idaho. Because of their association with the Palouse River and the tribes that lived along it, white settlers were said to have referred to the spotted equine as "a Palouse horse," thus their name. In 1938, the Appaloosa Horse Club was formed to promote and preserve the breed.

Appaloosas are versatile horses, used in all equine sports, from jumping and roping to racing and trail riding. Appies in the United States tend to be more of the stock horse type, typically of Quarter Horse lineage. In Europe, they are distinctly more inclined toward the warmblood type and, therefore, often score well in dressage tests.

The Appaloosa is identifiable by four distinct characteristics:

- Spotted coat pattern
- Mottled or parti-colored skin (flesh color mixed with dark pigmentation)
- White eye sclera (white rings around the edges of the iris)
- Vertically striped hooves

To be accepted in the registry, the horse must possess either a spotted coat pattern or mottled skin and either white eye sclera readily visible and not associated with a white face or black-and-white striped hooves. If the horse's lineage is of Appaloosa stock but the horse does not exhibit these required characteristics, it can be registered as "noncharacteristic."

The leopard-like spotting can occur against almost any base color and variation thereof. A variety of coat patterns are possible, too, with the most easily recognized versions described as follows:

- **Blanket with spots:** a white blanket draped over the horse's hindquarters with darker spots within the white
- **Blanket:** a white blanket over the hindquarters with no spots
- **Leopard:** white with darker spots all over; these horses are rare and truly eye-catching.

Paints and Pintos

The pinto or Paint horse came to North America with the Spanish conquistador Hernando Cortés in 1519. One of the sixteen horses that accompanied Cortés was a sorrel and white horse that bred with Native American mustangs, whose offspring were the first of the American Paint Horse breed. These boldly spotted horses became favored by the Native Americans, and in the 1950s a group dedicated to preserving the breed was formed. With careful breeding, Paint horses can be bred to consistently produce color offspring.

QUESTION?

What's the difference between pintos, piebalds, and Paints?
Pinto and *piebald* describe color, while the term *paint* refers to pinto horses with Quarter Horse or Thoroughbred lineage. In the United States, the American Paint Horse is an established breed of spotted horses with the characteristics of a western stock horse. In England, the word *piebald* refers to a black horse with white spots, and the term *skewbald* commonly means a brown and white horse.

To be registered with the American Paint Horse Association, color pattern is essential, but there are also strict bloodline requirements that the sire or dam must be registered with the American Paint Horse Association, the American Quarter Horse Association, or the Jockey Club. Coloring of the Paint must be a combination of white and any other coat color in the spectrum, and markings can be any size and shape and located anywhere on the body.

The basic pinto patterns are described as follows:

- **Overo:** There is typically no white on the back, the four legs are usually dark, the head often has a lot of white, and the predominant color may be white or dark. Eyes are often blue.
- **Tobiano:** The legs are usually white, the head markings are often like that of solid color horses with a blaze, stripe, strip, or snip, and the predominant color can be white or dark. The white usually occurs across the back and down the withers.
- **Tovero:** A mixture of the tobiano and overo patterns, one or both eyes are blue, with a tendency toward dark coloring around the ears (called medicine hat markings), flanks, and chest.
- **Sabino:** This pattern is characterized by white markings going high up on the legs, white belly spots, splashes of white anywhere on the body, and prominent or irregular white facial markings that often extend past the eyes. There may also be roaning anywhere on the body and around the edges of the white markings.

Other Spotted Horses

When most people think of spotted horses, they think of Appaloosas and Paints. But there are some other breeds noted for their spots.

Pony of the Americas (POA)

The POA is a large pony with Appaloosa markings that, not surprisingly, resulted from an Arab/Appaloosa and Shetland Pony cross. A spotted pony named Black Hand was the breed's foundation sire. Arab blood is evident in the characteristic dished profile of the face. The breed was developed in the United States.

Knabstrup

Originating in Denmark, this European breed bears the same color genles and variations as the Appaloosa, with the all-over leopard spotting being the most prized. The breed registry is one of the oldest in Europe, dating back to the 1800s. Within the breed today, there are three distinct types:

- The sport horse type, crossed with warmbloods to produce horses that excel in dressage and jumping

- The baroque type, smaller and more compact and muscular in stature, and popular as a circus performer
- The pony type, standing at less than 14.2 hands

Horse Markings

Many horses have white on their faces and legs. Although these markings are hard to keep clean, many people prefer horses with lots of white. Foals are born with the markings they will have as an adult. These markings are called by specific names to allow adequate description when registering a horse.

Facial Markings

As with the names of colors, the names and descriptions of the markings of the horse can vary from region to region and even from registry to registry. Generally speaking, the names of the facial markings are as follows:

- **Star:** White on the forehead that may resemble a star or simply be an irregular patch of white.
- **Stripe or strip:** A narrow vertical stripe of white running down the face. It typically starts below the eyes and stops short of the nostrils.
- **Blaze:** A wide stripe of white running down the face, starting above the eyes and sometimes ending below the nostrils.
- **Snip:** A small irregular patch of white in the nostril or lower lip area.
- **Bald face:** This is a large, wide blaze that wraps around the eyes and extends down the entire length of the face, including the muzzle.

The horse's face may have one or more of these basic markings. For example, it may have a star and a stripe combined, or a strip and a snip.

Leg Markings

The names of the leg markings are as follows:

- **Stocking:** white covering the leg and extending from the hoof up to the knee or hock or beyond.

- **Sock:** white extending from the hoof only halfway up to the knee or hock; also called a half-stocking.
- **Pastern:** white from the hoof to the pastern.
- **Ankle or anklet:** white from the hoof to the fetlock.
- **Coronet:** a ring of white hair circling the area just above the hoof.

Of course, variations of these markings are possible. A horse may also have white marks on the heels or to the side of the heel without any of the markings.

Color Genetics

Color genetics is naturally of special importance to people who breed Appaloosas, Paints, buckskins, and palominos. Certain dilution genes turn chestnuts into palominos or cremellos, or turn bays into bucksins or perlinos. A knowledge of the science is especially important to avoid lethal traits, such as lethal dominant white. Color inheritance in the horse is extremely complex and not completely understood; however, more information is forthcoming on the subject all the time.

Dominant and Recessive Genes

While we may not know all there is to know about color inheritance in horses, you don't have to be a scientist to understand the basics of genetics. You just need to grasp a few simple principles. First, genes are what control inherited characteristics, such as coat and eye color, among other traits. A gene is either dominant or recessive. Often, several genes must work together to create the colors, patterns, and markings that we recognize in the horse.

A foal inherits one set of genes from its dam and another set from its sire. Generally speaking, a dominant gene tends to express its trait and suppress or mask the qualities of any recessive genes. A recessive gene is called such because its traits remain hidden in the presence of a dominant gene.

A horse with both a recessive and a dominant gene for the same trait is said to be heterozygous for that trait. A heterozygous horse does not show the trait hidden in its recessive gene, but it carries that gene and can pass it on to its offspring. A horse carrying two recessive or two dominant genes for the same trait is said to be homozygous for that trait.

On a genetics chart, dominant genes are written as capital letters, and recessive genes are written in lower case. So if dominant black is "BB," then chestnut, which is said to be recessive to black in horses, is designated as "bb." For a foal to be born chestnut, it must inherit two recessive genes for the color, one from each parent. Chestnuts are homozygous (bb) for their color trait, so a chestnut stallion bred to a chestnut mare will always produce a chestnut foal.

Black is a dominant color, but black horses can have either two dominant genes for their color or a single dominant gene coupled with a recessive gene. In other words, a black can be either BB or Bb. This means that two blacks can produce either black or chestnut foals, depending on whether they're heterozygous (Bb) or homozygous (BB) for the trait. If both parents are heterozygous (Bb), the foal can be either BB, Bb, or bb.

But if black is a dominant trait, why aren't there more true black horses? The answer is that bay, the most common color, is dominant to black. In a bay horse, there are other modifier genes at work that govern whether the black pigment fully expresses itself or restricts itself to the mane, tail, and points. That's where it all gets very complex, but at the same time it allows for the wonderful variety of colors and patterns we see in horses today.

The genes and modifiers that control white spotting and Appaloosa coloring in horses is not as well understood, although we do know that some patterns appear to be dominant while others are recessive. Several genes are also responsible for the white markings, such as the stockings, stars, strips, and snips.

The Silver Dapple Gene

The silver gene, also called the silver dapple or the "Z" gene, has nothing to do with the color silver. Rather, it dilutes black, changing it into a milk chocolate or grayish brown. Horses with this gene typically have light manes and tails, dark-colored faces, and dark lower legs. Many breeds do not carry this gene at all, but it is well known in the Rocky Mountain Horse, in which the resulting color is called chocolate, one of the breed's most popular colors.

CHAPTER 4

A Horse of Your Own

When you are ready to buy a horse of your own, there are many places to start your search—backyard sales, auctions, sale barns, and so forth. This chapter offers advice on how to look and what to look for when shopping for your first horse. But first, let's look at some of the ways you can be around horses even if you don't own one.

Living the Horse Life If You Don't Own One

You can arrange to be around horses a lot even if you choose not to own one yourself. The best way is to take riding lessons. Some barns have general equine lessons that include information on how to groom a horse, how to use tack, and how to handle a horse safely. If you are certain that you want to purchase a horse, you are wise to learn these things beforehand so you will be better prepared to handle your horse. You may be assigned a specific horse that you can get to know, or you may be assigned a new horse with each visit.

Perhaps your neighbor has a couple of horses in his backyard. He may not be willing to let you ride one, but he may be more than willing to have someone help with the chores. Realize, however, that it's easy to get hurt around horses if you don't know what you're doing. Liability is one reason why few horse owners will allow anyone else to ride their horses unless they know for sure that you are a skilled equestrian.

Sometimes you can trade stable work for lessons. Search around and pick a stable you are comfortable hanging around in. Maybe the stable specializes in an equine activity you are especially interested in, or perhaps you can discover a new equine sport that interests you.

If you live near a university with an equestrian program, signing up for their horsemanship classes can help you quickly move into the horse life. Many beginner university horsemanship classes include the basics of horse care, how to groom, take care of tack, and so on. They often have events and shows as part of the program. It can be an expensive way to go, but not as expensive as owning your own horse and educating yourself about horses on your own.

Bring a Trusted Advisor

If you are new to horses, the most important thing you can do when you start looking for one to buy is to bring an experienced horseman along with you. This person needs to be someone you trust, who knows your skill level, and who preferably has nothing to gain or lose from the transaction. If you must travel to visit prospects, you are generally expected to pay for this person's travel expenses, in addition to whatever fee they may charge.

Some people bring their instructor or their trainer, the person they plan to have work with horse and rider together after they buy it. Both trainer and instructor have something to gain in the long run; however, that doesn't make them a bad choice. What's important to understand is that their opinions will naturally be based on their own ulterior motives, good or bad, no matter how unbiased they try to be. That's a good thing, of course, if their primary motive is keeping you as a satisfied customer for a long time to come because that means matching you up with a horse that suits your goals and abilities.

Deciding What You Want

Before you and your trusted advisor start looking for a horse, make a short list of traits you would like in the horse you are planning to buy.

Age

As a rule of thumb, beginners should stay away from horses under four or five years old. Between five and ten years old, many horses seem to mellow in temperament, although this is not always the case. An older horse usually means the horse has some training and experience going to shows. Ultimately, age does not determine a horse's safety. There is a saying that a horse will always eventually rise up or come down to the level of his rider/handler. This means that even the best-trained horse can be spoiled by an inadequate rider. Many twenty-year-old horses are happy to run away with an unskilled rider if they feel unsupported in scary situations, which can include something as basic as leaving the barnyard.

History

Find out what you can about where the horse comes from, how many owners the horse has had, and the circumstances of each sale. The horse's current seller may not know much or may not wish to share what she knows so as not to sour your outlook on the horse, but it's worth asking. Having too many owners can cause behavioral problems in horses due to inconsistent handling—or the horse may have changed hands often specifically because of behavioral problems.

Education

One of the most important things for you to know about your prospective horse is its level of education. If possible, find out who trained the horse and how it was trained. Whips and gadgetry teach the horse to obey out of fear, while natural and classical techniques build trust, respect, and harmony between horse and rider. Riding the horse will give you clues about how the horse was trained and how he responds to the aids. If you aren't a skilled rider yourself, have someone with you who is evaluate the horse and try it out under saddle before you get on and ride it yourself.

Color

Color should never be the sole reason for buying the horse unless you just want a lawn ornament. If you're going to ride the horse or compete with it, it is more important to buy a horse for what she knows and what she can do. Some people are attracted to Paint horses and collect them for their color alone. It does help to like the color of the horse you'll look at every day, but when you finally find the horse whose temperament and education fits you, you won't even notice how much white she has until you have to clean her.

FACT

The Thoroughbred Man O' War was born in 1917, a product of careful breeding. The chestnut colt was 16.2 hands as a three-year-old, and he lost only one race in his career. He won both the Preakness and the Belmont—which he won by six lengths—and regularly beat world and U.S. records.

Size

Size doesn't have to matter, but it can. Most people with large builds like to have a horse of some substance under them. A tall person typically would like the horse to be tall, too, because they look better proportioned on a tall horse, which matters more in the show ring than anywhere else. A beginning rider who is short may gain more confidence starting out on a smaller horse. After all, it is a farther fall to the ground from a tall horse than a short one.

Conformation

Buying a horse that is well put together and built for its intended use makes everything easier. When the horse's way of going is normal and even, it's not as prone to wear out shoes as quickly. It's also generally easier to fit a saddle to a horse with good conformation.

If you know what you plan to do with the horse—such as jumping, dressage, or barrel racing—look for conformation specifics that lend the horse to that activity. Someone experienced in your chosen discipline can help you in this regard. Any sound horse is suitable to do almost any basic riding activity for fun, but if you intend to compete seriously and move up in your levels of challenge, your equine athlete needs to have the appropriate physique and some innate ability in your chosen discipline. You may find that you need to change up horses as your own abilities progress. Few serious competitors stay with the same horse their entire riding career.

Cost

Price is of primary importance for most people. Chances are, you have a top limit of how much you can spend on a horse. Although there are some market standards, the seller will have his own reasons for setting a price, including how much he has invested in the horse's training.

Expect to spend up to $10,000 for your first pleasure-riding horse. If you're looking for a good show or performance horse, expect to pay a lot more. Lower-level dressage horses can start at $30,000 or more. That's because someone has invested a lot of time and expertise in the quality of training it takes to develop a good dressage horse. Don't let the numbers scare you, however. If your top price is, say, $5,000, there are horses out there for you, depending on what you want to do. It just may take a little longer to find exactly the right one.

Remember, if the horse is priced really cheap, there's probably a good reason, usually a soundness, behavior, or training problem. On the other side of the coin, just because you pay a lot of money for a horse doesn't guarantee that she's healthy or that you'll be able to ride her after you get her home.

Places to Buy Horses

Now that you have a general description in mind of the horse you are looking for, it's time to start scouting around.

Classified Ads

If you live in a horse-oriented part of the country, you may find a lot of horses for sale in the classified section of the daily newspaper. You can also find classified listings in any regional equine publication. Classified publications usually have a horse section. Most state agriculture departments have a similar publication. Keep your horse-to-be profile in mind as you read the listings, and circle any that come close. Don't make calls on horses that don't fit one of the major points in your profile. It just wastes your time and money, as well as the time of the person who is selling the horse.

If you're going to look in the classifieds, be aware that there are often hints in the wording that offer clues about the horse's usability. Here are some commonly used veiled phrases you may run across in the classified ads:

- **Broodmare only:** This usually means a mare has soundness problems that prevent her from being ridden, but she can still be used for breeding.
- **Companion horse only:** This typically means a horse cannot be ridden and is of no use other than to keep another horse company.
- **Good foundation; needs finishing:** This usually describes a horse that has had the fundamentals but is in the advanced beginner stage of its education as a riding horse. A novice rider would not want a horse at this stage of training.
- **Grade:** Grade describes a horse of unknown ancestry or one that displays the characteristics of a specific breed but whose breeding history doesn't allow it to be registered.
- **Green broke:** Typically this means the horse has had a saddle on and tolerates being ridden but hasn't had many hours under saddle and doesn't know all the cues or aids a rider would give.
- **Husband horse:** A husband horse is a nice, calm horse that tolerates inconsistent riding, tends to take care of its rider, and is a horse you would be comfortable with as a beginner or part-time rider.

- **Prospect:** This is a horse that the owner feels has the potential to excel in a particular type of activity after he has been trained to do so.
- **Rides E/W:** This means the horse has been ridden in both English and Western tack.
- **Ring sour:** This typically describes a horse that has been shown competitively for a number of years and is exhibiting signs of being sick of the show ring.
- **UTD on shots and worming:** This means the horse is up-to-date on her annual vaccinations and deworming program.
- **Willing over fences:** This horse has been jumped successfully and doesn't tend to balk.
- **Needs advanced rider:** One phrase that novices should definitely avoid, this more often than not means the horse is difficult to ride and handle in some way for anyone except the most skilled and experienced horseman.

Breeders and Show Barns

If you are interested in a specific breed or type of horse, you will definitely want to visit reputable breeders and show barns within the range that you feel comfortable traveling. Breeders often have young animals because, logically, they breed and sell the offspring. To keep a wide selection, many breeders sell other people's horses on commission. Show barns do this as well.

QUESTION?

What is a show barn?
A show barn is a facility where owners of a specific breed or discipline board their horses and keep them in training for competition. The riders also school here in their chosen area of competition. For example, you may find hunter/jumper barns or facilities that cater specifically to gaited horses.

Auctions

Horse auctions work like most auctions—people bring their horses, a professional auctioneer sells them, and a percentage goes to the auction house. The horse is led and/or ridden in front of the audience, and the highest bidder wins. Usually there are contingencies for vet checks and for you to test ride the horse, but you need to know these details before you hold up your bidder's number. Auctions are not the best places for beginners to buy a horse.

Sale Barns

Some horse facilities are set up in the business of buying and selling horses. They typically are not breeders and do not breed their own livestock, nor do they specialize in any one breed of horse or riding discipline. They are an outlet for people who want to sell a horse but don't have the time, expertise, or interest to sell it on their own. Typically, a wide range of breeds are offered at a wide range of ages and prices. This is a place where you definitely need some horse knowledge and experience to make a suitable selection.

The Internet

Many horse sites on the Internet have listings of horses for sale. This can be a great way to educate yourself about what's available and the pricing ranges; plus, you can see photos of prospects. It also can give you a sense of what the horse market is like. Ultimately, you should see the horse in person and try him out. Either limit your search to your state or region, or be prepared to fly or drive some distance to see the horse.

Professional Trainers

People who train horses for a living often know about horses up for sale. Making a few calls to barns where horses are trained may bring up a few prospects. Expect these horses to be on the higher end of your price range because the seller must pay the trainer a commission in addition to board and any ongoing training while the horse is there for sale.

Equine Rescue Shelters

Getting a horse from a rescue shelter can be inexpensive up front, but less experienced people can find themselves with more problems than they bargained for. Horses often become rescue cases because inexperienced people bring home a horse and unintentionally foster bad habits that eventually develop into dangerous habits, making the owner afraid to handle the horse. Other cases are the result of abuse or neglect.

Shelters usually work with the horses to bring them back to health. Some attempt to retrain the horse to increase the chances of a successful placement. If you are experienced enough to carry through with the work the shelter has done or to re-educate the horse yourself, getting a horse from a shelter can be an extremely rewarding experience. Some horses simply need better handling from the start and will do fine after they are placed under the care of an owner who understands them.

Visiting Your Prospects

Once you've found a horse that fits all your criteria, arrange time for a visit. During the visit, ask the seller to ride the horse for you. This allows you and your trusted advisor to see how the horse moves and how it is accustomed to being ridden. Then, your advisor should ride the horse and evaluate its abilities under saddle. Lastly, you should mount and ride the horse yourself to evaluate how it feels to you.

FACT

Under no circumstances should you ride the horse before seeing it ridden by the owner or someone else. Watching someone else ride the horse helps you determine if your skill level is high enough to handle the horse. Your trusted advisor should be able to tell you whether she thinks the horse would be a good match for you.

It's best if you can observe how the horse behaves being tacked up—and even caught in the field. You could also tell the seller you'd like to saddle the horse yourself. You need to find out how the horse behaves when having its feet picked up, how it accepts the bridle, and so forth. If the horse doesn't have good manners on the ground, don't expect good manners under saddle.

Unscrupulous sellers may use tranquilizers or some other substance that temporarily calms or masks the horse's ill behavior. That's why popping in unexpectedly to see the horse a second time can sometimes be educational. Substances are more likely to be used at an auction, where you have no chance of going back for a second visit.

In the excitement of the moment, you can forget to ask some important questions. Discuss what you need to ask with your advisor and write a checklist to follow when you visit prospects. Don't put your money down until you have learned the answers to your questions. For example, has the horse had any health problems or chronic illnesses? Ask to see the medical records. Is the horse up-to-date on its vaccinations and deworming? Ask to see the most recent Coggins test results. Does the horse require any regular medication, special feeding, supplements, or corrective shoes?

After you look at the horse, give the seller a sense of your interest level. If the horse isn't what you're looking for, say so. If you are truly interested in the horse, let the seller know, but you don't need to commit to anything until you've had the horse checked out by a vet. If you are interested enough to worry about whether the horse will be sold while you look at your remaining prospects, ask if you can have first refusal on the horse. This means that if someone else shows interest in the horse, the seller will call and let you know that you need to make a decision.

The Prepurchase Exam

Whether you want the horse checked by a vet before you finalize the sale is up to you—and it will be at your expense. Prepurchase exams are money well spent, especially if you're planning to use the horse for a particular sport or discipline. It's sort of like a home inspection before buying a house. All large-animal veterinary practices have a standard exam they administer. If the seller won't allow a prepurchase exam (also known as a vet check), suspect something fishy and walk away. Any reputable seller will expect you to do a vet check. Also, choose the veterinarian to do the exam yourself; do not find a vet based on the seller's recommendation. If possible, arrange to be present during the exam.

In a prepurchase exam, the vet checks the horse's temperature, heart rate, and other vital signs, and also performs some general lameness and range-of-motion tests. You may request other tests as well. For instance, if you are buying the horse with a specific performance activity in mind, such as jumping or dressage, you may want the vet to X-ray feet and leg joints. If you plan to use a mare for breeding, ask the vet to check the horse's reproductive system.

There are no perfect horses and no perfect scores. What you are asking the vet to determine is whether the horse is healthy, sound, and fit enough to do what you plan to use it for. The vet will share the results of the exam with you and the seller and provide you with a written copy. If the vet finds something out of the ordinary, you must determine whether it is something you can cope with or whether it will prevent you from doing what you want to do with the horse.

The Big Purchase

When you inform the seller of your decision to buy, you will probably be required to give a good-sized deposit to hold the horse. When you are ready to take him home, you pay the balance in full, unless you make other arrangements with the seller.

Getting Your Horse Home

The seller may be able to deliver the horse to you for a fee, or perhaps you have an experienced horse friend with a trailer who will help. If you are not yet ready to take your horse to her final destination, the seller may be able to board her for you for a short period of time, depending on the situation. For example, a seller with a boarding barn may be happy to have her on as long as you pay to board her, but a trainer may need to get her out of the barn as soon as possible to open up a stall for a new student.

Registration Transfer

If the horse is registered, you will need to transfer the registration papers to your name. Breed associations all operate a little differently, but generally the current owner sends in the transfer information, and then the breed registry sends the new papers to you with your name added to them. Sometimes the owner (who may or may not be the seller) will simply sign the papers over to you, and then you will need to send them to the breed registry. Transferring registration usually involves a small fee. You should get this done immediately, as this is an important part of the monetary value of your horse. If the horse is not registered, a simple bill of sale including a description of the horse should suffice.

A Smooth Transition

Be sure to stock up on the same brand and type of food before your horse comes home. Eventually, you will develop your own likes and dislikes when it comes to brands and types of feed, but for now you should feed him what he's been accustomed to.

Have a place prepared for her—a shelter or clean stall with fresh bedding. She'll also need her own water bucket and feed tub ready for her. Other items you'll need include a mineral block, a supply of grain and hay, a wheelbarrow and manure fork, and a solidly fenced turnout area. If you are boarding your new horse, the facility will already have these things, but you'll need a halter, a lead rope, and a few grooming supplies.

When you get your new horse to his new home, let him settle in and get to know you and his new environment for a few days. Don't throw a saddle on him the minute you get him out of the trailer. Spend some time with him, groom him, and walk him around and let him look at things. Some horses adapt readily and will settle easily, while others will be restless.

Don't turn the new horse out with other horses right away. Keep her separate for at least a week, but let her stay within sight and smell of the others so they can begin to get accustomed to one another. When you do put her in with other horses, watch closely to make sure no one gets kicked or hurt while they readjust their herd pecking order.

Leasing

Leasing is a way to acquire a horse without actually owning it. Sometimes the current life circumstances of a horse's owner—pregnancy, health problems, temporary relocation for a job, a new job—make it impossible for the owner to give the horse the attention it needs.

Why Lease?

A short-term lease is a good way for you to try out a horse before you consider buying him. If you are not in a position to buy a horse right now, a lease can make a lot of sense. Sometimes a free lease (one without a monthly charge) drops in your lap—for example, you are taking lessons at a barn, and someone tells you about a horse there that the owner never comes to see and is thinking about free leasing so the horse can get exercised.

Another logical reason for leasing is so you can trade up as your skills advance, especially if you compete. Say, for instance, you plan to learn dressage. If you spend the time and energy to get to the top levels of dressage competition, you will probably go through three or four horses on your way there. The horse that is laid back enough to be a beginner dressage horse may not have what it takes to be the Grand Prix candidate you want when your own skill level gets that advanced. If you have the space, you can collect these horses in your barn as you progress up the ranks. More likely, you will need to sell them and put the money toward your next prospect. However, if you lease a horse, you can simply give it back to the owner when you are ready to move on.

There are also shared leases, in which you lease a horse, probably at a riding stable, with someone else. You each are assigned specific days or even times that you can ride the horse. Typically, the stable owns such a horse and is responsible for all its care but uses partial leasing to cover a portion of the horse's upkeep. This is a reasonable way for boarding stables that keep a string of lesson horses to have the lesson horse pay its own way.

The Lease Agreement

Be sure to sign a lease agreement, or at least a letter of agreement, outlining the following details of the arrangement, plus anything else that you can think of:

- Who pays for maintenance items such as shoes and vaccinations?
- Is there an end date? Leaving the lease open-ended is probably not a good idea. It is better to make the lease easy to renew by inserting a phrase that allows the lease to continue for the same period of time simply by having both parties sign new signatures on the existing lease.
- Where can the horse be kept? What kind of shelter is sufficient? You may think a run-in shed with 24/7 turnout is perfect, but the owner may expect the horse to be in a box stall at night.
- Can the horse be turned out with other horses?

- Are you allowed to trailer the horse to a horse show or trail ride? Can the horse be trailered out of state? Can it be kept overnight?
- What happens if the horse needs emergency veterinary care? Who makes decisions about that care, and who pays for it?
- What happens if the horse dies while it is under your care? No one wants this to happen, but it certainly could and has.

If you are a parent buying your child's first horse or pony, follow all of the same advice given in this chapter. Don't mount your child with a horse beyond his abilities—even the most gentle horse is still a large and unintentionally dangerous animal.

CHAPTER 5

Boarding Your Horse

Before purchasing a horse, decide where you will keep the animal. You are fortunate if you own land and live in an area zoned for livestock. If not, you basically have two other options: a boarding facility or the property of a friend, acquaintance, or neighbor. Each option has its complications and benefits.

Choosing a Boarding Facility

The basic premise of boarding a horse is simple: You pay money to someone who has gone to the expense of constructing fencing and a barn that holds many horses, and that person takes care of housing and feeding your horse and the everyday chores, such as mucking out your horse's stall. Simple? It can be. However, boarding can also be extremely complicated and sometimes more than a little expensive.

FACT

Daily stall cleaning is important to your horse's health. Start by picking out the large piles of manure with a rake, and then sift through the bedding for scattered chunks. About once a week, strip the stall of all bedding and let the stall air out for as long as possible.

Location

Consider the proximity of the boarding facility to your home or job. How far will you have to drive to visit your horse? In some cases, the travel time may be worth your while, particularly if you are interested in the kind of horsemanship offered at a certain facility, and there is no place closer that provides the same environment. Some barns cater to a particular riding discipline, such as dressage, jumping, or Western, offering instruction and other activities related to your chosen style of equitation. The camaraderie at a barn where everyone shares the same interest can be extremely valuable and educational, especially to a novice horse owner.

Housing Arrangement

Facilities offer different housing arrangements, but the most likely scenario is that your horse will have a box stall in which he will spend a good deal of time. The larger the stall the better—10' × 10' is considered a minimum requirement, a 12' × 12' stall is better, and larger is even better, especially if you have a big horse.

Another good arrangement for a horse is a run-in shed with twenty-four-hour turnout, but facilities that offer this are few and far between. The reason is convenience—it is much easier to feed horses and clean stalls that are all under one roof than it is to trudge through adverse weather to attend to many outside run-in sheds.

Some barns with numerous stalls under one roof are set up with small turnout corrals off the outer wall of each stall, essentially creating a run-in situation. This, along with turnout in a larger area during the day when you aren't exercising your horse, can be an ideal arrangement. Horses seem to be more content when they have at least some control over where they spend their time—for example, being in the sun or in the shade, out in the snow or in a cozy stall with deep bedding.

What does turnout mean?
Turnout refers to the period when your horse is out of the confinement of a stall and loose in a larger fenced area—either outside in a corral or pasture, or in an indoor arena if the weather is bad.

QUESTION?

Turnout

Facilities differ greatly in what they offer for turnout for each horse. You should know whether daily turnout is offered, and how many hours a day each horse gets out. In ads for boarding stables, you might read "half-day turnout," which generally means each boarder's horse gets approximately four hours of the day out of its stall—which is perhaps okay if you ride every day, but not nearly enough if you don't. Other questions you need to ask include:

- Will your horse be turned out with other horses? Being herd animals, horses are happier when turned out with companions, if everyone gets along well together without a lot of kicking and fussing. If your horse doesn't socialize well with other horses, you will need to make this clear to the facility manager.

- Are the horses all turned out in a big pasture ("pasture turnout") after feeding in the morning and spend the day out until they are brought in for evening feeding and for the night?

The more time your horse is out of its stall, the better. Being penned up in a stall twenty-four hours a day is an unnatural condition for an animal that has evolved over centuries to be out grazing all day. Unfortunately, many show horses are kept this way solely as a convenience, for fear they'll get injured, throw a shoe, or mess up a tail set. If you own a horse like this, you have an obligation to see to it that the horse receives ample exercise everyday, whether you ride, lunge, hand-walk the horse, or pay someone else to do it for you.

The Facility Itself

You'll want to choose a boarding facility that has a riding arena for schooling your horse. Some facilities provide both outdoor and indoor riding arenas, which is a plus if you live in a cold climate where good footing is a concern during the winter months. If there is no indoor arena, does the outdoor arena have lights? This is important if you work and can't get to the barn until after dark. Find out how early in the morning or how late in the evening it is okay for boarders to come and use the facility.

Also, find out how many boarders the facility has or can take on. Are the barn aisles and riding areas big enough for the number of boarders, and are they often crowded? Are there riding trails nearby that boarders have permission to use?

FACT

Halters have been known to catch on other objects, which can cause potentially fatal injuries. It is safer to remove the halter when the horse is turned out or put up in her stall. All-leather halters, which will break under stress, are a good option. As an alternative, use a breakaway nylon halter with a leather headpiece that will break when stressed.

The Boarding Agreement

You will be expected to sign an agreement of some sort when you bring your horse to stay at the facility. Read the agreement closely and take note of anything that you are expected to supply or do. Also note when board payment is due and what happens if you are late with your payment. Some facilities will refuse to release a horse until overdue board payments are made. The signing is a good time to ask other questions that may come to mind, such as whether there is a limit on the number of riders allowed at one time in the arena.

Liability Release Form

Any place where you board your horse or take lessons will require you to sign a liability release. Although it covers standard things—that you are riding your horse on their property at your own risk or that you are taking lessons on one of the stable's horses at your own risk—you should nonetheless read a release carefully. Equine legal books often do not include contract forms because the authors realize that every situation is different. Therefore, stables are encouraged to tailor their release to their specific setup.

Other Boarders

Before signing on the dotted line, you should spend some time hanging around the facility, meet some of the other boarders, and watch them work with their horses. Ask them whether they like boarding there and how long they've been there. Boarders come and go fairly regularly for all sorts of reasons, but if there is a huge turnover at a place, you might want to find out why.

It's hard to discern everything in a couple hours, but you should be able to sense any major problems or personality conflicts after a few visits. What you hope to find is a congenial group of horse enthusiasts who welcome a new horse and rider into their fold and who will be willing to share their knowledge and interest with you.

Another good way to find out whether the atmosphere and folks at a facility suit you is to take riding lessons there if instruction is offered. If you don't already ride, you should take riding lessons for at least six months prior to buying a horse to find out if you really like it. This helps prepare you with some of the skills you'll need to handle your horse more safely after you acquire her.

Cost

The expense of owning a horse is a huge consideration, and boarding costs are a big part of it. Expect the cost to vary widely from facility to facility. The closer you get to more populated areas, the more boarding will probably cost. A thirty-acre horse facility in a highly desirable real estate market with limited open land left means the facility probably cost a lot to construct, and the monthly board will reflect that.

For a comprehensive directory of hundreds of interesting and unusual horse-related websites, go to *www.thehorse.com/source/thehorse*. The directory is organized by categories such as "barn and farm equipment," "clubs and associations," and "harness racing." It also lists newsgroups, classifieds, and publications.

Services will cost you as well. Some facilities include riding lessons with board. Some offer such things as holding your horse for the farrier or vet, or blanketing against winter winds or summer sun. Some facilities offer deworming programs to keep all horses on the same schedule. Expect a higher cost for more amenities—such as a wash room for horses, a tack shop, a nice tack storage area with personal lockers, a heated lounge area, food to purchase, full bathrooms with a shower, maybe even a vet or farrier on the premises of larger facilities. There is a cost associated to the owner to provide these things, and in order for the facility to stay in business the cost must be passed along to the boarders.

Type of Riding

If you are interested in learning about a particular type of riding, you might want to find a facility where the concentration is on that kind of riding so that you can really expand your knowledge in that one area. A barn concentrating on jumping will probably have a nice cross-country jump course, some good low-level training jumps in the arena, membership in the local hunt club, and some jumping clinics that you can participate in without having to leave the property. This type of arrangement is one of the big bonuses of boarding.

Other Details

Don't overlook the details when choosing a place to keep your horse. There's much more to good horse keeping than just providing food and shelter.

Safety and Tidiness

Does the stable practice good safety habits? Look for a neatly kept barn with things such as water hoses coiled up and out of the way of horses and people. Aisles should be clear of debris and not used as storage areas. Grain should be stored in an area separate from the horse stalls, behind a latched gate or door, and neatly kept in rodent-proof storage bins. Find out whether the driveways are clear of junk and quickly cleared of snow in the winter.

Stalls

Are the stalls constructed safely and without protrusions that could injure your horse? Look for feeders for hay and grain that are appropriate to horses. They certainly don't have to be fancy, but they should be without sharp edges or holes. Are the stalls clean on your visits? Stall doors should open and close with ease and latch securely.

Recordkeeping

It's nice when boarding stables put name cards on each stall door telling who the horse is, what she eats, any peculiarities such as allergies or unusual habits (such as the ability to unlatch a stall door), and how to contact her owner in case of emergency. Name plaques aren't an absolute necessity, but at the very least, the barn management should keep such detailed records on hand in the office for every horse.

Water Provisions

Do the horses get ample water in their stalls and out in the paddocks or pastures? The stable should have a good plan for providing ice-free water in the winter and for ensuring an ample supply of fresh water in hot weather. Look for clean water buckets and containers that are large enough for the number of horses turned out together in one area.

Shelter

Are there places in the pasture for horses to get away from flies or cold wind? A nice row of hemlock, spruce, or thickly planted shrubs will block the wind during the coldest times of the year if they are placed in the right spot. Tall pines and hemlocks and other evergreens can provide some overhead shelter from light rain and snow. In the peak of fly season, horses need either a place to escape to or plenty of attention with fly sprays, sheets, and masks. Is the pasture run-in big enough for the number of horses turned out there? Typically, one horse can guard a surprisingly large area, leaving no shelter for any other horse. Horses can be switched around so that those that don't compete so much with each other can share.

Supplements

Will the facility add supplements to your horse's feed at your request? Some boarding stables charge extra per supplement per day. Twenty-four horses that require an average of two supplements each added to their feed twice a day, can add up to a lot of extra time for caretakers.

Medical Care

What about those times when your horse needs medical attention? Will the barn management call a veterinarian for you if you can't be reached? When ongoing care is needed, can you pay someone to fill in for you if the horse needs to be walked three times a day or needs a bandage changed and you can't make it out to the barn to do these things yourself every day?

Security

Is there good security for your horse and your tack? You should be comfortable leaving your saddle and other equipment in the tack room without fear of theft. Otherwise, you'll have to tote it back and forth in your car or truck.

Night Checks

Does anyone perform a night check? It can be as simple as a walk through the barn, peeking in each stall. Does the night check include an evening snack for everyone or topping off the water buckets? If it is a large facility that houses many horses and has lots of people milling around all the time, you might want to make sure there is someone on the premises at most times and that the stable can be seen from the home of the owner or manager.

Fire Prevention

Are there good fire prevention measures, such as No Smoking signs, fire extinguishers, and up-to-date electrical wiring? Is there an evacuation plan in the event of fire? Many stables offer owners the choice of having a halter left on their horse in the stall for quicker evacuation in case of fire or hanging on the door.

Keeping Your Horse with a Friend or Neighbor

Aside from boarding at a stable, another viable and common option is to keep a horse with a friend who already has a horse or two. Usually, the financial arrangements work great for both of you. Your friend will probably charge you a lot less than the going rate at the local boarding facility. He might charge just enough for his time and to cover the feed costs for his own horses.

Dogs and horses don't always mix. Some dogs love to chase horses. If the pursuit is hot enough, they can chase them right through fences, causing all sorts of damage. Your dog can get hurt as well, so teach your dog early on that the horses are off limits. Never take your dog to the barn unless you have permission from the owner.

Working Out an Arrangement

As with a boarding facility, your friend would probably be the one doing all or most of the work, since he will want to clean stalls and such according to his own schedule and standard of care. Unlike a boarding facility, the two of you are free to agree on a different arrangement, depending on your situation. If your friend is close enough to your home, you could share feeding responsibilities. In exchange for relatively cheap (often referred to as "rough") board, you could offer to provide all your own feed and to muck out your own stall. Of course, the owner of the barn will have the final say in how any arrangement is set up.

Aside from cost, there are several advantages to boarding your horse at a friend's house. For one thing, you have a built-in riding buddy. Also, during hay season, you can chip in and help each other bring in the year's supply. In addition, you have someone to help you as you learn about caring for a horse if you are new to horse keeping.

Disadvantages

There are, however, some disadvantages to consider before you decide to board at a friend's house:

- If this person has been a friend for a while, you could run into a disagreement or financial dispute that could end your friendship.
- If the person was not so close a friend in the past, you may find you simply don't get along as well as anticipated, and you may be faced with having to move your horse as a result.
- In a setting more private than a boarding stable, you may sometimes feel like you are intruding on family activities when you want to go see your horse.
- You may not get a lot of the perks that a full boarding stable offers, such as access to a bathroom, a riding arena, and some of the anonymity that comes with the larger arrangement.

It all depends on the situation. Many people have multistall barns at their private home and board the horses of friends or neighbors. The barn is usually a bit away from the house and has a rustic bathroom, and the situation can work out just fine. The important thing is to communicate openly with the barn owner and be up front about your needs and expectations. Be businesslike in your dealings, and by all means, pay your bills on time. Money issues generally cause the most grief in such situations.

CHAPTER 6

Keeping Your Horse at Home

Perhaps you planned all along to keep your horse at your own home. This is the best arrangement of all—if you have enough land to accommodate a horse. It takes about three acres of grazing to support one horse. By keeping your horse at home, you get to decide everything about how your horse lives and to do things your own way. And you get to spend the maximum amount of time with your horse. If you have just fifteen minutes and can't fit in a ride, you can groom your horse without having to travel to do it.

In the Zone

Before you commit to keeping a horse at home, the first thing you need to know is whether zoning laws in your area permit a horse to be kept in your neighborhood. If it is permitted, find out the particulars of the regulations. For example, you may be required to keep the horse on a certain number of acres. Once you've established that it is legal to keep a horse at your home, here are some other things to consider as you set up shop.

Give 'Em Shelter

If you plan to have a barn built, your options are limited only by the amount of space you have to construct your building and, of course, your budget. If you have a minimal amount of space, plan to have just one or two horses, and would like to leave most of the space for your horse(s) to run around in, consider a three-sided run-in shelter. Horses can live absolutely fine in this situation even in the most severe weather, as long as you tend to their needs.

FIGURE 6.1:
Run-in shelter

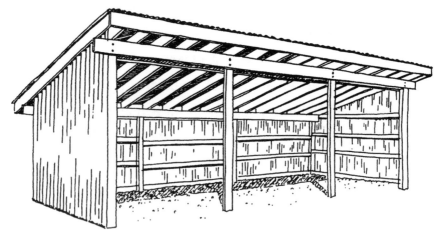

Ideally, the run-in should have a standard stall space for each horse that will use it—that is, two horses should ideally have a run-in that is 12' × 24', or a 12' × 12' stall space per horse. The nice thing about this setup is that you could put a temporary panel down the middle and create two stalls with turnout areas for nighttime or emergencies.

The only problem with using just a run-in shelter is the inconvenience for the caretaker. It leaves no space to do things such as groom or tack up your horse, or a wash rack for bathing and hosing off after a hot ride. You will need a space somewhere to store hay, grain, tack, a wheelbarrow, and so on.

If you plan to build a full-fledged barn, you can go two-stall, four-stall, ten-stall, whatever you have the space and money for. A four-stall barn with a couple of stalls used for horses, one for a tack/grain room, and another for hay storage or as a spare stall if you need it for a friend, can be just the right size.

Builders who specialize in equine shelters know the details of how high and wide the doorways need to be and how to safely install light fixtures for horses, and they are extra careful about picking up nails and taking care of all those little things that are hard to remember until you are in the midst of the project or, worse yet, after you are done. Equine barn builders offer everything from run-in sheds to multistall barns with tack rooms, washrooms, sprinkler systems, and overhead hay storage to indoor arenas with ten stalls, mirrors on the wall, and a heated viewing area. The amount of money you have to spend is your primary limitation.

FACT

There are always things to repair or replace when you keep horses, as they can be quite destructive. Plan to have extras of your most commonly used supplies to replace broken ones without having to make a special trip to the supply store. Replace or fix worn-out items before they give out.

Using an Existing Structure

If your property already has a barn that was used for horses in the past, your start-up will be a little easier. Get rid of protruding nails, replace or cover glass windows that will be within reach of the horse, and look for anything that might cause a horse's hoof to get caught. Are there any electrical wires or other such items within reach of the horse's stall—old rusted chicken wire, for example? If so, move it or block the horse's access to it. Be sure stall doors and such are high enough to contain a horse. Be sure stall doors and exterior doors open wide enough to get a horse in and out without the horse constantly hitting his hip on the doorframe.

FIGURE 6.2:
Floor plan
of a 30' × 30'
four-stall barn

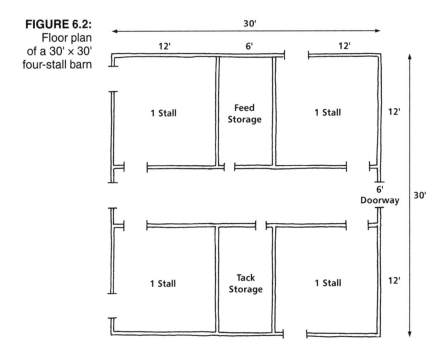

Do not underestimate the strength of a horse! When building walls, hanging gates, creating fencing, or constructing anything that is to contain a horse, consider whether they will be able to hold if the horse leans all its weight on them. Wooden fencing is safest for a horse. Most people run a line of electrical wire or tape across the top rail, just to keep horses from chewing or rubbing it.

Ideally, stalls should be well ventilated and have at least a little bit of sun exposure during the day. The advantage to this is that urine spots get baked by the sun for a few hours every day and dry out quickly. Sunlight also helps destroy certain types of molds and bacteria. However, if your horse stays in its stall a lot, you won't want the stall to bake in the sun all day, and you'll want to be sure the horse has a shady area to retire to.

Flooring

The type of flooring you choose for your stalls is important to the health of your horse's hooves, especially if the horse is going to be confined for long periods. There are basically three possibilities for stall flooring: wood, concrete, or dirt.

Wood

Wooden floors have the obvious disadvantage that they need to be exceptionally sturdy to support a horse's weight. Keep in mind that your horse isn't going to tiptoe around the stall. The floor must be able to withstand the occasional jumping of an excited horse or the thrashing of a horse rolling in her nice clean bedding and hoisting herself to her feet again.

Urine and manure will rot wood floors amazingly quickly, and the odors will linger in the material. Although wood tends to be the least desirable choice for horse stall flooring, it can be a solid choice. Wood floors need to be very sturdy and must have a solid foundation underneath, but they can be swept completely clean, which is a huge advantage for you. You can put down rubber mats or other synthetic floor coverings designed for use with horses. These help cushion the floor and, after being covered with some type of bedding, they prevent most of the urine from making contact with the wood, thus preserving the life of the floor. However, urine will still find its way between the mats, so once or twice a year, strip out the bedding, pull up the mats, wash down the floor and the mats, and let everything dry out in the sun.

Concrete

Concrete floors are definitely hard on a horse's legs because they don't give much. If this is the type of flooring you already have, it doesn't make them unusable, but covering the floor with rubber stall mats and a deep layer of bedding to cushion your horse's legs will help. Rubber mats will also help if the concrete is smooth and potentially slippery. On the other hand, concrete has two major advantages: It holds up incredibly well, and it can be hosed down and easily cleaned and disinfected.

Dirt

Obviously, dirt is the most natural material for horses to stand on. It is sturdy enough to support a horse's weight but not hard enough to cause damage to a horse's legs. Depending on the type of dirt used, the urine doesn't settle on the surface for the horse to lounge around in. However, the urine does sink into the dirt, and the odor builds up. You don't have the advantage of being able to hose down a dirt floor without turning it into a mud pit. If stalls with dirt floors are deep inside the barn where they never get any sun or air circulation, the urine odor problem can become bad.

If the dirt floor does not get a lot of sun exposure, you will need to be extra diligent in cleaning out wet spots daily. It may help to strip stalls more frequently than is needed with other types of stall flooring. From time to time, you may even have to dig out some of the dirt and replace it with fresh dirt. Whenever you strip the stall and put down clean bedding, you can help the odor problem by spreading some lime or other odor-reducing products on the urine spots before putting fresh bedding down. And don't forget that urine odor is not just unpleasant; the fumes are bad for your horse's respiratory health.

Different Kinds of Bedding

Like almost everything with horses, you will develop your own preference for the kind of bedding you prefer to keep in your horse's stall. Your horse may display its own preferences as well. Your choices are sawdust, shavings, or straw. Sawdust can be the cheapest to use, depending on what part of the country you live in. Sawdust is easy to clean, since it slips easily through the manure fork, leaving the bedding in the stall instead of in the manure pile. The main drawback is that is can be dusty and aggravate respiratory problems.

Shavings

Bagged wooden shavings are more widely available, both at mills and at your local feed store. Wooden shavings that are bagged for use with horses consist primarily of dry pine shavings. Make sure the shavings you buy are intended for use with horses. Avoid other kinds, as they can contain shavings from types of wood that could make your horse ill if they are consumed.

Both shavings and sawdust can dry your horse's feet. The key here is to get your horse out of its stall and onto natural grass for as much of the day as possible for both its physical and mental health!

Straw

Straw is another bedding alternative. It is often used in the stalls of foaling mares, since fine sawdust will stick to the wet newborn foal. Many horses will eat straw, but usually they only try a few bites before they decide it is not very palatable.

Alternative Options

Many other types of bedding, from chopped corn husks to recycled newspaper have come on the market. Some materials are synthetic. Some may be more available in some parts of the country than others, but none seem to have caught on as much as the old standbys of sawdust or shavings. If you are unsure about what's best to purchase in your area, ask your veterinarian or a knowledgeable horse person for a recommendation.

Fencing

There is a rule of thumb that recommends never bringing home farm animals until you have your fences up. Safe, sturdy fencing is critical. For horses, electric fencing is often best, but you will probably find that you end up with a mix of fencing.

Electric Fencing

Electric fencing is probably the most commonly used for horses in the backyard setup. It is inexpensive, easy to install, and easy to move and reconfigure. If your horse has never been housed in electric fencing before, it is important to teach him about it. Usually, it is necessary for the horse to experience being zapped for him to get the idea that he needs to stay away from it. This may seem mean, but in order for electric fencing to be effective, the horse needs to know the wire means business. If horses have been fully introduced to electric fencing, you can generally feel comfortable with them behind it for the rest of their lives.

Wire Fencing

Several different kinds of fence wire can be electrified: barbed wire, twisted wire, flat tape, smooth wire, and high tensile wire. Forget about barbed wire for horses. Horses can get badly torn up when they get tangled in barbed wire, and it's just not worth it. Similarly, high tensile wire is so strong that it can literally saw through bone if a horse gets tangled up in it. Each type of fencing has its advantages and disadvantages to consider. Whatever you choose, it needs to be strong and highly visible to help deter horses from running through it.

Board Fencing

White board fencing of the type that goes on for miles and miles in Kentucky racehorse country is beautiful, but painting and maintaining it is a high-maintenance chore. It is, however, one of the safest types of fencing available for horses, and that's why you see so much of it in Kentucky, where very expensive and valuable racehorses roam. Even board fencing that's left natural is expensive and time consuming to replace when the horses chew on it or kick it, which they will. People who use board fencing often add electric wire across the inside top to keep the horses from chewing or rubbing against it, so it becomes double fencing.

Vinyl

Vinyl fencing that resembles regular boards comes in two-, three-, and four-rail designs and averages around $4 to $5 per linear foot with posts included. Companies often offer lifetime guarantees against breakage. This kind of fencing is very durable and safe. It is advertised as a low-maintenance product and easy to install, but the initial outlay is considerably more than other kinds of fencing.

Metal Panels

For small corrals, metal pipe panels that link together with pins can be convenient. The configuration can easily be changed and divided in new ways for different situations. Look for panels that are made for horses. There are some stock panels that have a vertical brace made of flat metal that can really cut up a horse's leg if it gets caught in the panel. Pipe panels suitable for horses usually come in eight-, ten-, or twelve-foot lengths and are typically five feet high.

Food, Water, and Equipment Storage

Shelter and fencing are crucial for your horse, but it doesn't end there. You must have a safe, secure place to store a supply of your horse's food. Your horse also needs fresh, clean water at all times. Finally, the equipment you use for riding your horse and keeping her stall clean must be stored properly.

Feed and Hay

Store your horse's feed in a place that is not easily accessible to the horse if she happens to get loose. Grain takes up little space—a covered garbage can in the corner of the garage can work just fine, with perhaps a shelf next to it for a container of supplements, a scoop, or other paraphernalia.

FACT

Don't forget to think about manure management before your horse walks onto the property. Your horse will start generating it immediately, and the supply will be constant. Some communities have strict environmental regulations about manure disposal. Check out any regulations your area might have before the manure production begins.

Hay also needs good storage space, free from dust and dampness, and definitely not open to the weather. Count on storing at least a one- or two-week supply of five or ten bales at a time. Most barns store hay in the loft. Because of hay's combustible nature, however, it is preferable to store it in a separate building from where horses are housed. Hay that has not been properly cured can spontaneously combust after prolonged storage, so it is important to inspect the hay you buy and make sure it is not green, damp, or moldy.

Water

Your horse needs access to fresh water day in and day out every season of the year. In warmer weather, this is a piece of cake—just hitch up the right length of hose and fill a large container such as a muck bucket or livestock trough once or twice a day depending on how many horses you have and their sizes.

If you live in an area that gets below freezing in the winter, getting fresh, unfrozen water to your horse can be a chore for the entire season. If you have electricity in your barn, there are many bucket heating options available on the market. However, if you have only one horse, the expense and potential fire hazard of these heaters may not be worthwhile. It may be simpler to just check the bucket or trough throughout the day to make sure it hasn't frozen over. If it has, break up the ice so the horse can drink.

Before you bring a horse home, think about where you are going to get water from, and make it as easy for yourself as possible. It is important to keep fresh water in front of your horse all winter to avoid serious problems such as colic.

Tack/Equipment Storage

You will have some storage needs for your tack and other equipment. If you have a horse trailer with a tack area in it, you can simply leave your saddle, bridle, brushes, and other materials there where they are always handy. If you have an existing building, consider where you could carve out some space to keep your tack. Be sure it is accessible to the area where you will tack up your horse—you don't want to have to carry your saddle 100 yards every time you ride, or stand in the rain or cold wind next to your garden shed to tack up.

The Law

It's true, if for no other reason than their sheer size and weight, that horses are inherently dangerous. Getting hurt—stepped on, kicked, bucked off—is always possible when you handle and ride horses on a regular basis. As a horse owner, you are liable for any personal injury or property damage your horse may cause to someone else.

Liability Insurance

To protect yourself, you should consider purchasing equine liability insurance. Many people who keep their horses on their own property assume that their homeowner's insurance will cover them in such situations, but this may not always be the case. Check it out ahead of time to be sure you're covered.

If you allow neighborhood kids to come around your horse, establish some ground rules—no hand feeding and no visiting when you aren't home—and have their parents sign release forms. It's generally not a good idea to let others ride your horse, especially people who have no knowledge or experience with horses.

Occasionally, you may need to construct a liability release form of your own. For example, if you own property with lots of riding trails, friends may ask to come ride their own horses on your land. If you allow them to, you would be wise to ask them to sign a release, freeing you from any liability should they have an accident on your property. It can be uncomfortable asking a friend to sign a release form, but any real friend is going to understand your reasoning and should be willing to sign it.

Equine Limited Liability Acts

Most states have equine limited liability laws specifically designed to help horse professionals, from instructors to trainers, conduct their businesses without fear of frivolous lawsuits. The laws vary from state to state and do not take the place of responsible and professional actions or good insurance. They also do not allow horse owners and equine professionals to be negligent. If you choose to take riding lessons, you accept the fact that you may fall off or otherwise be injured while handling and riding a horse.

But if an instructor puts a beginner on a three-year-old colt for her first lesson, the instructor is acting negligently.

The website for the American Association for Horsemanship Safety has a list of the states with a limited liability law and a link to each one (accessible through *http://asci.uvm.edu/equine/law*). Find out how horses are viewed legally in your state and become active in your state horse organization to help keep the horse industry viable.

Loose Horses

Legal issues commonly arise in the area of loose horses, especially if they are involved in traffic accidents. Don't dwell on the worst-case scenarios, but do understand some level of the law as it pertains to horses. While bad things happen even under the best of circumstances, you are responsible for keeping your horses in an appropriate setup. If you feel you can't do that, perhaps boarding your horse until you get your place properly set up is the thing to do.

CHAPTER 7

Nutrition

Feeding the backyard horse can be a delicate and demanding task. The horse's digestive system is an amazing yet poorly constructed vehicle for processing the amounts of food it needs. Although it may sound simple when you hear that grass, grain, hay, and water can provide the essentials of a horse's diet—energy, protein, carbohydrates, fatty acids, minerals, and vitamins—there's a lot more to know about what's good and what's not good for your horse.

First, There Is Water

Clean water provided in clean containers day and night, spring, summer, fall, and winter is critical to the health and well-being of your horse. Without it, food cannot make its journey through the system, nutrients cannot be transported to and through the bloodstream, body temperature cannot be regulated, and waste and toxins cannot be eliminated. Without a steady supply of water, horses risk colic from food sitting in their digestive tract and fermenting or packing up and preventing the passage of manure.

How Much Water?

The average horse weighing approximately 1,000 pounds drinks about ten gallons of water per day. That amount increases if the horse works more than an hour or so a day. Also, if temperatures are extreme in either direction, hot or cold, the horse will require more water to replenish lost fluids and keep his interior temperature constant.

As a rule of thumb, a horse needs one gallon of water per 100 pounds of weight each day. Using this ratio, an average 1,000-pound horse will drink approximately ten gallons of water each day. This amount varies widely, of course, and depends on many factors, especially how much exercise the horse gets.

Keep Those Buckets Clean

Clean your water buckets and troughs regularly. If the buckets sit where they are exposed to the sun, algae and scum form quickly. Make bucket cleaning an easy task so that you won't mind doing it. Find your favorite bucket and water tub cleaning tool—a rag, a cookware sponge, a brush made just for bucket washing, a toilet bowl brush, and so on—and keep it handy (but out of reach of the horses). Once a week or so, round up all the five-gallon buckets, including feed buckets, give them a good washing, and let them dry in the bacteria-killing sunshine.

Hay: The Basics

Aside from grass, hay (which is dried grass) is the horse's next most important foodstuff. The digestion of hay keeps the horse warm in winter, from the inside out, and provides the roughage to keep the digestive process moving along. Hay is complicated, especially during severe droughts, when hay shortages are common. Feeding hay involves finding a source, determining what type of hay you want, figuring out how much to buy, having a dry place with adequate ventilation to store it, and making sure the supply you get is good quality and free of mold. If you board your horse, of course, you don't need to worry about most of these details. That's part of what you pay for.

What Makes Good Hay

"Making hay" is not a matter of hacking down a field and scooping it up into bales—there is a fine art to timing the cutting and curing of it, and weather is a constant variable. Hay should be cut at the optimum growth period—late enough that it has leafed out and absorbed the maximum amount of nutrients but early enough that it doesn't go to seed.

After cutting, hay must stay on the ground long enough to "cure" (around three days), but the longer it sits in the field, the more the sun bleaches nutrients out of it. If hay gets rained on after it has been cut, precious nutrients are leached out. The hay will have to lay on the field longer to dry out again, and the farmer may drive around and fluff it up to prevent it from molding underneath.

ALERT!

Never lay a plastic tarp over your hay to protect it from rain and roof leaks. While the hay is curing, the plastic tarp will prevent moisture from escaping, and your hay will spoil.

Too much moisture in hay causes mold and mildew, which can be a source of chronic respiratory damage to your horse. It also presents a serious fire hazard. If hay is baled before its moisture content has lowered enough, the high moisture level in the tightly packed bale builds up heat, which can result in spontaneous combustion. Many a barn has burned to the ground from hot hay. You must be able to trust your suppliers and their haymaking abilities. Hay that gets wet after it is baled is not as likely to heat up, but it is definitely going to mold and spoil.

Hay Quality

If you buy a few bales here and there from any number of different sources, it will not be effective to have your hay supply tested. But if you get your full year's supply of hay from one source, testing your hay for nutrient content can give you the basis on which to feed the right amounts of grain and supplements to your horse to balance the nutrition your horse is getting from his hay. Most grain stores have access to the sales representative of the particular kind of grain you buy, and they can often help you with testing your hay so that you can get a feeding plan for your horse.

Some traits of good quality hay include the following:

- **Leafy:** The leaf contains the nutrition, and by digesting leafy hay, the horse generates the heat she needs to keep warm in winter.
- **Green:** Hay fades as it ages; don't feed last year's crop too long into the new haying season. Even if the edges of the bale have faded from being exposed to light, the inside should still be green.
- **A good smell:** Although different grasses smell differently, good hay should basically smell sweet, fresh, and pleasing to your nose. If a bale smells musty when you open it, set it aside to use in the garden for mulch.
- **Dust free:** Some dust on the outside of the bale is almost inevitable, but the hay should absolutely not be dusty inside. Likewise, hay should be free from mold, dust, and mildew. White mold can be commonly seen in hay; when it dries, it is simply white dust. Again, set it aside for garden mulch.

Different Kinds of Hay

There are two basic kinds of hay that are commonly used with horses: grass and legume.

Grass Hay

Most backyard horses that are being used for recreational riding will do best on grass hay. It can be fed in reasonable quantities without the consequences of overeating that rich legume hay such as alfalfa can cause. Timothy, brome, orchard grass, wheatgrass, bluegrass, and fescue are different kinds of grasses that are used in mixed grass hay. Some horses do have a preference, and there are some grasses that some horses don't like. You may want to keep track of which hay your horse ate voraciously and which he picked at and wasted.

Legume Hay

Alfalfa and clover are legumes. The resulting hay contains more protein, essential amino acids, calcium, phosphorus, and beta-carotene than grass hays do. High performance horses do very well on alfalfa and need the extra energy it provides. Alfalfa may, however, provide a little too much energy for backyard horses that are ridden recreationally only a couple of times a week. Sometimes hay is part legume and part grass, which is a good compromise.

QUESTION?

What are amino acids?
Amino acids are the group of organic compounds that form the structure of proteins. Hay from alfalfa and clover is rich in amino acids and gives horses extra energy.

Hay Feeding Plan

Feeding your horse smaller more frequent meals is better for her digestion than feeding her two large meals a day. However, horse owners usually need to work to support their horse habit, so your horse is probably on the nine-to-five feeding schedule, where she gets fed half her meal in the morning before you go to work and half in the evening when you get home. While this is not ideal for the digestive function of the horse, thousands of horses survive just fine on this kind of schedule. Perhaps a neighbor would be willing to throw your horse a flake of hay in the middle of the day, or a responsible neighborhood kid would love to do it when he gets home from school. The size of a flake of hay can vary almost from bale to bale, but the average-sized horse should be fed around 2.5 percent of its body weight each day, with at least half of that in the form of hay. A 1,000 pound horse requires roughly twelve to fifteen pounds of hay per day.

With Grazing

Perhaps your horse is lucky enough to have some pasture to graze in during the day while you are gone. If the pasture quantity is small or the quality is unknown, you should feed your horse hay, too. The pasture can still provide good entertainment. Your horse can feel more natural as she wanders around the field, even if she can't get her full nutrition out of the pasture. However, you will want to be careful that your horse doesn't become overweight eating grass of little nutritional value.

If the pasture is lush and large, you may not need to feed your horse hay during the growing season, or you may only need to give your horse one hay feeding each day. Overeating of forage often produces a rounded belly in horses, fondly referred to as a "hay belly."

Horses put on pasture for the first time or at the beginning of the grass-growing season need to be introduced to it gradually, perhaps for an hour the first day and an additional hour per day over the course of a week. Horses can founder and get very sick from overeating rich pasture before their stomach bacteria is adjusted to this new item.

If your horse stays out on good pasture most of the time and appears to be getting fat, you may need to fit him with a grazing muzzle to restrict his intake, especially in spring when the grass is most lush. These devices attach to the horse's halter and have an opening that allows the horse to drink water but will not allow him to bite off as much grass as he normally would. Another alternative is to limit the number of hours he spends in the pasture.

FACT

A horse can deplete a pasture very quickly, eating the grass right down to the dirt and never giving it enough time to grow again. A rule of thumb for grazing pasture is an acre per horse. If you have room, rotate your pastures to allow the grass to recover.

Without Grazing

If your horse spends the day in an area larger than her stall that provides turnout but no grazing, spread two or three flakes of hay in different places so that she can wander a little to eat her hay, even if it is only a few feet. During the winter months in cold climates, you should give your horse enough hay to keep her warm, but do not allow her to become overweight by overfeeding her during her least active time. You will need to observe your horse's body condition carefully and adjust your feeding amounts accordingly, always making any changes gradually.

Finding a Supplier

Owning a horse puts you in touch with the agricultural community, as finding and keeping a good hay supply introduces you to local farmers. Ask other local backyard horse owners where they get their hay; farmers like good customers who pass their names along. On the other hand, if it was a bad hay year and supplies are low, horse owners can be reluctant to pass along their source, for fear of running out of their supply.

Advertisements for hay will have some terms and phrases that tell you something about the hay:

- **First cut:** The first cutting of the year includes any growth that has wintered over.
- **Second cut:** The second cutting is more nutritious, includes shorter and softer grass, and is more expensive because it takes more of it to make a bale.
- **Alfalfa mix hay:** This often refers to a mix of grass hay that contains some alfalfa.
- **Horse hay:** Farmers will advertise hay as "horse hay," which typically means it is higher quality than the hay that people will buy for other livestock.
- **Mulch hay:** Hay that has gone bad for whatever reason is advertised as mulch hay.

- • **Never been rained on:** This statement typically refers not to hay bales getting wet but to hay that was not rained on while on the ground drying, waiting to be baled.

The Grain Store

The grain store is one place to ask about local hay farmers, and most grain stores usually carry baled hay. It is often high-quality hay, but their supply can be spotty, and it is probably going to be one of the most expensive ways to buy hay. If you have only one horse, then this may be a perfect source for you—you can get hay, shavings, feed, supplements, and any other supplies all in one monthly or twice-monthly shopping trip, and the additional cost is made up in convenience.

The Farmer's Barn

Farmers who have hay fields almost always end up with excess hay in the barn that they sell off over the course of the year. This method is usually a little cheaper per bale than the grain store. But the more the farmer has to handle the hay, the more expensive it gets per bale. When trying a new source, ask if you can take a look at the hay and try just a few bales to determine the overall quality.

FACT

It's important to make feed changes gradually, over a period of a few days. Make sure to have a few bales left from last year's supply when the new supply comes. If you don't have any older hay left to mix in with the new, feed your horse the new hay more frequently in smaller quantities for the first few days.

From the Field

Aside from having your own hayfield and cutting it yourself, the least expensive way to get hay is from a farmer's field during cutting season. Again, if you have one horse, this can be an easy method—you get on the local hay farmer's list and she calls you the morning she is planning to bale. A couple of round-trips with a pickup truck and you have your supply.

The hard part is that you need to be around when the call comes in. The farmer will probably be able to give you some sense of when cutting time is getting close, so it's not all a waiting game. Get yourself on the list of a few suppliers so if you miss one cutting you'll have another to fall back on.

Hay is typically baled in mid- to late afternoon, and you will need to be ready to pick it up. The farmer will direct you to the field. You can drive around and pick up the bales lying in the field as they come off the baler. Ideally, you'll have three other people to help you—one to drive the truck, one or two people to walk along the rows on either side of the truck and toss bales onto the back of the truck, and one in the back of the truck to stack the bales.

When you transport hay on the road, bring a tarp and plenty of rope. Take time to tie the hay down well. Don't underestimate how much hay bales weigh—a tiny rope with a flimsy knot won't hold a pitching load of hay. You don't want to be responsible for causing an accident by spilling hay all over the road.

Delivery

You can have hay delivered during the cutting season for an extra charge. Some sellers offer to load it into your barn, too, but again it will cost you more for the workers' time. Some people have hay delivered monthly to their barn, which sounds like a nice arrangement; however, you are unlikely to find a supplier who will do this for the amount needed for only one or two horses.

Grain

In the wild, horses live only on roughage, and they innately know how to get the nutrients they need by seeking out specific herbs and grasses—in other words, horses do not need grain to thrive. In the domesticated life of the horse, grain is more accurately a supplement, making up for what dry forage cannot provide in nutrition. Except for the horse that cannot eat hay for health reasons, such as allergy or heaves, hay should be the main source of nutrition for the horse.

However, horses typically cannot eat enough dry, bulky hay in the course of a day to get the nutrition they need if the hay is of mediocre quality or if the horse has a heavy workload. This is where grain steps in to fill in the nutritional and energy gaps. In some areas of the country, horses are fed oats, corn, and mixes of whole grains. Most backyard horse owners rely on commercially manufactured horse feeds that have been designed to balance the nutrient intake when added to a recommended amount of hay.

Mixed Grain

Grain mixes can come with or without molasses (the addition of molasses gives the grain the designation of "sweet feed"). Manufacturers usually have many different mixes in their line of premixed grain. The major difference is often in the percentage of protein. Some are actually "complete" feeds that, if forage is not available, could be fed as the horse's entire ration if given in sufficient quantities.

What Kind of Grain?

You should pick a brand of grain that is easily accessible. When you buy your horse, find out what he is eating. If he seems to be doing well with it and maintaining good body condition, you may as well stick to it. If you have other horses or if you cannot find the brand he was eating through your nearby grain store, you can switch to a different brand. You will probably find a similar mix in all brands. Always change gradually over the course of a week, mixing the new brand with the old brand, and slowly increasing the amount of the new until you've made a complete switch.

Complete Feeds

Most grain manufacturers offer a feed that contains some roughage and can be fed as a complete feed without hay if it is fed in sufficient quantities. Complete feeds often come in pelleted or extruded form, but they also can come as loose mixes.

A horse that relies on complete feeds as her entire ration with no hay may be more prone to exhibit unwanted behaviors, such as chewing wood. This is thought to result from the frustration caused by an innate need to eat roughage and simply keep busy by grazing. After all, horses evolved to be grazing herd animals.

When a Horse Isn't Thriving

If you don't think your horse is thriving on a particular feed, talk with your veterinarian and your feed supplier. They can help you make some new decisions about grain choices and help you determine whether your horse needs a supplement. In making recommendations, they will consider his breed, size, age, living arrangement, and amount of use.

A Checklist

Of course, with your veterinarian, you should rule out certain diseases and illnesses that can contribute to poor digestion. Consider the following:

- **Are your horse's teeth in good shape?** Have an equine dentist inspect and file her teeth if necessary. Sharp points develop from uneven wear, making it difficult to chew grain and causing considerable amounts of grain to drop on the ground instead of being ingested by the horse.
- **If your horse is eating in a group, is he getting his full ration,** or is another horse eating part of his meal?

Weight Control

Being overweight or underweight can pose health problems for a horse, although a slightly underweight horse is probably a little better off than an overweight horse. However, it takes very little—illness, overwork, stress—for the slightly underweight individual to become too thin.

ALERT!

Many plants and flowers are poisonous to horses, including rhododendron, milkweed, foxglove, laurel, yew, nightshade, bracken fern, ragwort, buttercup, lily of the valley, narcissus, and larkspur. If you see a sudden onset of diarrhea, colic, extensive salivation, staggering, or muscle weakness, or if the horse collapses, suspect poisoning and call your vet immediately.

Overweight individuals tire easily, and obese broodmares can have breeding difficulties. Some horses, like people, easily gain weight and need to be carefully monitored for food intake. They may need to be taken off pasture, placed on restricted turnout, or fitted with a grazing muzzle and given a more controlled feeding program. They will probably be more inert, so the owner will have to take responsibility for getting the individual the exercise it needs to maintain a good weight. Keep close tabs on your horse's weight, and work with your health care team to address any weight issues.

Feeding Differences

The nutritional needs of a growing horse compared to an adult horse that gets light work are very different. Horses need to be fed according to age and use. All grain manufacturers give recommendations on the bag or in supplemental literature. You can also talk directly with the feed sales representative.

Mature, Idle

"Mature" refers to the horse that is beyond growing age, which varies from breed to breed but is usually around four years old. The idle horse is one that is ridden only a couple hours per week and spends the rest of his time hanging out with pals in the corral or field. This horse does not need to be stuffed full of food. Often, he can exist on high-quality hay alone; however, always have the hay tested to be sure it contains all the nutrients a horse needs. If it does not, you will need to include grain in his feeding program.

Mature, Light Work

An adult horse of five years or older that is ridden three to five hours per week most likely will need some supplemental grain to meet her nutritional needs. Again, you need to be sure of the quality of your hay and consider your horse's individual characteristics to feed her enough but not too much.

Mature, Medium Work

The horse that is ridden five or six days out of seven days a week will definitely need to have his hay supplemented with a grain ration to get the proper amount of nutrients.

Mature, Heavy Work

The horse under heavy work, typically a performance horse ridden a few hours every day, will need to be fed hay, grain, and probably supplements. Her feeding program should be carefully constructed and constantly re-evaluated. The type and amount of feed the horse gets will depend on the type of work—jumping, dressage, eventing, trail riding—that the horse does.

Broodmares

The broodmare should be fed according to her age and activity level except during two critical periods: in the last three months of pregnancy, when the fetus is under rapid growth, and while nursing a foal. During the last three months of pregnancy, her need for protein, calcium, and phosphorus increases dramatically and these will probably need to be given to her as a supplement rather than simply by increasing overall grain ration. Continue the same sort of regimen while the mare is lactating, but pay particular attention to the mare's decrease in lactation. As the foal begins to eat grain and hay more seriously (in two to three months) and starts to wean, begin to decrease the mare's feed accordingly.

The Growing Horse

Nursing foals, weanlings, and yearlings all need access to high-quality hay. They often need to be fed grain to supplement hay, and they may need additional supplements beyond that. And like all horses, these youngsters will need twenty-four-hour access to fresh water and mineralized salt.

Supplements

Look in any equine supply catalog or tack shop, and the array of supplements you will find can be mind-boggling. The catalog copy sounds appealing, and you can easily go a little overboard simply by your desire to provide the best for your horse. You can also drain your bank account paying for these supplements and add a host of complications to feeding time by having to pull from a smorgasbord of supplement buckets. Supplements may not be necessary, and they may not necessarily be good for your horse either. Remember, too much of a nutrient can be just as detrimental as too little.

As with all other health and nutrition concerns, consult your veterinarian to determine what, if anything, your horse might need for supplements.

Regional Nutrient Deficiencies

Sometimes a region has a known deficiency in a certain nutrient. For example, in many areas of the Northeast selenium is known to be deficient. That is a good reason to supplement feed with that nutrient. The local extension agency or the U.S. Department of Agriculture can provide specifics about your area.

Salt Blocks

Salt and mineral blocks come in small bricklike sizes or large fifty-pound blocks. If you feed commercial grain, your horse will probably get all the appropriate trace minerals he needs, so you could choose to use plain white salt blocks. Hang one in every horse's stall and keep one in the paddock so that horses can always have free access to salt, which is a key mineral in their diet. Place the fifty-pound block on a pan that keeps the salt block off the ground. If at all possible, keep it under some sort of cover since it will deteriorate fast if it is rained on.

QUESTION?

What does esophageal choke mean?
This is a condition that is often caused when horses gulp down pelleted feeds too rapidly. To deter this, place a couple of stones or half a salt block in the feed bucket. Having to eat around them makes the horse slow down.

Multivitamins

According to Griffin and Gore's *Horse Owner's Veterinary Handbook*, all vitamins except A and E "are synthesized by bacteria in the horse's large intestine." Only A and E need to be supplied through the diet, so giving multivitamins to a healthy, properly fed horse is probably overkill.

Supplements for Older Horses

Most supplements directed at older horses are to relieve arthritis and joint pain and include a glucosamine/chondrotin mix for joint flexibility (with names like Glucomax, Flex-free, etc.). Some are digestive aids and include bacterial cultures, such as acidophilus, that are critical to digestion, since older horses often don't process their food as efficiently as younger horses do.

Hoof Growth Supplements

The horse's hoof is important. If the hoof is not growing properly, it probably wouldn't hurt to add a supplement to the horse's diet. However, as always, consult with your equine health care team, especially your veterinarian and farrier, to determine the need of supplementation of this kind. Hoof problems may also be caused by environmental factors, and it may be the bedding that needs to be altered, not the horse's nutrition.

Calcium and Phosphorus

Calcium and phosphorus are extremely important to the health of a horse. However, they also are dependent on each other, and their ratio is as important as their quantity. The perfect ratio is between 1:1 and 3:1 calcium to phosphorus, but should always consist of at least as much calcium as phosphorus. This can be an important issue if, for instance, you decide to add rice bran to your horse's diet. Rice bran is high in phosphorus and low in calcium, so a calcium supplement would be needed to maintain an appropriate ratio.

Coat Supplements

These are supplements intended to enhance coat shine and maintenance and are usually fortified with fatty acids as well as other vitamins and minerals.

Colic Preventatives

These supplements contain high-fiber ingredients, such as psyllium seed husks, that are a natural laxative needed to reduce the potential for colic in horses who consume sand and dirt while feeding from the ground or on short pasture. These preservatives are intended for prevention and are not to be used in the event of a colic episode, in which case you should promptly call a veterinarian.

CHAPTER 8

Grooming

Grooming your horse is good for both his physical and mental health. If you've never done it before, you'll find the activity also provides a good physical workout for you. Being brushed can be an enjoyable activity for your horse, like getting a massage and beauty treatment. Grooming also offers an opportunity to bond and build trust with your horse, to discover his ticklish spots and the places where he likes being petted and scratched the most.

Grooming and Riding

Before and after riding, it is necessary to brush the dirt and debris out of your horse's coat and pick out her feet. Picking out the feet removes any stones and debris packed in there that might cause discomfort or damage during the ride. Brushing the dirt off the horse's back removes any foreign debris that might contribute to rubbing and skin irritation under the saddle pad. Some people clean only where the saddle goes, but it is important to clean the dirt out of the rest of the horse's coat as well because the dirt will irritate the skin when the horse gets hot and sweaty from exercise. If your horse gets only a quickie brush job before your ride, you should follow up with a thorough cleaning afterward, to make sure she is free of irritating dirt and sweat before you put her up.

Cooling Out

Always cool out a horse after a ride by walking the last fifteen minutes. Don't let him eat or drink until his breathing returns to normal. If his chest feels hot and sweaty to the touch, walk him or let him stand until he cools down. If the air is chilly, cover him with a cooler.

In hot weather, hose off the sweat. Occasional bathing with an equine shampoo is okay, but not after every ride. Too frequent shampooing can strip the coat of essential oils and dry it out. After hosing, use a sweat scraper to remove the excess water from the coat, followed by a good toweling off.

FACT

Competition in the horse show world is stiff, and you will want to give your horse every little edge to stand out. Perfect grooming is just one more notch in your favor on the judge's card. Even if grooming isn't an official aspect of a particular class, it never hurts to have the judge look favorably upon your team.

If the temperature is too cool for hosing off your horse, at least wipe your horse down with towels in the sweaty areas, and wipe off any mud or wetness from snow, puddles, or wet roads. Use a clean towel to wipe the face and ears. These places will be especially itchy from sweat, and if you don't rub them off, the horse will rub against fence posts or any other available object that serves as a good scratching place. Take a few extra minutes to give the horse's back a gentle rubdown—your horse will definitely appreciate it. When the sweaty areas are dry, brush the coat out thoroughly.

Grooming Tools

First, set up a tote or tack box with the basic grooming tools you need to give your horse an average grooming. If you have more than one horse and want to keep their grooming tools separate, you can color-coordinate their individual totes and brushes.

Combs and Brushes

As you wield the brush and curry comb, check your horse for nicks, cuts, bites, skin problems, and other things you might not see or feel unless you get hands on and up close. While daily grooming is highly recommended, many people only do it before and after riding. However, your horse will really appreciate it if, on occasion, you retrieve her from the corral or pasture and just groom her, instead of always preparing her for work.

Curry Comb

Curry combs are typically made of stiff rubber or plastic, with a ring of pointed edges around the outside. They loosen the surface mud from your horse's coat. They come in round or oval shapes and are designed to be used in a gentle circular motion. Always begin your grooming routine with the curry comb, going over the horse's body to loosen the dirt. Then whisk away the loosened dirt with a body brush.

You can spend as much or as little as you want on horse brushes, as they come in all price ranges. But if you can afford it, buy good quality natural horsehair brushes from the start. Nice brushes make the task of grooming easier and much more pleasant for both you and the horse.

Body Brush

A body brush is made of somewhat stiff fibers designed to really get down to the skin and brush dirt to the surface. Be careful not to get a brush with bristles that are too stiff, as you may inadvertently cause your horse discomfort. After all, we're talking about an animal with skin sensitive enough to feel a fly land on its butt, so imagine how a really stiff brush feels! You certainly don't want your horse to learn to resent grooming out of discomfort. Instead, get a brush that's stiff but still flexible, and learn to use a flick of your wrist to get that loose dirt to the surface.

Finishing Brush

This type of brush is the last you'll use in your grooming routine. That's why it's called a finishing brush. It is very soft and used to brush away the last remnants of loosened dirt while leaving a polished shine to your horse's coat.

Face Brush

Brushes for the face are also very soft and come in different sizes. You will want a fairly small one to do the delicate areas around your horse's nose, eyes, and ears. Avoid using a brush with stiffer bristles on the face, as the skin here is quite thin and delicate.

Mane/Tail Brushes

Mane and tail hair grows slowly, so you should be careful to pull out as little as possible. If the mane or tail becomes knotted, use your fingers to loosen the knots before you run a brush through the hair. You can also buy a style of comb with teeth that rotate to help untangle knotted hairs without pulling them out.

Hoof Picks

Simple hoof picks come as steel picks with vinyl-coated handles of differing colors. Also common are hoof picks in a pocketknife style that folds in half and is handy to carry in your pocket out on the trail. One particularly handy variety has a stiff brush on the other side of the hoof pick. The brush allows you to brush mud and dirt off the horse's hoof before picking it up and to brush off the remnants of what you pick out of the hoof.

Pick out your horse's hooves both before and after riding. Doing so before you ride allows you to pick out anything that might bother the horse's feet on the ride and perhaps cause him to go lame. Cleaning feet after riding allows you to inspect for and remove any stones or pieces of sticks or anything else that the horse may have picked up and gotten stuck in his hoof while on the ride. You don't want to put him away in his stall or pasture to stand all night with a rock in his shoe.

Electric Clippers

If you plan to show your horse, you will need clippers. Even if you don't plan to show, clippers are nice to have on hand to remove the shaggy hairs around the face and fetlocks and give your horse a neat, trimmed look. Also, if your horse is amenable to clippers, they are more efficient to use than scissors for trimming a bridle path behind the horse's ears.

FACT

Buy clippers intended for horses, not dog grooming. Clippers need to be sturdy and suitable for a horse's coat and mane hair. Keep extra blades handy, since clipping coarse horsehair dulls them fast.

Most horses don't like the whirring sound of clippers, so get yours accustomed to the noise gradually. To do so, let your horse see and sniff them, check them out and feel them. Turn on the clippers and let the horse hear them from nearby. Talk quietly and reassuringly to the horse while the clippers whir. If the horse handles this well, she may be ready to feel them against the coat while they are on. At first, have your horse on a lead rope, not on crossties. You may even need an assistant to help hold the horse until she learns to stand still while being clipped. It also helps to use cordless clippers so that you can easily move around the horse and not worry about where the cord is.

Don't punish or reprimand the horse for moving away from the clippers at this stage. Simply take the clippers away when the horse stops moving to let him know that standing still is what you want.

You may choose to clip the winter coat on a performance horse to help him get less heated during winter workouts. A clipped coat is also easier to cool and dry out after a ride, which is why many people clip. Just remember that you're clipping off the horse's primary protection against the elements, so you may need to compensate for that lack by blanketing him for the rest of the season.

If it is too cold to bathe a horse, she probably needs a heavy blanket if she is clipped. A full-body clip in the northern climates in winter means heavy blanketing, indoors and out. Watch for sore and chafed areas where the blanket rubs the horse. Check the horse several times throughout the day to make sure the blanket isn't coming loose and posing a danger of entanglement.

Types of Clips

The level of clipping you choose depends on how hard and how often your horse will work in the winter, how cold the winters are in your area, how much blanketing you want to do, and how much you want your horse to go outside in the winter.

- **Trace clip:** Just the areas on the lower part of the body from the middle of the side to the top of the legs are clipped.
- **Blanket clip:** A blanketlike area of unclipped hair is left on the horse's back from the withers to the croup.
- **Hunter clip:** The entire body is clipped except an outline of the saddle. (Set the saddle or saddle pad on the horse's back while clipping to serve as a template.)

Shedding Blades

If your horse grows a nice winter coat, you'll need a shedding blade in spring when that coat starts to shed. The traditional shedding blade comes as a long, thin metal blade with a leather handle on either end that can be folded and bent to form a loop. The blade is smooth on one edge and has small teeth on the other to get that loose hair out. A flat rubber mitten with little bumps on both sides helps lift mud and loose hair, and you can really scrub at the mud without hurting your horse.

Towels, Wipes, and Miscellaneous Items

Always have plenty of clean towels and washcloths around the barn. They are useful for any number of things, from grooming to first aid to cleaning tack. A roll of paper towels and moisturized hand wipes also come in handy.

Another handy item is a grooming apron, especially at horse shows. The apron protects your clothing from getting covered in horsehair, dust, and mud. One with pockets in front holds your brushes, hoof pick, or braiding equipment.

Vacuums and Blow Dryers

Yes, you can buy special vacuum cleaners for horses that suck mud, dirt, and shedding hair off the horse. You can also use the reverse end of the vacuum hose or a regular hair dryer to blow-dry the horse when he is wet. Of course, you have to get the horse accustomed to the sound and feel of these mechanical tools, just as you do with electric clippers. If you show your horse or have several horses to groom, these can be time-savers. Otherwise, elbow grease and good brushes do the trick just as well.

Bathing Items

Horses shouldn't be shampooed too often, although for the show ring, it's almost inevitable that they will be bathed regularly. Choose a product that's labeled and intended for use on horses. Some equine shampoos are moisturizing or conditioning, intended to make your horse's coat shine. Some are specifically antifungal. Others include fly-repellant products such as citronella. Shampoos also exist especially to clean and brighten gray and white horse coats. Rubber mitt-style brushes are great for shampooing. The rubber bumps give the coat a good scrubbing without harming the horse's sensitive skin.

Braiding Kit

The turnout tradition for many horse show classes requires you to braid your horse's mane in a certain style. The braiding style depends on the equitation discipline. In general, the more braids you put in a mane, the longer the neck appears to be. Just a few thick braids make the neck appear shorter and thicker. Mane braids can be left hanging, tucked up into themselves in neat little bobs, or looped into the next braid in chainlike links. Braided manes are often, but not always, accompanied by braided tails, which can be left in one thick long braid or woven into tight, smaller braids.

Braiding kits, available at most tack shops, typically include rubber bands, a three-pronged fork that splits the hair into three even sections for easier braiding, and instructions. Making nice-looking braids takes a lot of practice, so don't wait until the night before a show to try your hand at it the first time and expect good results.

QUESTION?

What does hogging mean?
Hogging, also known as roaching, refers to a mane that has been completely shaved. Some gaited horses are shown with roached manes in certain horse show classes to accentuate the neck and topline.

Sweat Scrapers

As the name implies, the sweat scraper scrapes excess sweat and moisture from the horse's coat after a ride or a bath so the hair can dry out faster. They come in numerous styles in plastic or aluminum.

Grooming Products

Many products exist to make grooming a little easier. Some just smell nice and make the horse look more polished. Others have practical or specialized purposes, such as detangling manes or making braiding easier.

Mane/Tail Detanglers

Detanglers do their job well, and they smell great, too. They come in spray or gel form. Be aware that some of these products are slippery, so be careful not to get any on the saddle area. If you get it on your hands, you will find it difficult to keep reins from slipping through your fingers without wearing gloves.

FACT

One product that has long been on the market for horses—Straight Arrow's Mane and Tail shampoo and conditioner—became so popular with horse people that they began to use it on their own hair. The company caught on to the product's secondary use and got FDA approval to market the shampoo and the conditioner to humans. Now it can be found on drugstore shelves.

Coat Gloss

Coat gloss makes your horse's coat shine. It is a topical product for coat enhancement only and doesn't provide any deep-seated benefit for coat health or condition.

Hoof Dressings and Conditioners

Horses in the show ring have their toenails polished with special hoof dressings. Black has always been available, but now you can choose copper, silver, and many other colors, depending on what the class traditions allow. Such dressings are just for looks and can dry out the hooves, so don't use them excessively.

Hoof conditioners, on the other hand, are typically used two or three times a week as part of regular grooming. They help restore or maintain the natural moisture content in your horse's hooves so that the walls are more resistant to cracking. Always read product labels to determine what the product is designed to do and how it is supposed to be applied.

Grooming How-To's

Everyone develops their own style and rhythm to grooming, but the main thing is to work with the lie of the hair, not against it. Pay attention to your horse's body language for signs of pleasure, pain, or annoyance during the process. He'll tell you what he likes or doesn't like simply by the way he reacts.

Body

To give your horse's coat a thorough grooming, follow these steps:

1. Begin with a curry comb of your choosing and brush up loose hair and underlying dirt. If the horse is shedding, use a shedding blade first and get as much loose hair as possible out before you begin brushing. Use these tools only on the horse's main body, not in areas where bones stick out, such as in the flank or shoulder area, and not on the legs and face.
2. Use your stiffest body brush to brush out all the loose dirt and hair the curry brought to the surface. Use this brush to get the mud off the horse's legs. Don't forget to brush under the mane. Brush gently but firmly, using a flicking motion as the brush leaves the horse's body to help lift up the deeply embedded dirt.
3. Use the soft finishing brush to brush out any remaining hair and dirt and to give your horse's coat a nice shine.
4. Finish by rubbing down your horse's coat with a clean, soft towel.

As you groom your horse, inspect for cuts, parasites, or other skin problems. Be aware of any tenderness she may exhibit as you touch her. While picking out hooves, sniff for foul odors (indicative of thrush) and look for any bruises or sensitivity in that area, especially if you picked out a stone or stick that was caught in her foot.

Hooves

Some horses stand quietly and pick up their feet for you for cleaning. They aren't born knowing how to do this; it requires some careful and consistent training. Other horses can be quite nasty about having their feet touched and will kick. Regardless of your horse's typical behavior, you should always exercise extra caution when doing anything around a horse's feet. A kick from a horse can kill or seriously injure you.

The proper way to pick up a horse's foot is to stand beside him, starting on the left and facing toward the rear. Lean your weight against his shoulder to make him shift his weight to the other side. As you bend over, run your hand down his leg and gently squeeze the back of his leg to encourage him to lift it. When he does so, cradle the hoof in your hand and clean it out with a hoof pick, working from heel to toe.

Gently dig the packed dirt, manure, and bedding out of the grooves (bars) around the triangular-shaped protrusion known as the frog. If your horse is barefoot (without horseshoes), the rest of the dirt will pop right out. If your horse has shoes on, remove other packed dirt that has stuck to the inside of the shoe, and inspect the shoes for looseness and wear.

FACT

Avoid shaving your horse's whiskers. They are tactile instruments. However, if you're going to show, you will need to do this. You can use small electric clippers designed for delicate areas. Some people use disposable human razors, especially for touch-ups. Don't shave the inside of her ears. Ear hair keeps out dirt, water, and insects. If her ear hair is long and unruly, you can tidy it up with a small pair of scissors.

In winter, digging frozen snow out of your horse's hoof can require a little muscle. To avoid the problems of ice adhering to metal horseshoes, many people have their farrier pull off the horse's shoes for wintertime, when they ride less often.

Grooming for Show

The manner in which you turn out a horse for a show varies widely from one discipline to another. For example, some horses are shown with long, flowing manes, while others are shown with short, roached, or braided manes. You can find all the information you need about show appointments and requirements by asking your riding coach and by reading the *U.S. Equestrian Rule Book*, published annually by the U.S. Equestrian Federation (USEF). USEF is the national governing body that regulates horse competitions in the United States. At one time, this organization was called the American Horse Shows Association. The website is *www.usef.org*.

Giving a Horse a Bath

Horses live outside, so being dirty is natural to them. But if you're going to show your horse, you want him to look his best to catch the judge's eye. Grooming a horse for show involves some extra effort, including a bath, that you wouldn't normally put in during your daily grooming sessions.

When bathing your horse for the first time, don't just turn the hose on him. As with anything new to a horse, take the time to introduce it to him slowly. Turn the water on just a bit and begin by spraying the ground near him. Spray the water on his feet and lower legs and let him know the noisy thing isn't going to hurt him. Keep working up the body and stay at each level until he accepts it. It may take a few sessions, but if you introduce the hose gradually and calmly, he will come to enjoy bath time. If your horse refuses to tolerate spray from a hose, use buckets of warm water instead.

If you board, most large facilities will have a wash rack equipped for the purpose. If heated water is available in the wash area, so much the better. Wet the horse's coat first, then squeeze a thin line of shampoo the length of the body and give him a little shampoo massage. Do one side at a time, including the legs, and rinse it thoroughly. Leaving shampoo behind to dry in your horse's coat is worse than never bathing him at all because it will eventually cause itching and possibly even hair loss in spots where the horse rubs the itch.

If the outside air temperature is cool, cover a wet or sweaty horse with a cooler before walking him out to dry. Coolers are made of a special fabric that helps wick away the moisture. The cover also keeps cool drafts off the horse's damp back.

Rinse until the water runs off clear, not foamy white. Few horses are amenable to being sprayed in the face with a water hose. When you wash the horse's face, use warm water (no soap), a damp washcloth or sponge, and some gentle elbow grease. Take care not to get water down in a horse's ears. Once the horse is thoroughly rinsed, use the sweat scraper on his upper body to scrape off the excess water. Then rub the entire horse down with clean, dry towels.

It will probably take about thirty to forty-five minutes for the coat to dry, so plan enough time for this step. This isn't a problem on a hot summer day if you can turn the horse out in the warm sunshine to dry. But in chilly weather, you must keep a damp horse out of cool drafts and make sure he is dry before turning him outside.

Of course, if you've just bathed and groomed your horse for a show the next day, keep him in a clean stall overnight. If you turn him out in his pasture, the first thing he's likely to do is to get down in the dirt and roll. Bed down the stall with fresh shavings and blanket him with a light blanket if the weather warrants one.

Pulling Manes

If the horse show classes you compete in call for your horse's mane to be braided or kept short and trim, you'll need to start pulling the mane long before the show date to get it in presentable shape. Pulling the mane is exactly what it sounds like. You work on a small section of mane at a time over a period of many days until you've covered the entire length of the mane. Comb each section of hair straight down with a metal mane comb, then backcomb or push up the majority of hairs, as if teasing it. This leaves behind a few strands of the longest hairs underneath, which you wrap around the comb and yank out straight down. It doesn't hurt the horse as long as you pull only a few hairs at a time over a period of time. Obviously, this isn't a chore you can wait until the last minute to do.

Why not just use scissors? Cutting the mane with scissors gives it a chopped up, artificial look with a thickened edge, kind of like what a kid's crop looks like when you set a bowl on his head and trim the hair around the rim. Pulling the mane shortens and thins it at the same time and gives it a more natural and neat appearance. If you keep the mane short, it will also be easier to braid because you have less hair to manage.

Special Grooming Problems

Perhaps the most distasteful grooming chore of all to most people is cleaning the horse's private parts. Regardless of the sex of your horse, it's a task that needs to be done, not necessarily on a daily basis, but at least from time to time. It is, however, a task that needs to be approached with great caution, as some horses don't like being touched in their tender areas and will kick you if you try. Part of every foal's early training should include being touched in these areas so that they become accustomed to it. However, if you don't know how your horse will react or if you don't feel safe in cleaning your horse's privates, ask your veterinarian or a more experienced horse person to assist you the first time.

Cleaning the Udder

Mares especially need to become accustomed to having their udders cleaned. You don't want them to be so touchy in that area that they won't allow a foal to nurse. Some mares are more sensitive about it when they are in heat. If you neglect cleaning in this area, a waxy substance can build up between the teats that can be irritating and unsanitary to both mare and foal. After your rides, make it a practice to either hose off her udder and backside with lukewarm water or wipe the sweat away with a clean, dry towel. Don't use the soiled towel on other areas of the body.

Cleaning the Sheath

The sheath houses and protects the penis in stallions and geldings. If it isn't cleaned from time to time, a nasty, smelly, black cheesy substance called smegma builds up and can cause considerable discomfort. If the accumulation is significant, the sheath may become sore and swollen, and the horse will be unable to let down his penis to urinate. To clean the sheath, wear gloves, and soak a sponge in mild soapy warm water. Stick your hand and the sponge into the sheath and clean it. Obviously, this puts you in a very vulnerable position to be kicked if the horse decides to be uncooperative. Some horses simply won't tolerate this and need to be restrained or sedated for the procedure. That's why many people ask their veterinarian to do it during routine visits.

CHAPTER 9

Horse Anatomy

Knowing a little about how the horse is put together can help you understand when something is wrong and what the problem might be related to. Understanding the various systems can also help you understand proper equine management and avoid many problems. This chapter provides a brief overview of a horse's anatomy, but it is no substitute for your veterinarian's advice. There are many more comprehensive books on horse health and anatomy that you should own in your library if you have a horse. For a list, see the resources in the back of this book.

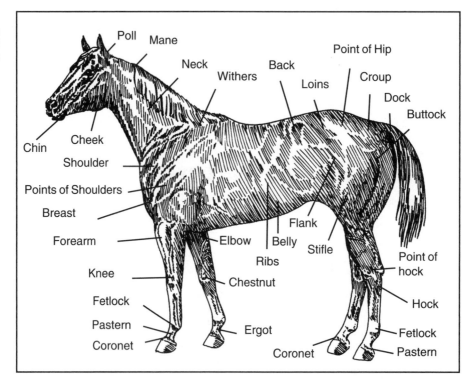

FIGURE 9.1:
The Parts of
the Horse

The Teeth

Foals begin to show teeth within a couple weeks of birth. Between the ages of two and five years, baby teeth begin to shed and are replaced by permanent teeth. The horse has at least thirty-six permanent teeth—twelve incisors and twenty-four molars—and some horses have four wolf teeth (essentially premolars) and four canine teeth (behind the incisors). Because wolf teeth can interfere with the bit's placement in the mouth, they are usually removed.

FIGURE 9.2 (a):
One Year

FIGURE 9.2 (b):
Five Years

FIGURE 9.2 (c):
Fifteen Years

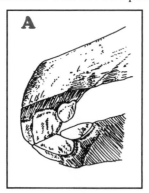 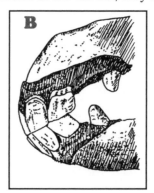 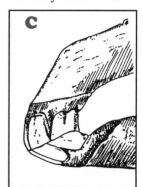

Underbites and Overbites

Also known as sow mouth (underbite) or parrot mouth (overbite), these malocclusions of the incisors are genetically based. Some dental issues can be corrected if they are caught and dealt with early enough in a foal's life. That's why it's important for the young foal's mouth to be inspected early and regularly by an equine dentist.

FACT

As much as four inches of the horse's tooth is imbedded in the jawbone. The horse's teeth keep growing out from that base throughout its life.

Galvayne's Groove

This groove starts at the base of the tooth, making its first appearance at around ten years of age. The groove grows out with the tooth and recedes off the bottom as the tooth elongates. At around age thirty, the groove disappears off the tooth. The Galvayne's groove is often used to estimate the age of the horse. The old sayings "long in the tooth," and "never look a gift horse in the mouth" originate from the practice of looking at the horse's teeth to determine its age.

Tooth Wear

If the molars wear unevenly, they can develop sharp edges, called points. As a result, the horse may experience discomfort, lose food out of his mouth, have difficulty chewing, or perhaps even drool. A horse that cannot chew properly may not get the full nutritional benefit of his food. Observe your horse's eating habits routinely so you will know what is normal for him. If you notice that he begins to spit out bits of food while chewing or leave partially chewed bits behind in his meal bucket, have his teeth inspected by an equine dentist.

The adult horse's teeth should be checked annually for proper wear. A veterinary dentist will examine the teeth both visually and manually using a speculum to keep the mouth open. Sometimes it is necessary to sedate the horse to carry out the inspection. If the vet finds sharp edges from uneven wear, she will rasp the teeth with special tools. Rasping brings the teeth back to an even grinding surface again. This procedure is called "floating" the teeth.

The Digestive System

Horses have a huge digestive system but a stomach capacity of only about four gallons. In the wild, the horse grazes almost continually, passing food through its digestive tract all the time, emptying out the stomach and processing the food through to elimination. If you've ever cleaned out horse stalls on a regular basis, you're all too familiar with how much food comes out the other end in a day's time. The volume and consistency of manure can be a fairly reliable barometer of health. That's why it's important to become familiar with your horse's elimination habits and always be observant, so you'll notice right away if anything changes.

FIGURE 9.3:
Digestive System
of the Horse

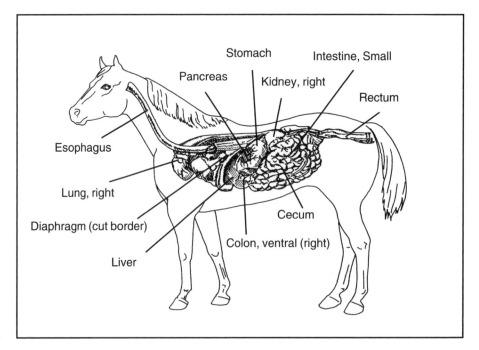

Maintenance

To approximate natural conditions as closely as possible, domestic horses should ideally be kept on pasture all the time, or at least turned out to graze in a paddock for several hours a day. The horse's digestive system is a large, complex machine that needs to constantly process food but can't be stuffed too full. The horse without access to pasture relies on good management practices of his owner to feed him small amounts a few times a day. If the horse receives grain, it should be divided into at least two and perhaps three meals per day. The quantity depends on the level of work required of him. Hay can be fed free choice, but many people also split this up into three or four feedings a day.

Many things can go wrong in the horse's digestive tract. For one thing, the horse cannot vomit and rid herself of something that upsets her stomach. Because the horse evolved to graze with its neck bent down to eat, the muscles in the esophagus only work to move food in one direction. A one-way valve at the entrance to the stomach prevents the contents from moving backward.

Overall, the equine digestive system is poorly equipped to process the huge amounts of food needed by an animal its size, especially in the manner that domestic horses tend to be fed. It is also full of kinks and turns that increase the potential for blockage.

ALERT!

Smaller, frequent feedings are best; otherwise, the stomach will move food before it is fully digested. This can mean that the horse isn't getting the full nutritional value of its feed. A greater risk is that the food may become impacted at one of those odd kinks and turns in the system.

The Intestinal Tract

The small intestine is approximately seventy feet long and has approximately a twelve-gallon capacity. Some food is processed by the liver and stored as energy. The cecum is a critical apparatus that holds a huge amount of bacteria. The bacteria break down cellulose and produce fat-soluble vitamins that are absorbed and used.

The large colon is around twelve feet long. It holds as much as twenty gallons of semi-liquid stool. The small colon is a little shorter, at ten to twelve feet long. In it, water is absorbed and stool is formed into balls. The rectum, around a foot long in the horse, is the channel through which the stool leaves the body.

The Muscles

The horse has muscles in every part of its body. Short, thick muscles provide short bursts of speed, and long, lean muscles are needed for both speed and endurance.

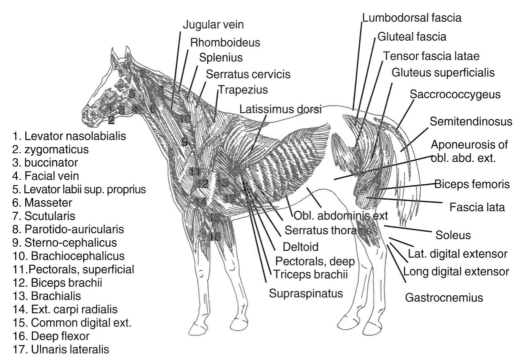

FIGURE 9.4:
The Muscles
of the Horse

Jugular vein
Rhomboideus
Splenius
Serratus cervicis
Trapezius
Latissimus dorsi

Lumbodorsal fascia
Gluteal fascia
Tensor fascia latae
Gluteus superficialis
Saccrococcygeus
Semitendinosus
Aponeurosis of obl. abd. ext.
Biceps femoris
Fascia lata
Soleus
Lat. digital extensor
Long digital extensor
Gastrocnemius

Obl. abdominis ext
Serratus thoracis
Deltoid
Pectorals, deep
Triceps brachii
Supraspinatus

1. Levator nasolabialis
2. zygomaticus
3. buccinator
4. Facial vein
5. Levator labii sup. proprius
6. Masseter
7. Scutularis
8. Parotido-auricularis
9. Sterno-cephalicus
10. Brachiocephalicus
11. Pectorals, superficial
12. Biceps brachii
13. Brachialis
14. Ext. carpi radialis
15. Common digital ext.
16. Deep flexor
17. Ulnaris lateralis

Types of Muscles

Muscles in the horse are classified as cardiac, smooth, or skeletal. Cardiac muscles involve the heart and operate involuntarily. Smooth muscles also are involuntary and involve specific functions such as digestion, breathing, and circulation. The skeletal muscles involve the horse's voluntary movements.

The contraction of muscles causes the production of lactic acid. Muscle fatigue results when there is too much of a buildup of lactic acid. Proper conditioning allows the horse to increase the muscles' ability to cope with lactic acid.

Skeletal muscles are made of different types of fibers, generally classified as slow-twitch and fast-twitch. Horses with more slow-twitch muscle fibers tend to possess greater endurance, while horses with more fast-twitch fibers typically display greater bursts of speed. Muscle makeup is one reason why certain breeds of horses are better suited to some tasks than others.

Sore Muscles

Like any athlete, horses need to be conditioned for the type and amount of riding you plan to do. Slow, simple, and step-by-step buildup is the key to adequate muscle conditioning. Dressage training provides a good foundation for any kind of riding for precisely this reason—it slowly prepares and conditions the horse's body for more complex maneuvers as it progresses from one level of training to another.

If you plan to enter your horse in, say, a twenty-five-mile competitive trail ride in August, spend a few months getting her into shape for the task, giving her muscles a slow buildup for strength and endurance. Proper conditioning is the best way to avoid long layoffs from strained muscles, tendons, and ligaments.

Also, be sure the equipment fits properly. For example, when saddles fit poorly, they contribute to bruising and straining of the longissimus dorsi muscle, which runs almost the entire length of the horse. Simply translated, this can create a sore back and result in behavioral problems if the horse hurts every time you ride it.

The Skeletal System

The horse's body is made up of 216 bones. The forelegs carry as much as 60 percent of the weight of the horse. By understanding the skeletal system of the horse, you can better understand how the horse moves and how movement may be hindered or aided when riding. For instance, in the diagram, you can readily see a huge bone at the shoulder just above and in front of the ribs. It isn't difficult to imagine that a saddle that rests too far ahead on the horse will interfere with movement of the shoulder structure.

FIGURE 9.5:
The Skeletal
System of
the Horse

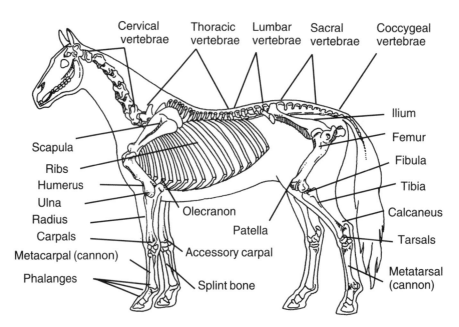

The horse's spine is composed of eighteen thoracic and six lumbar vertebrae. (Many Arabians have only five lumbar vertebrae.) The eighteen thoracic vertebrae have eighteen pairs of ribs attached to them. The neck contains seven vertebrae, and the croup (rear end portion of the spine) includes five fused vertebrae. The highest part of the back near the base of the neck is called the withers. The height of the horse is always measured in hands (one hand = four inches) from the highest point of the withers to the ground.

The Foot

The horse's foot is a complex and amazing apparatus. It not only holds a great amount of weight but also is able to withstand high impact from that weight. The hoof of a mature horse grows approximately a third of an inch a month. Routine trimming and proper shoeing by a good farrier is critical to the horse's soundness. That old saying "no foot, no horse" is all too true. A horse with sore feet cannot perform its job and is in constant misery. Some horses have to be put down because they develop painful foot problems, such as severe laminitis, that cannot be resolved.

FIGURE 9.6:
The Foot of
the Horse

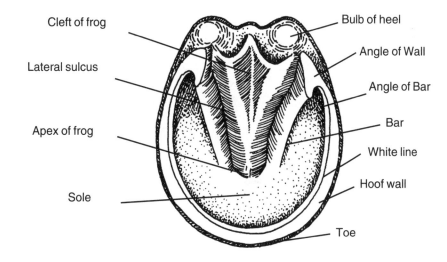

Cleft of frog

Lateral sulcus

Apex of frog

Sole

Bulb of heel

Angle of Wall

Angle of Bar

Bar

White line

Hoof wall

Toe

Five factors make it possible for the hoof to absorb shock:

- The digital cushion found deep within the foot
- The hoof wall, which is the key structural support designed to take impact and spread it to the other shock-absorbing areas
- The sole, which is (or should be) concave and, therefore, doesn't impact the ground
- The frog, a wedge of horn that is triangular in shape and presses into the digital cushion
- The bulbs of the heel, which form the back of the frog and the bars alongside the frog

If your horse loses a shoe, keep a rubber protective boot on hand to slip over the horse's foot. You can save your horse discomfort and yourself lost riding time by protecting that bare hoof and calling your farrier immediately. These boots are also handy when administering ointment to the hoof or for treating an abscess in the foot.

Vision

The horse's visual capabilities are unique and well suited to its needs. The uniqueness of the horse's vision contributes considerably to the horse's reputation for spooking easily. The horse's eye is not round and, therefore, the retina and cornea are not equidistant from each other across the eye. In order to focus on an object, the horse needs to turn its head and focus with both eyes.

FIGURE 9.7:
The Eye of
The Horse

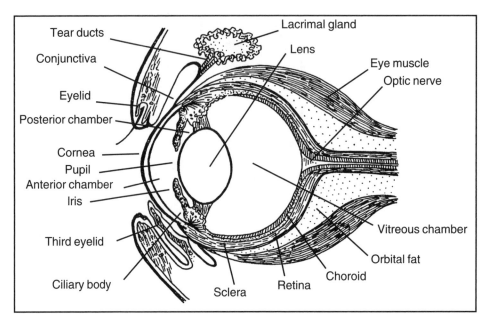

Tear ducts
Conjunctiva
Eyelid
Posterior chamber
Cornea
Pupil
Anterior chamber
Iris
Third eyelid
Ciliary body
Lacrimal gland
Lens
Eye muscle
Optic nerve
Vitreous chamber
Orbital fat
Choroid
Retina
Sclera

Aside from being an animal of prey with a built-in flight response, another contributing factor to the horse's tendency to spook is that the placement of the eyes on either side of the head makes the horse's vision largely monocular. In contrast, humans have binocular vision, which means that both of our eyes see the same image within the brain. But the horse has one view of the world on the right side of the body and a different view on the left side. The brain doesn't blend both images into one. This independent vision allows the horse to be on the lookout for predators while grazing.

Anyone who trains or rides horses needs to be aware of this fact. If the horse spooks at something on the ground, you need to let it walk up to the object, investigate it, and see it from both sides. If the horse hasn't seen it from both sides, the object will only register on one side of the brain.

FACT

The horse can see as much as 350 degrees around its body, with a blind spot directly in front and directly behind. Anyone who handles horses needs to be aware of this limitation and, for safety reasons, avoid standing directly in front of or behind a horse. You should also speak quietly to a horse when you approach it from behind to announce your presence and make sure it won't be startled by your sudden appearance within its visual field.

The Respiratory System

Comprised of the lungs and the air passages through which the horse breathes, the respiratory system is obviously vital to life. The respiratory health of the horse is greatly impacted by its surroundings and the quality of equine management. Horses that spend a lot of time locked in closed stalls are subject to respiratory problems caused by constantly breathing urine odors. Whenever a horse is exposed to lots of dust—from hay, indoor arenas, dusty oats, and so on—chronic respiratory problems can develop.

Heaves

Perhaps the most commonly known respiratory ailment is heaves. Heaves is a chronic problem usually caused by dust and mold in the feed. Many horses that develop heaves either have their hay soaked in water before eating it or have to avoid hay all together and instead eat commercially prepared complete feeds. Heaves is sometimes likened to COPD, or chronic obstructive pulmonary disease, in humans. It can be serious enough to cause permanent lung damage and is therefore considered unsoundness in the horse.

Pulmonary Hemorrhage

It is often shocking but not uncommon to see a racehorse bleed from the nostrils after a race. This is caused by tiny blood vessels that rupture in the lung tissue, usually as a result of strenuous exercise and exertion, such as high-speed galloping. Horses with this tendency are called "bleeders." In most cases, these nosebleeds are not serious and usually stop within a few minutes. Lasix (Furosemide) is a much-disputed drug used to control such bleeding in horses.

Skin

The best way to avoid skin problems is to groom routinely and take care to prevent broken skin from dangers in paddocks or stalls or from poor-fitting equipment. Practicing a solid equine management program to reduce exposure to flies and other external pests and parasites also protects the skin.

The Skin's Job

The skin of the horse has all the same jobs as the skin of any animal:

- Skin provides a barrier to foreign objects.
- It synthesizes vitamins.
- It provides insulation.
- It serves as a huge sensory organ.

The Layers of the Skin

The skin has two main layers—the epidermis and the dermis—as well as a layer of fat just below its surface. Regular grooming helps the horse maintain a healthy hair coat by removing dirt and matted material and by increasing the production of sebum, an oily substance that helps the horse shed water and makes the coat shine.

CHAPTER 10

General Health Care

This chapter is only an overview of general care. There are many books on the market that go into greater detail. Read and learn as much as you can about horse health. The more you know, the more quickly you are likely to recognize when something is wrong. This will allow you to call your vet right away and get your horse treated, saving you time, money, and anxiety.

The Horse's Environment

Horses seem to be simultaneously hardy and delicate. Proper nutrition does more to keep a horse in good health than almost anything else you can do. Well-maintained horses can withstand hot summers or cold winters, and the physical conditions under which they thrive range from cushy box stalls in barns rimmed with stained glass windows to three-sided sheds in rocky pastures. But when things go wrong, they can go wrong in a big way.

Feeding a horse moldy hay can cause colic or long-term respiratory problems. If you don't provide your horse with clean, ice-free water at all times, you have a colic situation waiting to happen. And when horses get caught in barbed wire or snag their halter in a stall, they seem to go for the gold when it comes to bodily damage.

The more you do to prevent horse health problems, the less it will cost the horse in stress and potential lifelong health issues, and the less it will cost you in time and money in the long run. The first step to protecting your horse's health is simple. Make the horse's environment as safe as possible and keep it clean and tidy.

Pick manure from stalls and turnout areas at least once per day, more often if more than two horses are turned out together. Horses that stand in accumulated manure and inhale urine odors are susceptible to hoof diseases, chronic respiratory problems, parasite infestations, and a host of other secondary problems.

Keep turnout areas clear of debris and keep fences in good repair to avoid physical injury to your horse. Fix damaged items—loose fence boards, downed electric fence wire, protruding nails—as soon as you see them. If you don't, your horse will surely find them, likely with devastating consequences. Lock up grain and keep stored hay out of your horse's reach. Close off any areas that aren't safe for a horse to walk in, and keep such areas free of tempting items, such as hay bales, that would lure a horse into that area.

As a horse owner, you are liable for any damages or injuries that your horse may cause to another's person or property. For example, if your horse escapes from his pasture and is involved in a traffic accident, you can be held responsible for the damages. It is wise to purchase equine liability insurance to protect yourself from such financial losses.

Use fencing and equipment designed for horses. Avoid barbed wire, as loose strands tend to snare and entangle a horse's limbs and cause serious lacerations. Gates must have secure or double-locking mechanisms to prevent your horse from escaping. Many horses are quite clever at figuring out how to open gates, especially ones fitted with simple latches that move up and down.

Your Horse Care Team

As soon as you acquire a horse, assemble a team of equine-knowledgeable people to help you with your horse's care. This team should include at least one equine veterinarian, a farrier, an equine dentist, the stable manager if you board your horse, and your group of horse-owning friends. You may also seek out a holistic practitioner, but if this person is not a licensed veterinarian, she should not take the place of your regular equine vet.

Yourself

You know your horse better than anyone, especially if you keep him at home, and you choose when and if to call in those other team members. You have a responsibility to your horse to educate yourself as much as possible about his care so you can respond appropriately when a problem arises.

Money, of course, is nearly always a factor in making decisions about horse care. It is up to you to decide the level of expense you can afford for your horse when disaster strikes. It can actually be less costly in the long run to spend some money up front to educate yourself about equine health, nutrition, and first aid.

Veterinarian

Your choice of veterinarian may be limited to the people who practice in your area. Years ago, most veterinarians treated both large and small animals, but not today. Vets who treat horses tend to specialize in equine care exclusively. If you live close to an equine clinic or a veterinary teaching hospital, you are fortunate. Whatever your situation, you should have one veterinarian who will come to know you and your horses well.

Farrier

Health problems with the foot can be common, and you should select a farrier who is willing to respond to an emergency and who is knowledgeable in foot health as well as in tacking on a shoe. Most people who take on farrier work as a profession have educated themselves in foot health as well as shoeing. Many also do corrective shoeing to resolve specific gait problems or to help make a horse with chronic lameness more comfortable.

FACT

You will see the farrier for general hoof maintenance more regularly than any other member of your horse's health care team—on an average of once every six to eight weeks. It's important to find someone whom you feel comfortable with and whose approach to your horse matches your own.

Equine Dentist

Equine dentists are veterinarians who specialize in the subject and who can treat specific dental problems. Tooth problems can affect the comfort of the bit in the horse's mouth and can even hamper his serviceability as a good riding mount. That's just one reason why good dental care is important for horses, especially the young and old. An equine dentist needs to monitor the eruption of a young horse's teeth closely. If any issues arise, the dentist can often correct them before they become a bigger problem.

A sound practice is to have your regular veterinarian check and "float" your horse's teeth (rasp away sharp points) in the spring when he administers spring vaccinations. Then, in the fall, schedule an appointment with an equine dentist who can check for any special problems.

Stable Manager

If you board your horse, the person who feeds or leads your horse out to the paddock and back to her stall every day will know a lot about your horse's normal behavior and when she is acting abnormally. The person who provides your horse's daily care and who is familiar with her routine behavior may be your first line of defense when it comes to realizing your horse needs medical attention. When this person can't be you, choose someone who is knowledgeable, experienced, and responsible. Someone who has been in the stable management business for a long time is ideal. If you're new to horse ownership, this person will be an especially important member of your team until you get up to speed on your horse know-how.

Finding a Veterinarian

Find a local large animal veterinarian before you even bring your first horse home. If you're planning to board your horse, the stable probably already has an established veterinarian, which can help save you money by splitting the farm call fees with other boarders. But you should be free to choose your own vet if you wish.

Establish a Relationship

Finding an equine veterinarian shouldn't be too difficult in most parts of the country. Simply look in the phone book or ask your horse friends for recommendations. If you don't find a large animal veterinary practice listed, call a small animal hospital and ask for a referral.

After you make a choice, call the vet's office and set up a farm call. Ask if you can stop by to see the facility. You should find a neat, clean facility with professional, friendly staff who know how to answer your questions and who seem willing to do so. Above all, you want to feel comfortable with the person and the practice you choose.

Finally, establish a relationship with the vet for routine vaccinations, deworming, and regular care before you need him to come in an emergency situation. Your relationship with your vet will be much smoother if you observe these simple rules about being a good client:

- Catch your horse before the vet arrives and have her waiting in a stall.
- Stick around to help your vet restrain your horse.
- Describe all symptoms and observations, no matter how unimportant they seem.
- Keep accurate records about your horse's health.

- Follow the vet's treatment instructions.
- Ask questions if you don't understand something.
- Pay your bills on time.

Establish a Baseline

Before you buy a horse, it is a good idea to have a vet check performed on the horse you want to purchase. The results of this exam can provide a baseline with which to begin to know your horse's health.

The prepurchase exam should include a temperature, respiration, and pulse report, which you can use as a standard if the horse was well at the time. At some point, you'll need to know how to perform these simple procedures yourself so you can do them when your horse is ill. Ask your veterinarian or stable manager to show you how. Practice so you feel confident in doing them and also so your horse becomes accustomed to these checks if he isn't already.

Here are four important vital signs to know about the horse:

- Normal temperature: between 99 and 101 degrees Fahrenheit
- Normal pulse: thirty to forty beats per minute
- Normal respiration: eight to twenty breaths per minute
- Capillary Refill Time (CRT): one to two seconds for blood to return to blanched tissue

While these statistics are average for the mature horse, they may vary slightly in some individuals. That's why you should establish a baseline for your horse.

Vaccinations

Annual vaccinations are the most crucial part of horse health maintenance. Besides the universal diseases that all horses should be vaccinated against, your veterinarian will know others that are common to your area and will recommend additional vaccinations accordingly. If you have show and travel plans that include crossing state lines, tell the vet what states you will be going through and what your final destination is. There may be diseases common to those areas, and some vaccinations may need to be given weeks ahead to offer your horse effective protection.

There are also other concerns when traveling across state lines. For example, a health certificate with a negative Coggins test is required for interstate transportation of horses and even for entry at most local horse shows. Certificates and test results often take a month or more to come back, so you definitely don't want to wait until a week before the show. Most people who show regularly have an annual Coggins test done with the early spring vaccinations.

FACT

A negative Coggins test is required to ensure that the horse does not have equine infectious anemia (EIA), a deadly, incurable disease that threatens the horse industry seriously enough for the U.S. Department of Agriculture to mandate testing and quarantine measures for horses imported from foreign countries.

Lameness

Lameness is one of the most common problems every horse owner faces from time to time. In most cases, it is only temporary lameness, caused by a hoof abscess or a stone in the shoe. Once the cause is remedied, the horse returns to normal. In other cases, lameness becomes chronic, requiring special shoeing or other treatments to keep the horse serviceable to ride. In the worst cases, lameness may result in having to put down the horse when the pain cannot be managed.

Causes of Lameness

The causes of lameness can be external or internal. The problem usually arises in either the leg or the foot, but it can also come from the shoulder, spine, or other areas. In some cases, lameness disappears on its own, and you may never know exactly what caused it. When the cause isn't obvious, diagnosis can sometimes involve a lot of guesswork.

Common lameness problems are typically seen in horses subjected to a lot of foot and leg stresses from racing, changing direction abruptly, or jumping. It's also more common in overweight horses or certain breeds like the American Quarter Horse that have been genetically manipulated to have heavy, muscular bodies supported by small legs and tiny feet.

If a horse suddenly becomes lame, the first place to look is the foot. Check the foot on the lame leg for a nail, stick, or stone. If nothing is readily visible, check the rest of the leg for tender spots, swelling, or warmness, all signs of inflammation. At the tender site, look for an abrasion or puncture wound. An abrasion would probably have to be significant and, therefore, very visible to cause lameness, but puncture wounds can be extremely deep and hard to detect. A puncture wound as high as the shoulder could cause lameness as well.

Navicular Disease

Navicular disease causes changes in the tissues and supporting structure of the small navicular bone in the foot. Repeated concussive injuries and metabolic disturbances are the most common causes of the permanent damage. The horse's conformation can predispose him to navicular disease if he has too-short pasterns, too-straight shoulders, or too-small feet to handle the concussion on the navicular bone.

A farrier can help make the navicular horse more comfortable with corrective shoeing. Medications exist to help manage the pain. Although some horses can still be used after they develop navicular disease, their use is often limited to light riding.

A navicular horse is considered unsound. Afflicted horses tend to shorten their stride and move off their toes to escape the pain in their heels. This causes them to stumble more, some so badly that they become unsafe to ride. The toes of the shoes on a navicular horse will wear down more quickly then the heels. X-rays of the feet performed during a prepurchase exam are done to rule out the presence of navicular changes deep inside the hoof when outward signs are not readily apparent.

Obvious Causes

You may witness your horse fall, get a leg caught under or in a fence, or slip getting out of the horse trailer. The injuries sustained in such accidents can cause lameness ranging from mild to serious, but at least you know what caused it and can tell your vet what happened.

Minor lameness from such mishaps is fairly manageable. Aside from treating any obvious cuts or swellings, a veterinarian will often administer phenylbutazone—commonly called "bute"—an anti-inflammatory pain reliever, for a few days to help relieve the horse's pain.

FACT

Be careful when using bute or other pain-masking drugs. They can make the horse feel good enough to move around too much, perhaps causing added damage. If the horse can remain calm in his stall for a day or two, bute combined with limited mobility may be all that is needed to help a minor problem resolve itself readily.

Sometimes a horse steps on a stone and bruises or cuts the sole of his foot, which will make him sore for several days or weeks. These injuries aren't always so readily evident, and your vet or farrier may need to pull off the horse's shoe and scrape around a bit to find the cause.

If the horse throws a shoe out in the field and rips off part of the hoof with it, he may be lame until his foot has time to grow out again. Some horses tend to go temporarily lame right after being shod. Such cases often resolve themselves in a day or two. Sometimes, however, the farrier may accidentally "quick" the horse with a horseshoe nail. Removing and resetting the nail properly usually resolves the problem.

Mystery Lameness

Sometimes a horse comes in lame from the pasture with no outward signs of kicks, knicks, cuts, bites, or other trauma. You'll see this most often with hoof abscesses. A horse that goes suddenly dead lame with only three good legs to stand on but with no signs of fracture, sprains, or swellings probably has a pocket of pus inside a foot. Try soaking the affected foot in warm water and Epsom salts to help relieve the pressure, and give your vet a call. Avoid giving bute in these instances, as you won't be able to tell whether the horse is improving because the drug masks the pain and symptoms.

To pinpoint lameness problems, your vet may want to administer a nerve-block test. This diagnostic tool numbs an area of the leg to see if the lameness disappears when the horse cannot feel pain from the affected area.

Lameness is a serious issue under the best of circumstances because it compromises your use of the horse. When you have no idea of the cause, getting your veterinarian on the scene as soon as possible can make the difference between a short-term layoff and chronic lameness. Your vet may want to take X-rays or perform a nerve-block test to zero in on the real issue.

Parasite Control

Because they live outdoors and eat from the ground, horses are subject to being robbed of nutrition and having their digestive tract damaged by many different kinds of parasitic worms. Your horse is going to get worms simply because of his environment, but prevention can protect your horse from a major worm infestation that could compromise her health.

Dewormers

Your veterinarian can recommend suitable deworming agents and set you on a schedule. Different parasites thrive in different climates, soil, and conditions, so you should follow a deworming schedule recommended for your area. Many deworming medications are in the same chemical class, but the way they're administered can vary from region to region, depending on the parasitic cycles common to a particular area.

Your vet can have a sample of your horse's manure tested to see what worms are present and select appropriate dewormers accordingly. Most horse owners learn to administer paste dewormers themselves, typically every other month, or as recommended by a vet. Paste dewormers have the consistency of ointment or gel, are flavored to a horse's taste (usually apple or molasses), and typically come in a syringe-like tube applicator. They are easy to administer simply by placing the applicator in the upper corner of the horse's mouth and squeezing the plunger. Your vet can show you how to do this. Some dewormers are available in pellet form so they can be mixed with feed. The major drawback, however, is that many horses won't eat them.

FACT

By squeezing the thick layer of skin on the end of the horse's nose with a twitch, you give the horse something else to think about besides that worming medication. Although it looks a bit barbaric, the twitch is used in an area known to be an acupressure point, one that releases natural pain-relieving, soothing endorphins that help the horse relax.

Environmental Control

Clean manure out of the horse's area as often as possible. Picking out stalls daily and paddocks once or twice a day is ideal. Fresh manure is the perfect environment for flies to lay their eggs, which, if left in the paddock, can be ingested by the horse.

In larger pastures where horses have plenty of room to move about and graze, they usually avoid eating near the areas where they defecate. These areas, called roughs, must be removed periodically to prevent the field from becoming sour. If you can't remove the droppings by hand, harrow the field at intervals to spread them.

Rotating grazing areas is a good idea if you have enough land to rope off the field in sections with electric tape and move the horses from one section to another. This allows the vacated area to rest and recover from the damage horses do to it. This practice also helps keep parasites in check by encouraging their numbers to die off.

Internal Parasites

Horses have internal and external parasites. For many, the life cycle is completed in or on the ground, but the host, the horse, is important in at least one or more phases of the process. Preventing internal parasites involves putting the horse on a regular deworming schedule, as recommended by your veterinarian. The choice of medication depends on the types of parasites that are most prevalent in your geographic area. Ivermectin, for example, is a common broad-spectrum paste dewormer, but several others are available. Your veterinarian may recommend rotating medications to avoid resistance, in which parasites build up a tolerance to a certain chemical.

Types of Internal Parasites

The following are the most problematic internal parasites that affect horses:

- **Small and large strongyles:** These bloodsucking worms attach themselves to the intestine and can cause anemia and ulcers.
- **Pinworms:** These live in the large intestine and cause irritation around the rectum.
- **Ascarids or roundworms:** These can cause coughing, inflammation, and gut problems if the buildup is large.
- **Tapeworms:** Once thought to be relatively uncommon in horses, these pests, when present in large enough numbers, steal nutrients and contribute to anemia, wasting, and colic.
- **Bots:** Bot flies lay tiny yellow eggs on the horse's body, usually the legs. The horse ingests the eggs, which cycle through the body and pass out through the manure, where the fly emerges, and the cycle repeats itself. To prevent these parasites, scrape the eggs off your horse with a bot knife or pumice stone.
- **Lungworms:** Rare in horses but usually associated with donkeys, lungworms live in the lungs.

Fly Control

The first step in controlling flies is getting fresh manure away from the barn. Resort to sprays to protect your horse from the biting pests. There are many fly control products on the market, from sprays and wipes to nematodes that devour fly larvae before they hatch. Each product or method controls some flies better than others. Try out several to determine what works best for you.

Using Fly Sprays

Small biting flies of different varieties really like to get along the horse's belly midline, in the ears, right at the top of the foretop, and in other places the horse can't reach with his built-in fly swatter, the tail. Spraying the horse every morning before turnout helps relieve some of the misery, but not all. Use fly spray especially before you saddle up and ride. This will prevent your horse from getting distracted by the biting bugs and possibly even bucking you off in a desperate effort to remove a fly from his butt.

During fly season, spray the legs before you start grooming and tacking up to prevent an accidental kick. Horses sometimes try to shake off a fly by shaking a leg, and if you happen to be in the way, you could get kicked unintentionally. Read the product label and follow the instructions on the bottle for how much and how often to spray your horse. Keep an eye on the horse for an allergic reaction, usually in the form of hives. Some products that didn't bother a horse last year may cause hives this year, so don't be complacent just because you use the same fly spray every year.

ALERT!

Never spray fly spray on the horse's face. Spray it on a mitt or a small brush reserved exclusively for this purpose and carefully apply it to the horse's face, avoiding her eyes. You could also use a roll-in pesticide for the face and around the eyes.

Nonchemical Methods of Fly Repellant

When the flies are really bad, put a fly mask on the horse to protect the eyes from the biting swarms that like to settle in the corners. These are made of a mesh material that allows the horse to see out but keeps flies from getting in.

You can also buy mesh fly sheets that cover the horse's body but are light and not hot in warm weather. Another tactic is to put your horse in his stall during the times of day when the flies are out in force—typically mid-day to dark—and turn him out overnight when the flies are not as bad.

Your Equine First Aid Kit

Be prepared for emergencies. Don't wait for something to happen before you gather some basic first aid supplies. Having a first aid kit on hand can be the best insurance against having to use it! Know what is in the kit and what each item is for. In cold climates, keep any liquids, lotions, or paste medications somewhere warm but handy. Like all medications, keep your equine meds out of reach of pets and small children.

What You'll Need

You can buy ready-made equine first aid kits in tack shops and from horse supply catalogs. Although items can be less expensive when they are purchased à la carte, the kit container itself offers a convenient way to keep everything together. Kits also often include a laminated information card about basic first aid. Once you figure out what kinds of bandages and other supplies you like best, you can tailor your first aid kit to your own preferences.

If you assemble your own first aid kit, here are some items to include:

- A few different kinds of bandages
- Traditional quilted leg wrap
- Tube of antibiotic cream
- Iodine
- Hydrogen peroxide
- Vet wrap

- Rubber and/or latex gloves
- Thermometer, either digital or heavy-duty ring top with string attached
- Scissors
- Adhesive tape
- Hand wipes
- Banamine, bute, bute-less, or other equine-approved pain relievers

Also, keep a cold pack in the freezer. Depending on how adventure-some and experienced you are in your equine self-care program, keep a supply of different size needles and syringes on hand, as well as a vial of antibiotics (make sure they are up-to-date), epinephrine (for allergic reactions, to be used only under the advice of a veterinarian), and perhaps some electrolytes. Ask your veterinarian to help you assemble these types of items and show you how to use them.

Surface Wounds

You can clean minor scrapes yourself with warm water and an antiseptic solution. If the wound is bleeding, dust it with a blood coagulant. In fly season, apply a dab of wound-healing ointment laced with fly repellent to keep out the bugs. Check the wound daily to make sure it isn't getting infected.

Deeper Lacerations

Call your vet immediately for deeper lacerations to determine the need for stitches. Control bleeding first, especially if the wound is squirting blood. Blood spurting from a wound indicates that an artery has been nicked. To control bleeding, get a clean bandage and apply pressure to the wound, either with your hand or by securing the bandage with an ace wrap.

Puncture wounds also need to be carefully examined to ascertain if any part of the object is still lodged in the wound. Puncture wounds are exceptionally susceptible to infection, as dirt gets trapped and the airless environment provides a perfect breeding ground for bacteria. Your vet will thoroughly clean the wound and will probably prescribe a precautionary course of antibiotics and a tetanus booster shot if necessary.

Hives

Hives are raised bumps that show up all over the horse's neck and body, or sometimes just in a certain area. Hives generally indicate a reaction to something, possibly something in the environment or feed. Figure out what has been introduced to your horse—a different fly spray, a new supplement—and avoid that product.

QUESTION?

What does proud flesh mean?
A wound that won't heal produces scar tissue that protrudes from the wound area. This unsightly scar tissue is commonly referred to as proud flesh.

Tying Up

Also called azoturia or Monday morning disease, tying up is essentially muscle cramps caused by a metabolic disturbance of some sort. It is a medical emergency requiring immediate veterinary care. The condition occurs most often when a horse has been out of work and is suddenly ridden aggressively. The afflicted horse will appear stiff and refuse to move. He may sweat profusely and breathe hard, and muscle tremors may be visible over his body. Urine may be dark brown in color, a result of substances released into the blood by the damaged muscles.

General Health Care for the Geriatric Horse

Because of better nutrition and veterinary care, horses can live into their late thirties or older these days. If your horse reaches a ripe old age, you can be proud of your equine management skills. By this age, the horse may be able to be ridden lightly—say, a little pony ride for your five-year-old nephew or a trip down to the mailbox each afternoon—but she probably won't be up to jumping fences or barrel racing.

Dealing with Arthritis

The ailment you will most likely have to deal with is arthritis. With medication and/or support from natural products such as glucosamine, you can probably keep your elderly equine partner quite comfortable. For the arthritic horse, your major concern is his ability to get up after lying down for a little nap or taking a little roll. If you stall your horses, give the older horse as large a stall as possible, as some movement helps alleviate stiffness. If he is getting either picked on or jostled around too much by the other horses, you may find it necessary to separate him from the younger horses.

Digestive Issues

The other ailment you will most likely have to deal with is digestion. Old horses have worn teeth that just don't work as well as they used to. Some commercial feeds are designed especially for senior equines. They are typically more palatable and easier to chew. It may be harder to keep enough weight on your horse. Try to avoid first-cut hay with the older horse, and give him later-cut hay, which is softer and more easily digested.

Keep a close eye on your old pal, especially during winter months if you live in the north. Offer her a few extras—warmed water, a blanket—to help her live a comfortable retirement.

When to Say Goodbye

Ultimately, the older horse will present you with that heart-wrenching decision of whether the time has come to euthanize him. If you can keep him comfortable, eating well, and enjoying life, that's great. But when the horse spends most of his day in noticeable pain and no longer cares about the world around him, it's time to be kind to your old friend and say goodbye. The unfortunate reality is that horses are large animals that must spend most of their time standing. When a horse can no longer stand without feeling constant pain in his feet or joints, it's an unkindness to delay the inevitable.

The disposal of a horse's body can be a problem. Generally, your options are to bury the horse on your farm if this is permitted or to call someone to take the body away. Your veterinarian or stable manager can explain the options available and help you make arrangements. The ordeal will be much easier on you if you plan ahead for the reality that will eventually come to pass for your senior pal.

CHAPTER 11

Equine Diseases and Disorders

As a horse owner, you must know enough about the most common diseases and disorders that afflict horses so you can recognize when your horse is sick and in need of veterinary treatment. This chapter provides a brief overview of the more common equine afflictions that you need to be aware of.

Colic

While horses get cancer, the truly frightening C word in the horse world is colic. If you own horses long enough, chances are you will experience a colicky horse at some point. Almost everything you do for your horse has some effect on the horse's potential for colic. Feeding schedule, feed storage, a change in feed, the feed itself, fresh water access, stress, hard riding, no exercise, trailering, medications, eating or drinking too soon after exercise, and overeating—you name it and colic can be the result! This is why careful, knowledgeable horse management and good feeding practices are so important.

What Is Colic?

Colic is not an actual disease; the term refers to general digestive upset in the horse. Put simply, it is a stomachache. Sometimes, it is a really bad, life-threatening stomachache. It can be many different kinds of stomachache—gassy, not gassy, causing diarrhea, or causing constipation. Colic is always cause for concern, as it can easily turn into a medical emergency.

One of the reasons for this is that horses cannot vomit and rid themselves of whatever is causing the upset stomach. If a horse consumes bad, moldy feed or some other toxic substance, the offensive material literally must go in one end and out the other. With an enormous intestinal tract to meander through, the material can cause a lot of damage along the way before it ever reaches the end.

Sometimes colic is a symptom of another problem. It may be an external factor such as overeating or moldy feed, or it may be caused by something internal, such as a strong heat cycle in a mare, an overload of parasites, or even a tumor. Sometimes the cause of a colic episode is obvious—for example, you found your horse in the grain room halfway finished with what was a full bag of grain. But if it is something less obvious, you may never know the real cause.

What Are the Signs of Colic?

Predators seek out the weak and the sick in a herd, so as animals of prey, horses are pretty good at hiding signs of illness until they become full-blown and serious. This is why it is important for you to come to know your horse's normal behavior. Being a picky eater can be a normal thing for one horse, but in another horse that usually gobbles down his food with gusto, picking at his meal or refusing to eat can be warning signs that something is wrong.

Other warning signs of colic to watch for include:

- Not passing manure
- Grabbing at the sides with the mouth
- Kicking at the belly with the back legs
- Unusual restlessness in the stall
- Sweating excessively for no apparent reason
- Lying down for a long period of time and not getting up when encouraged
- Frequent rolling

What Do You Do for a Colicky Horse?

The first thing to do is alert your veterinarian. If you just started to see signs of colic, you may not think it is necessary for him to pay a visit yet. However, your vet will want to get to you as soon as possible. Addressing colic immediately can mean the difference between a mild bellyache and a life-threatening situation.

The outcome often depends on the type of colic you're dealing with. Spasmodic colic is the more common and generally the milder type. *Impaction colic* is the term for an obstructed bowel, and *intussusception* is the term for when a loop of intestine telescopes inside itself. While colic is never good, the latter two types may require surgery to save the horse's life.

Not passing manure suggests an obstruction may be present, so don't hesitate to report this observation to your vet. In a mild colic episode, there are a few things you can do to try to encourage a bowel movement, such as getting the horse out and walking him around. This will also serve to keep the horse from lying down and rolling. If the horse's stomach is impacted with feed that won't pass through, rolling can cause a twist within the digestive tract, which you must try to avoid.

Another strategy is to try loading the horse into a horse trailer if he is generally a good loader. This may be just the stimulation he needs, as most horses, even those who walk calmly into a trailer, are still a bit on edge when they do so and will almost immediately pass manure after they get in. If your horse does not load well, even simply showing him the back end of an open trailer may be enough. However, if your horse is really afraid of getting into a trailer, or is typically resistant and difficult to load, do not add this extra stress to the already existing stress of colic pain.

Pain-relieving medications such as Banamine are often administered to relieve the pain of gas colic and can help relax the muscles enough to help the horse release gas and/or manure and relieve the colic episode. However, don't administer any medication without first discussing it with your veterinarian, and then only if you have lots of experience. If the drug masks your horse's symptoms, the veterinarian will not be able to make an accurate diagnosis or suggest the most appropriate treatment regimen.

Prepare yourself for the fact that colic is sometimes fatal and can involve some difficult decisions. You may be faced with the option of expensive surgery and follow-up care that may or may not have a good outcome. Or you may have to put the horse down to spare him a painful death.

Insect-Borne Diseases

Mosquitoes are among the most notorious carriers of some of the world's deadliest diseases. Because horses live outdoors, they are easy prey to these and other silent blood-sucking insect killers. Fortunately, we have effective vaccines to help prevent many of these diseases.

Equine Encephalomyelitis

Also known as sleeping sickness or the blind staggers, this mosquito-borne malady comes in three deadly varieties caused by different strains of viruses:

- Eastern encephalomyelitis (EEE)
- Western encephalomyelitis (WEE)
- Venezuelan encephalomyelitis (VEE)

The disease affects the central nervous system, causing inflammation in the brain and spinal cord. It is deadly in both horses and humans; however, only the Venezuelan variety can be transmitted from horses to humans via the bite of a mosquito. With the Eastern and Western varieties, the usual mode of transmission to either horse or human is from an infected bird or rodent via the bite of a mosquito.

The first symptoms appear within a few days after exposure. A sick horse displays a high fever, excessive depression, and a rapid heart rate. He may also refuse to eat—always a sure sign that something is wrong in a horse. As the infection progresses, the horse will begin to display marked behavioral changes, such as unusual aggression, aimless circling, and pressing or leaning against walls. You may see noticeable muscle twitching or paralysis as well. Eventually, the horse starts to have convulsions and collapses. The death rate runs as high as 90 percent, which makes vaccination with regular boostering imperative. Vaccinate annually and sometimes twice annually in areas where mosquito season runs well into the fall.

West Nile Virus

Similar to EEE, WEE, and VEE, this mosquito-borne viral disease causes swelling of the brain and spinal cord with all its attendant neurological symptoms. Mosquitoes get the West Nile virus from infected birds and pass it on to other animals, including people. Although humans and horses alike may contract the virus, there is no evidence that an infected horse can transmit the disease to a person or to other animals.

FACT

The disease is relatively new to the United States, first detected here in 1999. Since then, it has spread rapidly, possibly by migrating birds. It is now recognized as one of the major threats to horses, and it can also cause serious illness in humans as well.

Symptoms may include fever, stumbling, muscle incoordination, partial paralysis, appetite loss, head tilting, walking in circles, or walking blindly into things. Fortunately, a vaccine is available to protect horses from this deadly infection. Good mosquito control methods in and around your barn and pastures also help.

If you plan on hauling your horse into an area that has a heavy mosquito season, ask your veterinarian about boostering your horse's vaccine for added insurance, especially if some time has passed since he was last vaccinated.

Equine Infectious Anemia (EIA)

Also called swamp fever, EIA is another nasty disease transmitted by biting insects, primarily large horse flies. However, there is no vaccine for it, and the disease is incurable and has a high mortality rate. Horses that recover from a bout with the disease can become carriers of it and spread it to other horses. They either must be euthanized or quarantined away from other horses for the rest of their lives. Symptoms may also become chronic. Fortunately, rigorously enforced testing protocols have been instrumental in reducing the incidence of this difficult disease.

Symptoms include fever, loss of appetite, weight loss, anemia, and muscle weakness. However, some horses can carry the virus without showing any signs of sickness. Because of this, strict rules have been put in place to govern the transport of horses from state to state and from country to country.

The so-called Coggins test requires the drawing of blood, which is tested for EIA antibodies. Although proof of a negative Coggins test is required for a horse to cross state lines and is also usually required at all horse shows and other events where horses congregate, this test has drawn a lot of controversy in the past. If a horse tests positive, most states require the horse to be either quarantined or destroyed, as it may be a carrier even though it never exhibits clinical signs of the disease. The controversy stems from this fact: Only a small percentage of all horses in the country get tested. The ones that do—typically those that travel for shows and other events and need to produce a negative Coggins test for admission to the event's grounds—are thought by some to be unfairly penalized.

It is up to you to halter break your horse thoroughly enough for him to be gentle to handle. A vet should be able to give your horse a simple physical, administer annual vaccinations, and draw blood without difficulty. However, don't let any practitioner handle your horse in a way you don't approve of.

Lyme Disease

Carried by ticks, Lyme disease has become a concern in humans, pets, and livestock. The use of tick-controlling fly sprays can help prevent this disease, particularly in spring when ticks are most voracious. The very tiny deer tick is the culprit in the spread of Lyme disease.

Respiratory Diseases

Horses can get the flu, and their symptoms are similar to what people experience: fever, cough, sneezing, runny nose, and watery eyes. Sometimes horses may even have enlarged lymph nodes, stiff limbs, and difficulty breathing. The respiratory diseases seen in the horse are nothing to sneeze at, as they have the potential to lead to serious complications.

Equine Influenza

Several types of viruses are known to cause the equine influenza, which spreads easily from horse to horse by the droplets discharged during coughing and sneezing. Fortunately, the disease is not usually fatal, except perhaps for the very young, the very old, or for horses with compromised immune systems. But fatal complications, such as pneumonia, can develop if the horse isn't tended to properly or if he is overly stressed by travel and competition.

Horses that routinely come in contact with strange horses are most at risk. If your horse is often exposed to other horses at shows or at a boarding stable that has steady turnover, he definitely needs to be vaccinated against this disease at least once a year, if not more often.

Equine Herpes Virus

Also called equine rhinopneumonitis, this highly infectious viral disease is caused by a herpes virus. There are two strains, EHV-1 and EHV-4, both of which can cause abortion and respiratory illness in the horse. Obviously, the disease is especially hazardous among pregnant mares, although abortion may not occur until long after the infection has seemingly run its course, and often well into the pregnancy.

Symptoms include mild fever, nasal discharge, and coughing. Young horses are more likely to develop the respiratory form with flu-like symptoms, while older horses may carry the virus but show no signs of illness.

Strangles

Once you've experienced an outbreak of strangles in your barn, it's not something you ever want to have to deal with again. The disease affects primarily the upper respiratory tract, although it can go systemic. It causes copious globs of cloudy or yellow mucus to stream from the sick horse's nose.

The infected nasal secretions can readily spread the disease from horse to horse; however, not every horse exposed will come down with the disease.

Young horses are most susceptible and usually get the sickest. Older horses have had more time to acquire some natural immunity to the disease and often develop a much milder form. These horses may show only minimal nasal discharge and lethargy, symptoms sometimes mistaken for the flu. However, they can still spread the disease through a herd, so if there's any doubt, you should ask your vet to rule out strangles for sure with a test.

Aside from a snotty nose, a horse with strangles exhibits a high fever and depressed attitude. He may also cough, go off his feed, and experience difficulty breathing. Some horses develop abscessed lymph nodes under the jaws in the throatlatch area. The abscesses usually open and drain on their own, or they may need to be lanced by your vet. Otherwise, the swellings can become so enlarged that they actually block the horse's airway, strangling him to death, which is how the disease got its name.

Nursing a horse sick with strangles can be quite labor intensive when there are other healthy horses on the farm that you're trying to protect. You must adopt a workable strategy to prevent spreading the disease to the others. This may involve wearing gloves and sickroom clothes for handling the sick horse and removing them before you get near the others. Each time you exit the sick horse's stall, it's also a good idea to disinfect your shoes by stepping into a kitty litter pan filled with bleach.

After the horse recovers, you'll need to strip his stall down and disinfect it, along with any buckets, lead ropes, halters, grooming utensils, or other items he may have touched. Under the right conditions, the causative bacteria, *Streptococcus equi*, can linger in the environment and pastures for a period of time after an outbreak.

Also, recovering horses continue to shed the bacteria in their nasal secretions for a short while. Your vet may recommend doing a series of nasal swab tests on your horse every other week or so to determine when he has stopped shedding bacteria and become disease-free. Occasionally, a horse continues to be a silent shedder, or carrier, of the disease, although he has no outward signs of illness.

As a rule of thumb, it is wise to allow no horses to come onto the property or leave (except to go to a veterinary clinic) for about thirty days after the last horse on your farm is declared disease-free. Needless to say, if you run a boarding or riding facility where horses come and go all the time, your business can really suffer during a strangles outbreak. Other horse people will avoid your place like the plague, fearful that they may carry the contagion back to their own farms.

QUESTION?

What is bastard strangles?
When strangles moves from the upper respiratory tract and goes internally, it is called bastard strangles. It is a life-threatening complication of *Streptococcus equi*, caused when lymph nodes deeper inside the chest or abdominal cavity become infected and form pockets of pus that begin to drain inside the body.

Before the discovery of antibiotics, a significant number of strangles cases were fatal. Nowadays, most horses recover from the disease with treatment; however, some serious complications can develop, even months afterward. One of the more serious systemic complications is *purpura hemorrhagica*, an inflammation of blood vessels, first evident by sudden and pronounced swelling in the hind legs. This complication is thought to be an autoimmune response, or a type of allergic reaction, to the *Streptococcus equi* bacteria. A strangles vaccine is available, but it has some risks. For this reason, it's not included in your routine lineup of spring shots unless you and your vet discuss the need for it.

Other Diseases of the Central Nervous System

Equine encephalomyelitis and West Nile virus, two diseases of the central nervous system, have garnered headlines in recent decades. These two diseases were discussed earlier in this chapter. However, there are some other less publicized central nervous system disorders that are just as deadly. For example, most people have heard of tetanus and rabies, two diseases that have been around for ages and that terrorized people long before the age of vaccines finally reined them in.

Tetanus

Horses are quite susceptible to tetanus, a deadly disease caused by bacteria living in the soil. Their environment—old barns, rusty nails, dirt, manure—readily supports the bacteria that affect the nervous system and for which successful treatment is difficult at best.

When the bacteria enter the bloodstream, usually via a bad cut or a deep puncture wound, they release a toxin that targets the horse's nervous system. Afflicted horses display extreme stiffness and muscle paralysis, especially around the neck and face, hence the origin of the common name for the disease, lockjaw.

Like encephalomyelitis, tetanus has a high mortality rate, roughly 80 percent. Fortunately, the disease is easily prevented by vaccination and annual boosters. As a precaution, most veterinarians will also rebooster a vaccinated horse that suffers any serious wound, especially a deep puncture wound.

Rabies

Rabies is a problem throughout most of the continental United States. This horrible disease of the central nervous system has an outcome of certain death. It is not one to mess with—for your horse's sake and for yours, as rabies is communicable to humans from contact with the saliva of an afflicted animal to an open wound. Statistics are not high for horses contracting rabies, but those living in open situations with access to pasture are prime candidates because they come in contact with skunks, raccoons, foxes, bats, and other common rabies carriers. Furthermore, horses are curious animals, likely to go up and sniff a sick or dying animal that wanders into the field and end up getting bitten on the nose.

In most localities, rabies vaccinations are required by law for dogs, and in some places, even for cats. As more and more cases crop up, horse owners have taken notice and begun to vaccinate their animals routinely as well. It is a commonsense precaution, a small investment that could save you lots of grief if you were ever faced with the situation.

An animal suspected of having been exposed to rabies is either quarantined and observed for symptoms or destroyed and tested for the virus. Medical authorities, not the animal's owner, choose which option is best to take, depending on whether any human life has been placed at risk.

If your horse contracts the disease from a chance encounter, he will surely die or have to be put down. If that isn't reason enough to get your horse vaccinated, consider this. A rabid horse can spread rabies to anybody who handles him via a bite or by licking a wound. People exposed to animals even suspected of having rabies are usually given antirabies shots as a precaution. As the horse owner in this scenario, you would be responsible for any medical expenses, or worse, any human fatalities incurred as a result.

Because of the legal ramifications, always have your veterinarian give the rabies shots to your horse so there will be a documentation trail. Some savvy horse owners learn how to give their horses their shots themselves, to save money. This is perfectly legal in most cases. But with a suspected case of rabies, you want to be able to prove with legally recognized medical records when and how your horse was vaccinated. Even if you give your horse all his other shots yourself, leave the rabies shot for your vet to do.

Equine Protozoal Myeloencephalitis (EPM)

EPM is sometimes misdiagnosed as West Nile Virus because it affects the brain and spinal cord and causes similar symptoms. The disease is often difficult to diagnose because the symptoms mimic other health problems. Testing is the only way to be sure which disease you're dealing with, although an astute veterinarian can distinguish the two more readily if one side or one part of the horse is affected more than the other.

While West Nile is caused by a virus, EPM is caused by an entirely different organism called a protozoan. This organism is transmitted to the horse via the opossum, which acquires the protozoan from infected birds. Because of the source, EPM is often called the possum disease. Symptoms may include abnormal gait, lameness, stiffness, incoordination, weakness, muscle paralysis (especially around the face), head tilt, and unusual sleepiness. Treatment is long-term, expensive, and not always successful.

A vaccine is in the works but not yet widely available. As a means of prevention, you can discourage possums and other wild animals from coming around the stable at night by keeping all feeds in tightly closed containers and behind closed doors. This goes for cat and dog food, too, as possums love to find a steady source of these delectables; don't leave food out in the barn for Fido and Fluffy to munch on at will.

Disease Protection Based on Risk

Some diseases are more prevalent in some areas than in others. That's why there's no set recipe for what vaccinations every horse needs. While the so-called "core" vaccines protect against the deadlier and more widespread conditions (encephalomyelitis and tetanus, for example), a vaccination recommendation depends on where you live and on how great an exposure risk your horse has. Your veterinarian is your best resource for assessing the potential risk, based on the incidence of disease in the area where you live or plan to transport your horse. One of the most noteworthy diseases to fall into this risk-based vaccine category is Potomac horse fever.

Potomac horse fever affects the gastrointestinal tract and has a high mortality rate. If contracted, the disease needs to be treated immediately, or it can become quite serious. Symptoms begin with the horse going off his feed, followed by severe diarrhea and colic. Laminitis (founder) is a serious complication of the gastrointestinal upset and can lead to the horse becoming permanently unsound.

FACT

This disease was first diagnosed in the Potomac region of Maryland and named for the area. Now, however, it can occur anywhere in the country. Your veterinarian will know whether there have been incidents in your area and whether or not horses in your area should be vaccinated.

A certain type of bacteria harbored by freshwater snails has been identified as a cause of the disease. Some species of flies that spend their larval stage in the water are also thought to play a role in the cycle of disease. For this reason, it is recommended that you water horses from troughs or buckets instead of ponds and streams that may be contaminated by snails and insects.

Hoof Ailments

There's an old saying, "No hoof, no horse," which is all too true. The horse is a one-ton animal that stands on its feet most of the day and night. If something is wrong with one or more of the feet, the horse is truly miserable and unhappy. Just imagine yourself standing on a sore foot all day. While injury or abscesses account for most lameness, there are some specific ailments that afflict the feet.

Laminitis

Like colic, laminitis is one of the things horse owners hear about and dread a lot. By definition, laminitis is an inflammation of the laminae in the foot. Although typically used interchangeably with the term *founder*, founder is actually a result of laminitis that has progressed enough for the coffin bone to rotate, resulting in a chronic condition caused by permanent structural damage inside the hoof.

Many horses that have foundered can be kept fairly comfortable through drugs and corrective shoeing, but they will only be able to withstand extremely light riding, if any at all. Some cases are so severe that the horse must be put down. The great racehorse Secretariat was put down due to laminitis.

Common causes of laminitis are overeating grain or lush pasture (especially in early spring) and postpartum infection of the mare, both of which cause enterotoxemia (also called overeating disease, characterized by excessive bacterial growth in the digestive tract that reaches toxic levels). The following are the signs of laminitis:

- Hot feet caused by increased circulation
- Rapid pulse in foot area
- Preference for lying down to take weight off feet—when all four feet are involved
- Leaning back on its hind end to relieve the front feet or holding her front legs out in an odd stretched position—if just the two front feet are involved

Laminitis and founder are conditions that will require your farrier and veterinarian to work together to treat the horse. As with colic, prevention includes good horse management and careful attention to feeding practices.

What is thrush?
Thrush is a foul-smelling infection of the frog of the foot, evident by a blackish discharge. It is most common in horses that stand in damp, dirty conditions. It is easily treated with over-the-counter products available at tack and feed stores. If neglected, however, the condition can lead to lameness.

Scratches

This condition, also called greasy heel, is characterized by granular scabs and inflammation on the back of the pasterns, which can make the horse quite sore. It occurs most commonly when horses stand in mud, manure, tall grass dampened with dew, or other conditions of prolonged moisture. Interestingly, legs with white markings seem to be afflicted most often. Treatment involves removal of the scabs and daily applications of an equine skin medication containing antifungal and antibacterial properties until the area heals completely.

White Line Disease

White line disease is a deterioration of the inner wall of the hoof, specifically along the nonpigmented layer, referred to as the white line, where the hoof wall joins the sole. The first sign of the disease is a flaky, powdery white substance along this line when you view the sole of the upturned hoof. As the disease progresses, it causes separation of the hoof wall from the sole, allowing bacteria and other pathogens to enter the foot. If the separation occurs in the white line at the toe, the condition is called seedy toe.

Excessive moisture, recurring hoof cracks, improper shoeing, improper hoof angle, and chronic abscesses are all thought to contribute to white line disease. In its early stages, the disease can be managed with proper trimming and shoeing and treatment for any infection. You will need to work closely with your farrier and veterinarian to control the condition.

CHAPTER 12

Beyond Conventional Health Care

Holistic practitioners—many of whom are veterinarians—consider the whole patient and not just the disease, condition, or symptoms. The goal is to understand both the immediate problem and the contributing factors and then propose therapies that enable the horse to heal from within itself and prevent recurrences. This chapter provides a brief overview of the alternative therapies that can complement conventional medicine and sometimes even offer an improved outcome in a treatment plan. Always consult your veterinarian first in all matters related to your horse's health; alternative therapies are not intended to replace the wisdom of conventional medicine.

The Holistic Approach

Holistic approaches can be grouped into three categories: body work (massage, chiropractic, and acupressure); nutritional support (herbs, vitamins, and nutritional supplements); and energy work (acupuncture, homeopathy, magnetic therapy, lasers, Bach flowers, infrasonic therapy, and Reiki). But the list goes on: applied kinesiology, which uses muscle testing to pinpoint allergens; NAET (another allergen identification approach); aromatherapy, osteopathy, and shiatsu (similar to acupressure); and myofascial release (massage and stretching to release tight/restricted muscle and connective tissue) are among many.

QUESTION?

What is alternative medicine?
Alternative medicine refers to diagnostic and treatment approaches not commonly taught in depth in traditional medical/veterinary schools. These may include nutritional supplements, herbal medicine, homeopathy, chiropractic care, and acutherapies.

Here are some suggestions for finding a holistic practitioner:

- Ask your veterinarian for recommendations.
- Ask at local barns.
- Check bulletin boards at tack shops, feed stores, health food stores, natural pharmacies, and herb shops.

Contact holistic veterinary organizations, such as the following, to find local practitioners:

- Academy of Veterinary Homeopathy (AVH): *www.theavh.org*
- American Holistic Veterinary Medical Association (AHVMA): *www.ahvma.org*
- American Veterinary Chiropractic Association (AVCA): *www.animalchiropractic.org*
- International Veterinary Acupuncture Society (IVAS): *www.ivas.org*

Body Work

Body work includes massage, chiropractic, and acupressure. If you've ever had a massage, you know how good it can feel. The same is true for your horse. You can buy books that teach you how to give your horse a massage and that explain how chiropractic adjustments, acupressure treatments, and similar body work can help benefit your horse. If you think your horse might benefit from one or more of these therapies, discuss the notion with your veterinarian, who should be your first and foremost trusted advisor in all matters related to your horse's health.

Massage: Stress Point Therapy

The equine muscular system accounts for 60 percent of the horse's body weight and is responsible for movement. It is also the seat of most mobility problems, such as certain types of lameness and reduced range of motion and flexibility, which can diminish performance and cause discomfort. Whether your horse is a competitive athlete or accustomed to leisurely trail rides, it is likely that, at some point in his lifetime, he'll experience muscle strains and spasms.

Muscles create motion by contracting and folding over upon themselves. These folds then release so that the muscle can stretch to full length. Damaged, tight muscles cannot release completely. A muscle's ability to relax is reduced, and concussive stresses are transmitted down the line to other muscles, and finally to the tendons, which have limited flexibility and are thus vulnerable to serious, sometimes permanent, damage. Because the horse often compensates for a damaged part by increasing stress on a healthy part, restrictions in one area of the body can appear somewhere else. Adding massage therapy to your routine before you exercise your horse will help him maintain supple muscles and efficient motion and help avoid tendon damage and torn tissue.

The basis of Stress Point Therapy, used for decades by sports therapist Jack Meagher, is to locate and relieve the tight muscle that leads to the muscle spasm that leads to restricted motion before the muscle is torn. Spasms are areas of clumped attachment tissue that cannot release. They occur at the anchoring end of muscles, near the bone—the stress points for which this therapy is named.

Always consult a veterinarian any time your horse is ill, lame, or injured. If you're lucky enough to find a vet who is knowledgeable about the use of herbs and other holistic therapies, all the better for your horse.

The release process uses direct pressure from your fingers to dilate capillaries, cross-fiber friction to separate knotted muscle fibers, and compression with the heel of the hand or a loose fist to allow the entire muscle to relax and release the original spasm before exercise. Meagher's book, *Beating Muscle Injuries for Horses*, shows maps of all the stress points and specifics on identifying and correctly treating spasms and restrictions. It takes you through the process of identifying where motion is restricted, so you can provide the release that restores elasticity.

Chiropractic

Chiropractors focus on the relationship of the spinal column both to organic systems (nerves, organs, and immune system) and to the biomechanics of movement. The key approach in chiropractic is manipulation, and the key to success is the skill and training of the person using the technique.

The laws of biomechanics require that each part of the body interact with others precisely. When one part in the equine body loses its specific relationship with its coworkers, thousands of pounds of force can adversely affect the system. Long-term misalignments may be apparent in uneven muscle development or weight-bearing capacities. Even tiny structural changes can result in discomfort for the horse and will probably show up under saddle or in exercise.

Chiropractors use palpation—checking for pain or asymmetries with their hands—and flexion of the horse's limbs and joints to identify problem areas in the skeletal structure. Adjustments are made manually, using a brief thrust at specific locations or by manipulating the body of the horse to provide release in various joints. This should be a relatively gentle process, always without force, and it should be attempted only by someone who is well trained in the therapy.

Acupressure

Acupressure is an easy and rewarding therapy that you can use yourself to promote the well-being of your horse. The benefits seem to be so varied that you may decide to learn the basic principles and develop your skills. Acupressure is based on the meridian system at the heart of traditional Chinese medicine (TCM). Meridians are pathways in the body along which flow the energy that is considered vital to health, known as chi (sometimes spelled qi). In TCM, it is thought that any block or break along a meridian causes a chi imbalance that may appear as illness or discomfort. Therefore, the goal in TCM—and acupressure—is to maintain or repair interruptions in energy flow.

FACT

In TCM, the ear is considered a miniature representation of the entire body, making ear work useful to relax a tense horse or rebalance an injured or ill one. Rubbing the ears or forehead seems to help calm horses being shod or examined by a vet. Some basic ear massages involve gently rubbing the tips of the ears to help relax the horse and rubbing in circles at the base of the ear or on the forehead between the ears.

The meridian system contains twelve main meridians, each related to major organ systems. Other points outside the twelve meridians are also important to the strong flow of chi. Zidonis, Snow, and Soderberg's *Equine Acupressure: A Working Manual* is one good source for point location and provides a comprehensive overview and guidelines to using acupressure, including strategies for relieving many common problems.

Acupuncturists have used the Qi Gong Machine (QGM) in treatment for humans for years, and the device has now been proven effective with horses. Equisonic QGM is designed specifically for horses. The machine emits low-level (infrasonic) sound waves in the range of 8–14 hertz, at the opposite frequency range from ultrasound (20,000–100,000 hertz). Studies have shown that during hands-on healing, qi gong healers emit frequencies in this range. Because tissues do not heat up and there are no side effects, the QGMs can safely be used by anyone. It has helped provide relief or aid recovery in horses suffering from fractures, laminitis, chronic and acute inflammation, sprains, tendon damage, colic, puncture wounds, and navicular disease. Again, this approach may sometimes serve as a useful adjunct treatment, but it should not replace conventional medicine for these or other conditions.

The relationship between the acupoints and their effects may seem strange at first if you aren't used to Chinese therapies—the points used to relieve symptoms are often located at a distance from the apparent site of injury or illness.

Basic acupressure is typically done by gently applying and releasing between two and four pounds of pressure with the thumb to stimulate points. Watch your horse as you work to see whether you need to reduce pressure. He should relax, not tense, with your touch. Often, the horse's lips, chin, or eyelids will quiver as relief flows. He may yawn repeatedly. Work both the left and right sides of the horse from front to rear and top to bottom. Significant improvements are often immediately apparent, making acupressure a valuable adjunct to other more conventional therapies, improving recovery time and outcomes.

Herbs for Health

Always use herbs, vitamins, and other nutritional supplements with care, and make sure your veterinarian is aware of any such products that you're giving your horse. Too much of a seemingly good thing can be just as bad as too little. Overuse of certain vitamins and other substances can lead to toxicity. There's a big emphasis today on natural care, but *natural* is a largely misused term and, therefore, isn't always what it implies. Read labels carefully and ask your veterinarian if you have any doubts about a product.

Herbal Basics

Herbal medicine was a primary base of veterinary care until the twentieth century. Today many pharmaceutical drugs are based on natural and synthetic versions of the active compounds in plants. However, there is more value to herbs than just their active chemical compounds, and often much benefit is lost in the process of isolating active ingredients for the pharmaceutical version. According to Dr. Andrew Weil, a well-known proponent of natural medicine, plant-based drugs can be more toxic than the natural form of the plant.

FACT

Medicinal herbs can enhance conventional medical treatment, boost and support the immune system for preventive maintenance, and offer remedies for some common problems that plague horses and the humans who care for them. Most remedies are based on repeated observation of the choices animals in a natural environment make when they are ill or injured.

It is rare for horses today to have access to the range of plants their ancestors encountered in the wild or in country pastures, but if they do, they often will instinctively select the botanicals that contain what they need. Horses with ample free-range grazing will usually avoid poisonous fodder. However, hungry horses will eat just about anything they can sink their teeth into to survive, poisonous or not. Remember that, and keep your pastures free of plants and trees that might potentially harm your animals, particularly if the fields tend to get overgrazed.

Certain herbs can, in some instances, be added to the horse's feed, used as simple topical remedies, or applied as poultices for swellings, bites, or abscesses. As in other aspects of horsemanship, it's possible to spend a lifetime studying herbs and not have enough time to learn half of everything there is to know. However, you can find valuable resources from people who have studied extensively if you decide to add natural herbal support to your horse care routine.

Be aware that there are herbal answers for a wide range of questions about equine health, but not all of them are supported or proven effective by research. It's important to educate yourself or to find a knowledgeable source to be sure you're helping your horse, not creating problems. Not all herbs are safe for long-term use, and some are not safe in combination with other medications. Also, remember that many drugs are based on botanicals, and some herbs will show up as banned substances in horse show drug tests.

Garlic

Garlic proponents claim it does all sorts of wonderful things, from serving as an effective insect repellent to preventing colic. Supposedly, horses excrete the sulfur from garlic through their skin, which is said to keep bugs away. Garlic is also said to support the good bacteria so vital to digestion, which is why some say it may aid in preventing colic. Others say that, since antibiotics wipe out all bacteria, feeding garlic may be valuable to encourage the good bacteria after a course of antibiotics. Proponents also claim that garlic is effective with respiratory infections and for seasonal respiratory allergies such as hay fever, that it can prevent wounds from becoming infected by stimulating the production of white blood cells, and that it can strengthen general resistance to infection and improve the immune system.

If these claims sound too good to be true, they probably are. The main point to keep in mind is that there often is little or no definitive research to support such grandiose claims about garlic and many other herbs. It is known, however, that garlic and onions contain a potentially toxic element that can affect the red blood cells adversely and cause anemia in horses and some other animals. What is not known for certain is how large (or small) an amount must be consumed to create this adverse result. Therefore, if you are tempted to feed garlic to your horse, proceed with caution and ask your veterinarian about it first.

FACT

Dandelions are a rich source of vitamins A, B, C, and D and minerals such as potassium, magnesium, and calcium. Most horses love to eat them growing wild out in the fields, particularly when they are flowering. Some people dig them up out of their yards and offer them as treats; however, avoid collecting dandelions for your horse from lawns treated with fertilizers and pesticides, as these chemicals can be harmful.

Rosehips

Rosehips are the small red fruits left behind after the petals fall off a rose bush. Herbalists claim that the high concentration of vitamin C in rosehips is great for fighting infection and helping to restore health after a long illness. They add that botanical sources of nutrients provide additional benefits, such as fiber, that supplements don't always include, making rosehips a good choice over a vitamin C supplement. In her book *A Modern*

Horse Herbal, Hillary Page Self reports that she has found rosehips to be effective in promoting strong, healthy hooves. The reason for this may be that rosehips contain a small amount of biotin, a nutrient known to promote healthy hooves that is contained in many commercial hoof supplements.

Nutritional Supplements

Humans are discovering the benefits of adding supplements to their diets to support good health. If the majority of the food you eat is commercially grown and processed, you should be concerned. Growing evidence suggests that modern farming techniques, based largely on synthetic fertilizers and single-crop fields, have stripped much of the mineral content from the soil and thus from the foods we eat. Processing also destroys many vital nutrients.

If you have plenty of grazing land for your horses to forage on, you are fortunate, but you are also in the minority. Most horse owners must keep their animals confined to smaller acreage with limited year-round access to the grasses that could supply their needs. For at least part of the year, they must supplement those needs with commercial feeds and hay purchased elsewhere.

Antioxidants

When you leave iron tools out in the weather, they oxidize, which produces rust. A similar degenerative process happens in cells. In the metabolic process, the body produces oxides, which are known as free radicals. Antioxidants are key components in the free radical defense system. Familiar examples of antioxidants are vitamins A, C, and E. When all is going well, the balance between free radicals and antioxidants keeps cellular damage manageable. However, in times of illness and other stresses—including exposure to pollution, heavy metals, and chemicals—free radicals can overwhelm the body's immune system, leaving the body vulnerable to infections and illness, perhaps even cancer. The theory is that supplemental antioxidants can help return stressed bodies to health or prevent stress exposure from negatively impacting health. The body will use and store only the antioxidants it requires and eliminate excess levels.

Horses that compete on the show circuit endure a great deal of extra stress. Frequent trailering, disruption of routine, and the added athletic demands placed on them during show season all can take their toll. If you feel your horse may benefit from an antioxidant supplement, talk to your veterinarian. Ideally, your veterinarian can help you determine the need and the best strategy for supplementation.

MSM

Methylsulfonylmethane (MSM) is an organic sulfur used by the body to produce enzymes for digestion and antibodies to fight infection and to build connective tissue (e.g., cartilage, skin, and hooves). MSM, used in conjunction with glucosamine, is often recommended for arthritic symptoms to help rebuild the cartilage that cushions the bones. It also reduces allergic reactions. If your horse gets a case of hives, MSM can erase this allergic reaction.

ALERT!

If your horse's hives are unusually severe, aren't gone in a day or so, or if they worsen, call your vet immediately. Allergic reactions can be serious. Hives can also indicate more serious underlying conditions.

Glucosamine

Osteoarthritis seems to go hand in hand with an athletic life. When the cartilage that lines the joints to keep bones from rubbing together deteriorates because of wear and tear or age, crippling pain can result. Proponents claim that glucosamine can actually rebuild damaged cartilage, in contrast to anti-inflammatory drugs that mask the pain and, therefore, speed up the deterioration process from overuse. If you and your veterinarian suspect arthritis, try a joint supplement containing glucosamine, additional vitamin C, and MSM. (It is worth noting that there is evidence that glucosamine HCl is more absorbable than glucosamine sulfate.)

The supplier will provide a recommended dosage frequency and amounts based on your horse's weight. You may see some change in about a month, but it often takes several months before the full benefit of the supplement begins to kick in. If it's effective, you can keep your horse on glucosamine for the rest of his life if you can afford it. Although prices have come down a bit, joint supplements can still be quite an expensive addition to your feed bill.

Be aware that feeding an excess of certain nutrients and supplements can sometimes backfire and cause unintended problems. For example, you can undermine your efforts to improve your horse's health by creating an imbalance of phosphorus and calcium through over supplementation. Too much sulfur may actually inhibit hoof growth. That's why it's important to know exactly what's already going into the feed bucket and the hay bin, as well as the quality of your pastures, before you start adding supplements willy-nilly. If your horse maintains good health and body condition without them, save your money.

Probiotics

As an owner, your horse's digestive health is a primary concern. Colic (abdominal pain that can be mild or severe) is the number one killer of horses, and a variety of things can cause it, including:

- Dehydration
- Changes in feed
- Bolting feed
- Eating sand
- Eating moldy hay or spoiled feed
- Eating or drinking too soon after strenuous exercise

Anything we can do to keep our horses from being stricken with colic is worth knowing about. Aside from good horse management and feeding practices, that includes knowing about probiotics and when to consider their use.

Horses process feed with the aid of various digestive bacteria (intestinal flora). These friendly bacteria are greatly reduced in number when your horse is under antibiotic treatment or under stress caused by long-distance traveling, loss of a companion, a move to a new home, and so forth. Also, if you change feed (which should always be done gradually), new flora must develop to break down the new feed. Adding beneficial bacteria (called probiotics) to your horse's diet can help him recover more quickly from an illness or difficult adjustment and may even help reduce the chance of colic.

Horse-specific probiotics are widely available from feed stores and catalog suppliers, and dosage suggestions come on the package. Older horses or those prone to mild colic episodes may especially benefit from probiotics.

The list of dietary supplements is extensive, and as you become more involved with horses, you will find that you add them based on your horse's health and needs. You certainly won't need them all, and you may not need any if your horse is thriving and energetic. But we all age, and as time passes the body can't make or absorb some nutrients as efficiently as it used to. Used wisely and with a great deal of forethought, nutritional supplements can potentially add comfortable, useful years to your horse's life.

Energy Therapies

For thousands of years, Asian cultures have perfected techniques to improve the flow of life energy called chi. Energy practitioners enhance energy to improve total health through various remedies (homeopathics or Bach flowers), tools (needles, magnets, sonic devices, or lasers), or their hands, as with Reiki.

FACT

New uses for laser therapy are being discovered all the time. The modern low-level laser is gaining acceptance as an important adjunct to acu-therapies and has been used to treat a variety of conditions. You should never use one of these devices on your horse without first asking your veterinarian and becoming thoroughly trained in how to use it safely.

Acupuncture

Acupuncturists use extremely fine needles to release areas of blocked chi at specific acupoints along the meridians. After normal energy flow is re-established, circulation of chi increases to stimulate the nervous system to restore normal function in the body system that was depleted. Another benefit of acupuncture is the release of endorphins, the body's own feel good chemicals. As a result of these benefits, horses generally find acupuncture quite soothing.

Acupuncturists palpate the acupoints to make diagnoses and determine the best treatment. Because a specific diagnosis is involved, acupuncture is considered the practice of medicine and, therefore, can only be legally performed by licensed veterinarians. Growing numbers of vets are training in this ancient medical art, so it won't be impossible to find someone. If your vet isn't licensed for acupuncture, perhaps she can refer you to someone.

Homeopathy

Homeopathic remedies are gaining in popularity both with horse folks and veterinarians. Homeopathy has been practiced for about 200 years in Europe and the United States. The basic premise of homeopathic medicine is that like cures like, a theory first proposed by Hippocrates, the father of medicine. In theory, a substance that in large doses would produce symptoms can actually alleviate those symptoms when applied in smaller doses. Homeopathic remedies stimulate the body's defense system to cope with the problem very similar to the way vaccines operate.

Homeopathic remedies are subject to strict FDA standards. The natural animal, vegetable, or mineral substance a remedy is based on is present only at an electromagnetic level, which makes this branch of natural medicine difficult to understand. Homeopathic practitioners use individual symptoms and case studies to devise a strategy to treat chronic or complex problems. Success may depend on the experience the practitioner has prescribing remedies, so work with a veterinarian who has formally studied this art.

Bach Flowers

Bach flowers can be thought of as homeopathy for the emotions. Dr. Edward Bach developed flower remedies in the 1930s to help human patients restore the harmony between mind and body necessary for the well-being of each. Today, many holistic animal practitioners swear by the power of Bach flower remedies to help animals, including humans, to reduce or eliminate negative emotions so that they can better cope with stressful activities or events. If your horse is anxious, nervous, or fearful, you may want to consider using Bach flower essences as an appropriate complement to alternative and conventional treatments.

The power of these remedies comes primarily from flowers, although other botanicals and even minerals may be the basis for the remedies. Supposedly, they work not on the cellular system but on the subtle energies of the body. There are thirty-eight individual remedies, plus the combination remedy known as Rescue Remedy. With the assistance of brochures that are available where you purchase the flower essences, you can select the appropriate remedy based on your horse's personality and behavior. For example, walnut is said to be useful in helping horses cope with changing circumstances, as when moving to a new home.

FACT

Rescue Remedy is the most famous of the Bach flower remedies. It contains a blend of five flower essences said to help reduce the effects of trauma and shock. If your horse suffers a loss of a barn buddy this remedy can purportedly help reverse the effects of the emotional shock and panic. This remedy is said to be good for people, too.

Magnetic Therapy

Magnets have been used in health care for centuries to improve circulation, oxygen absorption, and cell function. The theory is that the iron atoms in blood corpuscles respond to magnetism to enhance blood flow, which aids in the elimination of waste products and in cellular regeneration. A similar action is thought to carry calcium ions to broken bones.

Magnetic fields are created by the flow of energy between a north and a south pole in static magnets. In pulsed electromagnetic field magnets, the field is created by electric pulses, but static magnets are more common and are found in the leg wraps, hoof wraps, and blankets recently developed for equine uses.

By following a few basic rules, magnets can safely be used by anyone. (As always in cases of serious injury or illness, call in a professional for evaluation and treatment recommendations.) Magnets should only be used under veterinary supervision and for a few consecutive hours a few days at a time.

Equine product manufacturers recommend that you don't use magnets on open wounds or burns, on injuries that are less than forty-eight hours old, injuries that are hot, or over liniments or chemicals such as fly sprays.

TTouch

The Tellington Touch (TTouch) was developed by Linda Tellington-Jones from work she did with Moshe Feldenkrais in the 1970s. Feldenkrais developed a system of gentle, nonhabitual movements and manipulations (the Feldenkrais Method of Functional Integration) to redirect human body patterns that had been established in response to dysfunction, tension, or pain. These new patterns of movement were said to awaken unused brain cells and establish new neural pathways. People from all over the world have used the Feldenkrais Method and found relief from pain and new freedom of movement. With TTouch, the primary goal is to enhance the health, performance, and well-being of the horse, as well as to foster communication and trust between horse and handler. It is recommended that the owner or primary handler of the horse be the one to use TTouch on the horse to increase the connection between them.

Here are the four basic TTouch techniques:

- Stroking with your flat hand to increase circulation and calm the horse
- Cupping the hand and using the fingertips to move the horse's skin in small or large circles one and a quarter revolutions
- Cupping the hands and patting the horse over the entire body to stimulate blood circulation
- Taking up a roll of skin between the thumbs and fingers and sliding it along the muscle surface in straight lines

TTouch for horses incorporates stretches, mouth work, tail work, and ear work to release tension and increase the horse's sense of security. TTouch is often part of a program that includes ground exercises and bodywork called TTEAM (the Tellington-Touch Equine Awareness Method). These techniques promise to increase willingness, horse-human rapport, and athletic performance. Tellington-Jones also has a riding component based on her thirty years of experience.

Learn about TTouch techniques from Linda Tellington-Jones's books (see Appendix A), videos, and nationwide clinics. You can also check out her website at *www.tellingtontouch.com*.

Reiki

In some human hospitals in the United States, trained nurses now offer Reiki to surgical patients. Recovery can be easier and faster when the patient receives this gentle therapy before, during, or after surgery. In the past decade, as more horse owners and holistic practitioners have discovered the benefits of energy therapy themselves, they have shared these healing techniques with their animals, too.

Using their hands, Reiki practitioners boost the body's own energy flow to open pathways where chi may be blocked. Once students have been attuned by a Reiki master, they find that suddenly they can sense areas where energy is blocked. These areas supposedly feel warmer than surrounding areas, in response to the greater draw of energy there. Hands-on energy work requires no diagnosis because the body will simply take the energy it needs from Reiki treatments to re-establish healthy chi movement throughout the body. As internal energy resumes its vital flow, healing can begin.

If you get the chance to watch a Reiki session, check it out. Generally, a treatment lasts forty minutes to an hour, depending on the horse's needs. Reiki soothes emotional unrest and can help a horse recover from physical illness or injury. As energy pathways open, the horse's response can be dramatic. The eyes close and the head drops. The horse may yawn or work its mouth. His breathing deepens and gut sounds often increase. The horse's entire body reflects the deep level of relaxation, usually within ten to fifteen minutes. Some horses even fall asleep!

Of course, Reiki won't replace your veterinarian, but it may provide relief and make a difference in certain situations. It may also help minimize sprains and strains (especially in conjunction with homeopathics and cold hosing or ice), maintain chiropractic adjustments, and soothe sore feet, among other benefits.

Your Horse's Mental Health and Happiness

Much has been written about natural horse keeping, but there really is no such thing anymore. Horses under truly natural conditions run wild and free, without fences to stop their migrations. They live in herds and spend their lives foraging for food, fleeing from danger, and raising young. Unfortunately, the price for this lifestyle is a shortened lifespan, as the wild horse succumbs to disease, injury, and predators much sooner than her captive counterparts.

As Natural as Possible

Your horse will be happier and mentally healthier if you can keep him under as natural conditions as possible. This means keeping him on pasture with ample grazing when weather permits. Unfortunately, many people keep their horses confined to stalls most of the day, either for convenience or because of limited land resources. This circumstance is quite unnatural for horses, and the ensuing boredom and pent-up energy can lead to all sorts of behavioral problems. To simulate more natural conditions, give your horse as much turnout time as possible so he can graze and stretch his legs.

Provide Companionship

Horses are herd animals and are happiest when living with other equine companions. If you can afford to own only one horse, keeping him at a boarding facility offers the advantage of other horses for him to socialize with. If boarding isn't an option for you, then consider owning more than one horse, if at all possible. If you can't afford to buy two horses, perhaps you can adopt a homeless horse from a rescue shelter. If you have enough land, consider keeping someone else's horse on your property so that both animals have a companion and you have a riding buddy.

CHAPTER 13

Horse Behavior

Your horse's behavior is perhaps the most important thing for you to understand and know how to
influence for the two of you to have the most satisfying relationship. How your horse behaves around
you and in the barnyard is the key to your safety, as
well as that of your horse and everyone who interacts
with him.

Herd Behavior

Horses are herd animals. In the wild, they survive by roaming in groups. Herds consist mostly of mares, called harem bands, which are serviced by one stallion that protects and defends the herd. The patriarch is the sole adult male horse in the herd. All other males are young colts that will be driven out to live in a bachelor band when they are mature enough to become interested in breeding and, thus, represent a threat to the patriarch.

Alpha Mares

There are also young fillies in the herd who will remain with the herd until they are either stolen by another stallion trying to start or increase his harem band or are bred within the harem by their own father or by a new stallion who takes over the herd, which happens on an average of every two to three years.

The dominant member of a herd, however, is always an alpha mare. This mare decides where the herd goes and, as the high-ranking member, gets first choice of food and water. Through a process of testing and retesting, all herd members come to understand and accept this as standard. If a herd member does not submit to the lead mare, the lead mare drives the disobedient horse outside the group, which leaves the horse vulnerable to predators, a fearful situation for any horse to be in. The horse may learn from this experience and be accepted back, join a bachelor band if it's a young stallion, or be scooped up by another stallion's harem if it's a mare.

QUESTION?

What does alpha mean?
The term *alpha* refers to an animal's personality type. Alpha animals are usually more aggressive, curious, protective, and bossy in a herd. They are leaders, not followers. The proud attitude of an alpha mare can make her an exceptional show horse and an intelligent mount to ride. However, she must be trained and handled with knowledgeable care and respect, so as to mold these qualities into desirable, rather than dangerous, behaviors. It is a huge mistake to try to bully such animals into submission.

In domestic horse life, stallions have the reputation for being dangerous and going after what they want—which tends to be to mate with any mare in sight—whether or not there's a human being in the way. However, anyone who owns mares knows that little compares with the bossiness of an alpha mare and the danger she can pose, especially if she is protecting a foal.

The stallion keeps the herd together, and newcomers are not allowed into the established herd without the stallion's okay. With the mare and stallion dominating, all other members of the herd are part of a pecking order and must show submission to the ones that rank above them. As the herd dynamic changes—members die, foals are born, and youngsters age—the pecking order constantly adjusts. Age typically determines rank, with the youngsters being at the bottom, but as they grow older, these young horses constantly challenge and, thus, alter the status quo. The herd members may change, die out, or move on, but the herd laws remain the same. Such consistency gives the horse a sense of security, as it helps him know his place in his world.

Domestic Herd Behavior

If you have more than one horse or if you keep your horse at a stable with other horses, you have ample opportunity to see horse-to-horse behavior in action. Of course, the domestic herd dynamic is different from that of a wild herd. In the wild, the herd grows and changes according to breeding season, and there is a natural mix of younger and aging animals. In your backyard or at a boarding stable, the herd changes artificially, directed by humans. New horses may be of similar age, size, or even of the same sex as the existing herd members.

You can learn a great deal about horses simply by watching groups of domestic horses interact in the field. You can learn more about your own horse and how she functions in her equine world by watching how she fits in with her pasture companions.

Turning Horses Out Together

If you've ever watched horses play in the field together, you know they can be very rambunctious, which is why people often are reluctant to let horses be together. Domestic horses, like wild horses, will establish a pecking order, and in determining their ranks, the scene can get a little wild, with biting, kicking, charging, and rearing. They can definitely hurt each other, but most of them wisely pay attention to each other's subtle signals and know when to avoid actual physical contact.

ALERT!

Horses in rental-type trail rides are usually well socialized to people and other horses, but they will still behave like normal horses. This can pose a danger for a novice rider who doesn't understand the warning signals that a horse gives to another one that follows too closely. Never ride too closely behind another horse, or you could get a good kick from the horse in front.

Not Enough Space

Horses confined together are more likely to get hurt when they don't have enough space to get away from each other. For example, if one horse chases another, and the horse being chased has nowhere to go but over or through a fence, that is where the horse will go. But if there is ample space, then the lower-echelon horse has room to move away and learn the lesson of boundaries, and it won't get hurt in the process.

Instead of chasing, some horses may back up and kick at their opponent with both back feet or lunge with bared teeth. If the space is big enough and there are no corners to get trapped in, the horse getting the worse end of the deal can stay out of reach of teeth or hind feet. But if the space is too small, the horse can easily be pinned in the corner of a corral and kicked badly. If given enough space, a horse's choice will almost always be simply to get out of harm's way. If provided with ample grazing, most horses will stay happily occupied with their nose in the grass and have less inclination for arguments.

Socializing Horses, Especially When Young

Horse owners sometimes make the choice to never put their horse in with another horse, for fear that they will hurt each other. Although this choice is understandable, especially if you own a valuable show animal, a solitary life is quite lonely and unfair to the horse. Horses crave companionship and need interaction with their own kind. If possible, it is better for their mental health and overall contentment if they can spend some time socializing with other horses. After all, they are herd animals by nature.

FACT

Imprinting is a specific desensitizing method used with newborn foals. Robert Miller, DVM, developed the technique, which involves handling the newborn foal extensively to accustom it to human hands. Learn more about imprinting by reading Dr. Miller's book, *Imprint Training of the Newborn Foal.*

Horses may hurt one another when two or more horses are suddenly thrown together without allowing them to see and smell each other first from nearby. If just one of them is unaccustomed to being with other horses, problems will develop fast. Some horses lack the necessary socialization skills to get along with and live among other horses, usually because they've never been allowed to live in a herd. These horses don't understand the nuances of the equine pecking order and are not likely to understand dominant and submissive standings in the herd. Nor do they understand the other horses' warning signals when they unknowingly violate the order by getting too close to a dominant member's feed.

Introducing Horses to Each Other

The best time to socialize horses is when they are young. Foals love to play and do so mostly without seriously hurting each other. At the same time, they learn to read each other's signals and coexist peacefully. Of course, the dam will teach her youngster some things, but that doesn't always translate into understanding the same signals from a horse that is not his mother. In addition, a horse that has learned only from his mother may not know that disregarding the signals can hurt, since the dam typically will not deliberately hurt her offspring.

Take It Slow

Although a well-socialized horse is more likely to fit in with others, you still need to allow the newcomer to blend into the established herd gradually. First, put the new horse in a nearby corral where the others can see him. Next, put the newcomer in a field adjacent to the herd. If the horses are stalled at night, put the new horse beside one of the other herd members. If all is going well at this stage, put the new horse out with one other horse in the herd (the most docile one), and finally, put the entire group together. At each stage, observe the reactions before you move on.

When you finally do put them all together, set out piles of hay a good distance apart to give them something else to occupy their minds besides each other. It can work like a charm—by the time they finish the hay pile, they look up and say, "Hey, it's you, the horse I've seen over the fence for a few days," and go off and have a drink or nap in the sun. This blending process may take days or weeks, but when you finally put them all together in one herd, there shouldn't be too many fireworks other than some inevitable squealing, and maybe even some striking and a little biting. This sounds a whole lot worse than it typically is; however, if after a couple of days, two of the group just won't leave each other alone, you may have to separate them or experiment with some new groupings.

Horse Talk

Horses are masters of body language and the body cues they use among themselves are their primary means of interherd communication. However, like many other animals, horses also communicate by making sounds. These include:

- **Snorts and blowing sounds:** Horses make snorting noises— sometimes a short snort, sometimes an elongated sound—when they are afraid of or curious about something.
- **Nicker:** This low, friendly rat-a-tat-tat sound is one that horses use as a greeting.
- **Neigh/Whinny:** High-pitched, long, and loud, a whinny is another greeting that can be used for long distances.
- **Squeal:** This somewhat unpleasant short, high-pitched sound is the one you'll hear when two horses are getting to know each other or playing rough games.
- **Scream:** This sound happens in a true fight, often between competing stallions, something we rarely witness in domesticated horse life.

FACT

If you're a fan of the classic television show *Mr. Ed*, starring a talking palomino, check out *www.mister-ed.com*. This website includes sound clips, historical background, information about the cast, and any recent news mentions that the show has received. Also included is an episode guide of all of the 143 episodes broadcast between 1961 and 1966.

When They Just Don't Get Along

Boarding stables often shift horses around until they find the group that a newcomer is most welcome in. Domestic horses that spend most of their leisure time living in groups seem to be the most content, so it is definitely worth trying to figure out how to turn your horse out with others. However, there are certainly times when two horses just don't get along, and you never feel like you can trust them together. If this occurs, don't take a chance on one or both horses getting hurt. Separate them.

Grouping by Age and Sex

Some people separate the mares from the geldings, although there are not hard and fast rules about this. Doing so seems to help reduce the amount of rough play and dominance games that go on within a herd.

Grouping by age range is often more logical than grouping by sex. Putting a very young or a very old horse in with a group can sometimes have undesirable results. Youngsters can get hurt just because of their size differences. After the age of two or three, most horses (and definitely the stock horse breeds) tend to be of substantial size compared to adults and are a little less delicate. If at all possible, make sure a young horse has a couple of companions of similar age in the group. Elderly horses may get edged out of their feed by the younger, stronger herd members. You'll need to observe the interactions closely, to make sure your older horse isn't getting picked on or excluded from prime grazing opportunities.

FACT

Some people perceive horses as stupid because they exhibit fear of things such as a plastic bag flapping in the wind. However, an animal of prey must always be on the lookout for danger. No one knows for certain how horses think, but clearly they do make decisions relative to survival in the prey versus predator environment. Some of their decisions may be good, some bad.

The Stallion Dilemma

Stallions present a different issue and clearly cannot run with mares that you do not intend to breed. Although some well-socialized stallions may run with groups of geldings, this is the exception rather than the rule. In most cases, stallions are kept by themselves, usually in a separate paddock with higher, reinforced fencing.

Bring in the Human

Your horse should conduct itself respectfully in your presence. Most people would agree that this means a horse mustn't kick, bite, strike out with a fore-leg, or treat you like one of its pasture mates. Your horse must respect your personal space so that it does not step on you or knock you down. And no matter how cute it may look, your horse should not be allowed to rub its head on you or use you as a scratching post, as such actions from a one-ton animal pose a potential danger to a human.

Training Happens Daily

Domestic horses are products of their environment and the quality of training they receive from humans. Most people think of training as something someone did before they bought the horse to make it amenable to being ridden. But training involves a lot more than breaking to saddle and bridle. Training occurs every moment a human spends with a horse, for better or for worse. From riding to grooming to just picking out the horse's feet, the horse is learning from you what he can and cannot do.

For instance, if after you take his bridle off, your horse rubs his head up and down your arm to scratch his sweaty, itchy ears, and you think, "Oh, that's cute," and you do not push his head away to stop it, you've just taught him that it's okay to do that. Later, he does it several more times, and you proudly show someone else how much he adores you and how amazing it is that an animal so big could express his affection in such a manner.

Then one day, while using you as a rubbing post, he knocks your glasses off and accidentally steps on them, or he bangs the bridle into your cheek and the buckle cuts a nice line up the side of your face, barely missing your eye. Suddenly, his head rubbing doesn't seem so cute. Preventable accidents like this happen all the time because unwitting owners don't realize that the average horse's head is heavy because it contains a lot of bone. If that head bangs into your face with the right amount of force, it can easily knock you senseless or even kill you.

FACT

Clever Hans was a Berlin horse whose owner, Wilhelm von Osten, taught him to solve mathematical equations, answer geography questions, identify musical scores, and perform other tricks. The secret? Von Osten was giving signals to Clever Hans from a spot behind the horse. Horses can see almost completely behind them, but unless you knew this you wouldn't have guessed the trick.

Of course, there's nothing wrong with a nice rub around the ears after a workout. Just make sure you do the rubbing with a towel and a soft brush. Even if you've been giving your horse the wrong messages all these years— letting him rummage in your pockets for treats or move off before you are mounted and settled in the saddle—it's never too late to start teaching new messages. Although it's harder to undo bad habits once they're well established, horses are smart and can learn new things if you are consistent and persistent in what you ask for.

Learning the Signals

If you observe a herd interact in the field, you will soon realize that horses usually signal an upcoming action. For example, before a horse kicks out with a hind leg, it has to shift weight off the leg that kicks out. Often, a glance back with ears slightly pinned accompanies the weight shift. If you learn to be aware of these subtle signals, you can learn to anticipate what your horse is going to do next. Your increased awareness will greatly enhance your ability to safely handle and ride horses.

Leading by Respect, Not Fear

Horses naturally look for a leader to follow. It is the way of the herd animal. In the horse/human relationship, the human must assume the role of leader. For the safety of both parties, it can be no other way. Being the leader doesn't preclude having a partnership with your horse. It definitely doesn't mean establishing a relationship with your horse that is based on fear—in fact, that is exactly what you don't want. A horse can follow its leader either out of fear or out of respect. To the novice horse handler, the outcome of either approach may look the same; however, they are radically different.

As with people, some horses are natural-born leaders. Every herd needs a leader, and the alpha animals naturally assume that job. They can be the most challenging and the most interesting to work with. If you are a beginner, you will probably need some help from a skilled horseman if your horse has this personality type. These horses seem to think, "Well, if this human isn't going to be the leader, then I am." A horse that seems a bit of a rogue in the hands of a beginner can be a gentle horse when handled by an experienced horse person who knows how to establish leadership.

Move or Be Moved

Horses decide the position of other horse herd members and human members of their herd according to who the movers are. Higher-ranking herd members do not need to exert much effort to get lower-ranking herd mates to move out of their space (or to not move into it). Ears back or a leg barely raised can be enough.

If dominance is determined by who does the moving, the human needs to be the mover, not the moved. This is not easy—every interaction you have with your horse presents an opportunity to be moved. You always need to be aware of this, even when you are just going into your horse's paddock to fill the water tub or grooming him in the barn aisle. Some horses want to dance in the crossties while you brush and curry them. This is understandable for a young horse or one just introduced to the crossties. But eventually the horse needs to learn that he must stand still when you are working around him.

FACT

Pay attention to how your horse interacts with you. For instance, it is common for a young horse that is learning to lead to drop his shoulder into you and push you out of his way. If you allow this, he will learn that it is correct. Instead, you need to push him back and show him where he belongs.

Novice horse owners typically have no clue what dangers such behaviors can lead to; however, the horse with the personality type that will take advantage of this experience will present you with all kinds of related dominance issues to deal with later on. Even the most submissive horse will remember that he can simply move you out of the way when a real crisis comes up. For your safety, you must insist that the horse respect your personal space. Of course, this doesn't mean you must be aggressive or brutal to your horse. You simply need to be assertive, consistent, and aware of the consequences of your interactions with your horse.

How to Be Safe in the Group

Within a horse herd, the pecking order system will be in high gear at feeding time, especially around grain. The person feeding a group of horses needs to be on high alert to avoid being kicked or trampled. It is safest for you to bring each horse into its stall and feed it separately. If that isn't possible, set up your feeding area so that you can feed them from outside the fence, without going into the enclosure with the herd. If you must go in with the group, carry a big stick, a flag (a three- or four-foot metal or fiberglass rod with a piece of cloth attached to one end and comfortable handle on the other), a whip, or something that can help you establish your personal space and help them learn that you are not approachable at feeding time. Remember to spread hay piles far enough apart so that each horse gets a chance to eat.

Herd Bound and Barn Sour

Because horses are herd animals and territory is important to them, most are bothered by being separated from their group or taken away from the barn where they feel safest. Some horses exhibit this displeasure so subtly that only the most experienced horse handler would even notice it. Others exhibit it so graphically that you can't help but notice—say, after you're mown down by a distraught horse being led away from his pasture pals, or when you are on a runaway horse that comes to a screeching halt only after he reaches the barn aisle.

Chances are you'll experience something similar in between, and you might even attribute the behavior to another cause. Don't be fooled—the horse that plods along on the ride away from the barn but jigs on the ride home is not suddenly peppy for no reason. This is called being herd-bound and barn sour.

The important concept to grasp here is that your horse must learn to be comfortable and feel safe with you while away from his equine friends. Your horse must learn to trust and follow your lead. You must establish yourself as his herd leader by being reliable in your support and consistent in the boundaries you establish with him. You need to understand what is happening when barn sour behavior arises. Instead of being convinced by well-meaning but misguided advice to turn to new and bigger bits or changes in feeding programs, get to the root of the problem and up the level of trust in your relationship with your horse a notch.

Stable Vices

Stable vices are bad habits that horses develop from boredom or from being left in a confined area too long. Too much stall confinement causes a horse to become frustrated and stressed because it is completely against their natural way of existing.

Cribbing

Cribbing is perhaps the most insidious, most well-known, and most destructive of all stable vices. When a horse cribs, it grips its top front teeth on some hard edge, usually the top of a stall door or a fence board, pulls back, and makes a grunting noise—and does it over and over and over again. This is an addictive behavior that, once learned, typically can never be fully eliminated but only controlled. The addiction has been discovered to come from a release of natural stress-relieving endorphins that the horse experiences each time it does this.

Horses can either learn to crib accidentally or they can learn it from watching other horses. Cribbing can be expensive. When a 1,000-pound horse pulls back on a fence board, a stall door, or a feed tub screwed into the wall, that object takes a lot of stress and eventually breaks. Cribbing holds numerous potential major health issues for the horse as well. For example, the front teeth will show unnatural wear. Some horses are more interested in their addiction than in eating, so their digestive health and overall body condition may suffer.

QUESTION?

Are cribbing and wood chewing the same thing?
No. Although a cribber will certainly chew up wood fencing in the process of biting the boards, a wood chewer doesn't necessarily crib while it's destroying your fencing. Pica, or the habit of chewing wood or eating other unnatural substances (sand, dirt, gravel, feces), can indicate a nutrient deficiency. Sometimes a pasture deficient in phosphorus is to blame.

Some people don't seem to mind having a horse that cribs, but if you are in the market for a horse, you are wise to avoid a cribber. Although cribbing doesn't affect riding at all, it is technically considered an unsoundness, and anyone selling a horse is obligated to tell you about this habit. If you board your horse and notice a horse nearby cribbing, get your horse moved out of the cribbing horse's sight and preferably earshot.

If you have a horse that cribs or if your horse develops the habit, keep it outside all the time in an environment where there is little to crib on—electric fencing instead of board fencing; feed buckets loose on the ground, not attached to walls; a shelter that has no edges inside for the horse to grab onto, and so on. The most addicted cribbers will find amazing ways to satisfy their addiction. Anti-cribbing collars seem to be effective if they are perfectly adjusted.

Weaving
This vice is typically seen in a horse that is kept in a stall twenty-four hours a day. The horse stands at the door and weaves back and forth, back and forth, shifting its weight from one front leg to the other. This uneasy type of horse doesn't take confinement well. The problem will escalate if he develops any lameness issues that require immobility because weaving is almost impossible to control. If your horse starts to weave, you need to make him happier by giving him more time outside his stall.

Digging and Pawing
This habit is annoying, but it can also cause uneven foot wear for barefoot horses on hard ground. The horse may stand at her bucket, put her

head down, and paw like she is in a trance. Clean bedding gets dug up with the dirt floor almost immediately. Some horses paw anywhere in their stalls, sometimes digging up giant craters with both front feet. Some will paw right at the entrance to the stall, setting a nice booby trap for you. Like cribbing, this seems to be a learned behavior that horses pick up by watching others.

Encouraging Good Behavior

When you earn a horse's trust, you have earned a lot. However, once you have that trust, don't ever betray it—it's hard, but the minute you let someone talk you into trying that bigger bit or whatever, you jeopardize your horse's faith that you are consistent and trustworthy. Go with your good instincts, and if you feel unsure, enlist the aid of people whose instincts are similar to yours. This doesn't mean you should avoid exploring new ideas. However, using your good instincts as a guide will help ensure your horse's trust in you.

The behavior of a horse that does not trust you can look pretty ugly, and yet the horse is not to blame. Find some mentors in the horse world that you can turn to before you reach the point where you can't handle your own horse. A trusting, respectful horse in the hands of a trustworthy, respectful human is wonderful to behold and even more wonderful to experience.

CHAPTER 14

Handling

When it comes to horses, handling is everything. Your safety—and often the horse's as well—depends on your understanding of the best ways to handle your horse. The basics of handling revolve around what horsemen refer to as groundwork: working with and educating your horse on the ground as opposed to in the saddle. Good groundwork will clearly translate into things that are also useful when riding your horse, such as teaching voice commands. This chapter provides the basic principles of horse handling, but there is much more to learn.

Why Is Good Handling Important?

The horse's world revolves around his innate need to belong to a herd and around his understanding of his place in that herd. Where he ranks in that pecking order isn't nearly as important as *knowing* where he is in that order. So, if you and your horse are attached by a lead rope and he decides you aren't running the show, he will put himself in charge. This is the point where you need to draw the line. You cannot let him drag you around. He's not a puppy on the end of a leash. He's a one-ton animal, and if you aren't in control, you place both your horse and yourself in a potentially unsafe situation.

You Must Be the Leader

The person on the end of the lead rope makes all the difference. The same horse in the hands of two different people may act very differently. Whenever you reach a point where nothing seems to be working, consult a professional trainer for help. Just as a dog trainer teaches you how to handle your dog and teach her commands, a horse trainer will work with you to help you establish leadership and understand the disconnects between you and your horse.

Keeping Their Distance

Beginners are usually taught to lead their horse by standing to the horse's left and holding the lead rope right at the clip, where it attaches to the horse's halter. This is potentially dangerous. If the horse spooks at something from the right side, he has no where to go but sideways, on top of the handler—he can't jump forward because his forward movement is blocked by the tight hold on the lead rope.

Instead, give the lead rope a foot or two of slack. That way, if the horse spooks from either side, he can jump without jumping on you. If he spooks forward, the freedom you are giving his head allows him to jump ahead to either side of you, which is what he will choose to do—if you've taught him that running you over is unacceptable under any circumstances. If you don't want your horse to run over you, you must first earn his respect.

In the wild herd, the horses on the lower rungs of the pecking order would never dream of pummeling a higher-ranking individual. But some domesticated horses are bolder than others and look to challenge the established pecking order. You need to show these individuals more presence than you might need to show others. If your horse doesn't tend to challenge your position as leader, you can probably just send some energy up the length of the lead rope when he comes closer than you want to make him back off. He will soon learn the rules of appropriate distance.

For the bold horse, you will need to do what it takes for him to understand that you are the boss and you mean what you say. Of course, this doesn't mean you should beat your horse—this is about leadership and safety, not submission—but it may mean a bop on the end of the nose with the lead rope, a slap from your hand on his shoulder, or a tap with the whip on his rump to get his attention. If your horse learns to run you over, that bop or whack will seem pretty mild compared to hoof tracks up your back.

QUESTION?

What does conditioned response mean?
Conditioned response is a training approach in which a horse (or any thinking animal, including humans) is conditioned to respond to the same stimulus the same way every time he confronts that stimulus.

If you get the horse as a youngster, you can teach him enough about respect so this won't happen to begin with. If you are trying to change bad behavior that has been instilled in the horse by other people, the more effective you are in your handling, the quicker the change will happen, and you can both be happier.

Groundwork in Earnest

Groundwork is teaching your horse while you are on the ground, not mounted. It should begin while the horse is a foal. Groundwork may involve teaching the horse to lead and stand still while being groomed, teaching her to tie, exercising the horse on a lunge line, and driving her with long lines. If you do the groundwork well, the good manners the horse has learned should transfer to her training under saddle.

Stepping over the Hindquarters

There are some key things you need to teach your horse to help ensure your own safety on the ground. One is respect for your personal space. Another is stepping over the hindquarters, perhaps the single most useful move your horse needs to know.

The goal is to have your horse learn that if you turn his head to the right and liven up some energy with your hand, arm, or the end of the lead rope (or eventually your mind), he is to step his right hind foot underneath him in front of the left hind foot, and step his whole hindquarters to the left—and vice versa for the left. This move not only expands your horse's bend and flexibility but also makes it possible, for example, to step your horse out of a corral full of other horses clamoring to get out, or to step him into his stall and turn him to face you while you remove his halter and step out to latch the stall door. The list of situations for which this step comes in handy is endless. As with all other groundwork you do, this move is pretty useful when you are riding as well.

Yielding to Pressure

Your horse also needs to understand that she is to yield to pressure, not brace against it or fight it. When your horse thoroughly understands this, you should be able to simply place your hand on her side with meaning to get her to step away from it. If she accidentally steps on the lead rope and pulls on her head, she will back up away from the pressure and free the lead rope rather than fight against it and rip it out from under her foot. The only time it is safe to tie your horse is after he gains a thorough understanding of yielding to pressure.

Understanding how to yield to pressure may also be helpful if your horse gets caught in, say, fence wire. There is a much better chance that he may not panic and struggle; instead, he may wait to be released and will not hurt himself too badly.

Yielding to pressure also means that when you put your horse's halter on, she drops her head and helps you get it in the right place. She doesn't throw her head up as high as she can, making it more difficult for you to reach. If you need to back her up one step, you can ask for one step. When you get it and release the pressure, one step is all she'll move. True yielding is not a conditioned response method; it is truly meaningful to the horse.

What's with the Left Side?

There are many myths about why most of what we do with the horse—including leading, saddling, and mounting—is done from the left, or near, side. The most logical one comes from the need to mount on the left because of the position of the soldier's sword in battle. Most of us aren't using our horses in battle or carrying swords when we ride, but the tradition continues. Problem is, the tradition has created many one-sided horses.

A good handler who wants to build a solid, reliable horse will be sure her horse is as two-sided as possible, exposing him to new things from both sides and not doing everything from the traditional left. For example, put the saddle pad on from the right side occasionally, just so your horse gets accustomed to it.

Interestingly, horses are often more pushy on the left side than they are on the right. That's because the left is where they are usually handled the most and where some learn to push their human handler around by stepping into your space or away from you. If your horse does this, it's not his fault; it's yours for allowing him to do it. It's up to you to teach him to stand still while being handled or tacked up. He must learn not to step into your space and lean or push up against you. If he does, don't step back or you will succeed only in teaching him that he can push you away. Instead, poke your fingers into his side, where the rider's heels would normally be, and push him back over where he belongs, with a sharp command, "Move over!"

Handling the Young Foal

Handling a foal is not something a novice horse person should attempt, at least not without the continued guidance of someone more experienced. Foals may look cute and innocent, but they grow strong quickly and can kick and hurt you like any other horse if you don't handle them with care and know-how. Many a spoiled foal has grown into an unmanageable, ill-mannered horse simply because her owner didn't know how to handle her and teach her good things instead of bad.

Good handling starts from the moment a human first comes into contact with a foal. This doesn't mean you need to halter up a three-day-old filly and drill her with groundwork exercises for two-hour stints. That is absolutely not a good idea. But what it does mean is that every time the human interacts with that filly—halter on or not—that interaction needs to be handling that is conducive to desirable behavior.

No matter what the foal's age, she does not need to step on you, knock you out of the way, or otherwise disregard you. Each simple interaction can teach the foal to yield and step away from your pressure. One touch and one step is the first building block, negative or positive. Even simply scratching the young horse can be an enjoyable and educational experience. By continuing to scratch only when the foal is behaving herself and moving her away (very important—move her away, don't move away from her!) when she is being obnoxious about it teaches her that only respectful behavior gets respectful and generous behavior in return.

FACT

Clicker training is a dog training method that has become popular in the horse world. It involves repeatedly asking for a specific action, rewarding the performance of that action with a treat, and marking the desired action with a click from a little clicker box or even a click of your tongue. The click is used to recall and reinforce that action.

Be ever mindful not to teach the foal to pull back against pressure. Although typically a very young foal does not need to be led (he will follow his mother anywhere), if you do need to lead him, run the lead rope around his rump to help encourage forward movement and avoid setting up a pulling match. Never engage in a pulling match with horses because even a foal is strong enough to win.

These are tiny steps taken over the six months or so that the foal is suckling. Get her used to being groomed and sprayed with a water hose. Give her a bath. Get her accustomed to having her feet touched and picked up. The earlier you start with these things, the better.

After the foal is weaned and more independent, it is time to take all the steps you've set up since birth and begin to build on them. Again, this doesn't mean taking a young horse and drilling her for hours each day. Let the horse be a horse for a while—once she is under saddle, she will spend the rest of her life working for you. Having the first three years to just play and grow up seems like a fair deal.

About Confinement

Humans seem to spend a lot of time concocting ways to confine and restrain horses—stalls, paddocks, halters, bridles, crossties, bits, side reins, tie downs—the list is endless. Horses that are confined too much without any turnout to run and romp like a natural horse often get depressed or develop bad behaviors from all that pent-up energy. The following are the two best things you can do for your horse from the beginning of your relationship, whether you are raising a foal or starting with a newly bought horse of any age.

Consider the Whole Horse

Consider the horse's happiness and mental fitness as important as her physical well-being. A horse with a calm mind will be able to listen to you and learn from you. Too many people concentrate on fussing with a horse's body because it is more accessible and, therefore, a little easier to figure out. If you don't understand the horse's mind, how she thinks, and what she needs, find someone more knowledgeable to help you, and read books on the subject to increase your understanding.

Your horse needs some freedom to be a horse, to graze in a field and socialize with his own kind. If he stays penned up in a stall twenty-four hours a day, he will almost certainly suffer some confinement stress—and your ownership and riding pleasure will suffer for it, too.

Establish a Bond of Trust

Develop a mutually respectful relationship that allows you to trust your horse enough to give her some space to be a horse. If the horse has to be on the end of a lead rope, then at least she can have two or three feet of rope instead of being gripped at the clip. Many people can't give their horses that much space because the horse will constantly dive for grass or prance around. On a trail ride, they can't give their horse a loose rein because she constantly eats the bushes and branches along the way. This is where it is your job to teach the horse from the outset that such behavior is simply unacceptable and will not be tolerated.

Give your horse a better life by teaching him to be respectful. This allows you to trust him, which in turn allows you to stop trying to confine him so much. A horse that knows he can move if he absolutely has to is more likely to be okay about standing still when you want him to.

Everyday Handling

When watching steeplechasers scale high fences and run at breakneck speed down steep slopes, no one doubts that equestrian sports are dangerous. Somehow, it seems a miracle when anyone finishes those perilous courses without taking a tumble. But the truth is, you are just as likely to get hurt during routine handling of horses if you let your guard down or get sloppy about safety. While accidents will happen from time to time, the best way to lessen the chances of one is to learn safe handling procedures from the get-go and adopt them as part of your routine.

Feeding Time

Feeding time places you in a vulnerable situation—big, hungry horse, little person holding flake of hay or pail of grain. A common problem is the horse that mauls you when you enter her stall with her meal. Teach the horse to stand aside until you fill her feed bucket. Halter her and ask her to stand back. If you have to hold her at bay by pointing the end of a whip toward her—don't actually hit her with it, just point it at her—do it until she understands she has to wait. Small transgressions in behavior build into big safety concerns if you let them slide.

Keep in mind that model behavior at feeding time can be a lot to ask of a horse in the domestic environment. They are confined to a space not much bigger than their bodies sometimes for extraordinary periods of time. Their eating is regulated, a process totally opposite of their wild instincts of roaming and grazing twenty-four hours a day. No wonder horses are a little anxious when their caretaker arrives with a meal! Be patient and understanding, but also be consistent about the way you want your horse to act when you enter his stall. Do only what it takes to insist on the behavior you want—just don't do too much and risk frightening the horse.

ALERT!

Feeding a horse treats by hand is perhaps fun for the human, but few people are capable of feeding a horse by hand without setting up obnoxious and pushy behavior in an animal with a very powerful jaw and head. If you want to feed your horse treats, put them in his food bucket!

Entering the Stall

Always speak softly to the horse as you enter her stall. When you step in, slide the door almost shut behind you so that the horse can't escape before you get her halter on. Leave yourself enough of a gap to get out if you need to. The horse should not be allowed to crowd you at the door. If she does, put your hand on her chest and quietly say, "Back up." Make her back up into the corner, but don't be loud and threatening about it. If your mannerisms are too forceful, she may feel trapped and become defensive.

Catching Your Horse in the Stall

If your horse turns his head into a corner and his rear end to you when you want to catch him in his stall, you have allowed a potentially dangerous situation. You need enough experience to know the fine line between what is enough to create change and what is too much for the horse. Your intention is to change the horse's mind about which direction he wants to face. To do so, you definitely do not want to frighten the horse. If you lack the experience to deal with this situation, enlist the help of a more experienced horse person.

A horse that is fearful of you entering her stall can put you in a dangerous situation, and you can easily make it worse if you overreact. For example, the horse turns her rump to you when you enter her stall, so you feel you need to do something about it. But if you do too much too forcefully, the horse may react defensively and kick out.

Remember, horses regard their stall as a place of comfort, but they can also feel trapped there. Their natural instinct to flee is not an option. The next instinct is to defend themselves. If they feel sufficiently threatened, they will position themselves to kick you or lunge at you with teeth bared.

Your horse should be ready and willing to be haltered when you enter the stall, and this is what you are trying to teach him. Do not expect the horse to turn and face you all at once. Look for small signs that he is making an attempt at figuring out what you want and that he feels okay about doing it. Look for an ear to turn in your direction or even for him to simply turn his head toward you but not his body. Step away from the horse the minute you get any sign he is becoming willing. By taking the pressure off him, you will give your horse the signal that his reaction is right and that you are giving him the physical and mental space he needs to make the turn. When he allows you to halter him, drop a treat in his bucket and allow him to eat it before you lead him out.

Catching the Horse Outside

The horse that turns her rump to you in the stall has the same problem as the horse that can't be caught in the corral or pasture, only the size of the space is different. The corral or pasture is probably less dangerous for you because the horse has room to get away from you and doesn't have to react defensively. But these games of catch-me-if-you-can are intensely frustrating. They steal your pleasure in horses and serve only to work up your anger—which is never a good thing with horses.

Don't get too cocky about your relationship with your horse—all horses will have spirited days when kicking up their heels with their friends will seem a better idea than anything you have in mind. But if you have built a solid, mutually respectful relationship, you will actually find these slight diversions more entertaining than frustrating because they don't happen all the time.

The horse that respects you and considers you supremely important will give you his attention when you step into his space—corral, pasture, or stall. He has learned that being with you is a good place to be, maybe even as good as being with his pasture buddies. When you have built this kind of positive relationship with your horse, he will position himself to be caught when you step into the corral rather than turn away from you. He may even go one step further and walk toward you because he wants to be with you. This is a relationship built on mutual respect.

Do Your Homework

Before you ever get to the point where the horse is in a larger space and you want to catch her, spend some time working on this in a smaller space, such as a corral or round pen. If the horse eludes you, then let her work for her avoidance. Keep her moving around the pen and, every once in a while, take a backward step and see what you get. If the horse stops, great. If she stops and turns her head toward you, even better.

Your ultimate goal is for him to stop and turn his whole body toward you. This is the sign that he is ready to be caught, and you had better be ready to take this opening and catch him. If you don't, your horse will think maybe this isn't what you want, and you will lose your opportunity, making the next try even harder.

FACT

To protect your personal space, a flag makes a good extender for your arm and can add to your presence. Use a length of stiff wire with a piece of bandana-sized cloth attached to the end. Bend the end of the wire over so it can't poke your horse. Make the handle comfortable and easy to grip, and make sure the flag is light enough for you to carry without getting tired.

Think Safety, Always

Always bear in mind that a horse can kick out a lot farther than you think. It is a good idea to let the horse know you are coming up behind her. Talk to her or, if you are going from the front of the horse to the back, keep your hand on the horse all the way around so she knows where you are. Do not put yourself in the line of fire.

Picking Up the Feet

Handling a horse's feet is something that needs to begin early in life. Like everything else concerning horses, the process should take place gradually and start with good handling in general. Trouble picking up a horse's feet sometimes indicates trouble in other areas of the horse's handling, especially in his attitude toward humans. Often, if the other problems are addressed, the horse's feet-handling problems clear up as well.

Start at the Front

Don't expect your farrier to teach your horse to stand still for foot handling. This is your job. Use grooming to get the horse accustomed to having her feet touched. Don't worry about picking them up right at the start. Instead, while grooming the horse, brush the legs with a soft brush, and get the horse used to having her legs touched, all the way down to the hooves.

Lifting a horse's foot off the ground the first time can be tricky. It's that self-preservation, always-be-prepared-for-flight thing! The front feet are often easier to pick up than the back, so start there. The human may also be more at ease with the front legs because they aren't the ones you get kicked with. Beware, however, that a horse can strike out at you with a front leg.

Stand beside the horse's leg and face the rear of the horse. Run your hand down the back of the foreleg. About halfway down, gently pull or squeeze to cause the horse to lift the foot. Hold the foot up for only a couple seconds at first. Then set the foot back down gently, before the horse snatches it away from you. The key is not to hold the foot so long that he simply can't stand it any longer.

Never drop the horse's foot and let it bang the ground. This is uncomfortable and will make the horse reluctant to have his feet handled. It may also teach him to snatch his foot away next time in anticipation of it banging to the ground. You definitely don't want this snatch-back behavior; setting the foot down must always be when you decide, not when the horse feels like it.

Later on, you can work on getting the horse to hold up the foot for longer intervals while you pick it out with a hoof pick. When you're done with the front, move on to the back feet. After they become accustomed to the routine, some obliging horses will pick up their feet in succession for you. Do not allow the horse to lean her weight on you. If she does, poke her in the side with your elbow or fingers to make her shift her weight off you.

Trailer Loading

Trailer loading seems to be one of those things people neglect to teach horses until they get ready to go somewhere. Then, in their rush to get the horse loaded, they succeed only in creating a bad experience for the horse. This training needs to start early in life and be carried out in a calm, gradual manner.

The Ultimate Test

Loading a horse onto a trailer is the ultimate test of how well you've refined all the groundwork you've done with your horse thus far. If you have done a thorough job of building trust with your horse, trailer loading should go pretty smoothly.

ALERT!

When loading young horses or any horse for the first time, it's wise to have someone around in case you get in trouble. You want someone there in case of a problem, but you should be the one to get your horse into the trailer. Make sure the person is patient and respects your approach to handling your animals.

Make sure the trailer you use is exceedingly safe. There must not be any sharp protrusions or odd places for a lead rope to get caught. It shouldn't make much of a difference if the trailer has a ramp or is a step-up type, although most horses seem to negotiate the ramp style better.

Before loading up, put a halter and lead rope on your horse. Put a bag of hay in the trailer. This is not so much as a bribe to get her in but a comfort item to greet her after she loads and to keep her busy during the trip. If the hay bag offers one more incentive for her to climb in, great, but you should be careful not to entice her onto the trailer physically before she's mentally ready to be there. The idea is to build trust so that the horse follows you up the ramp and loads willingly.

The way to do this is to lead your horse to the trailer and let him check out things. Have the gate open and let him look and smell inside. As long as his attention is on the trailer, let him investigate. If you sense that he is becoming interested in things other than the trailer, do what it takes to return his attention back inside. Send some energy up the lead rope or turn him around and lead him back to the entrance if you have to.

Don't Rush!

Horses are careful about where they put their feet, so that first step on the ramp will be scary to your horse because it feels different from standing on firm ground. Be calm and encouraging, but don't rush. Give him some time to get accustomed to this new experience, one step at a time.

If the trailer is big enough for more than one horse, it sometimes helps to load an experienced pasture pal to show the newbie that there's nothing to it. The last thing you want to do is frighten and betray the horse; if you do, you will probably always have problems loading.

CHAPTER 15

Types of Horsemanship

Riding or caring for your horse gets you outdoors and makes you exercise. That, along with the social environment of other riders, is what makes the horsy life so enjoyable. But for thousands of horse owners this is not enough. Whatever your interest or inclination, there is a horse activity and type of horsemanship to match it, including ones that don't involve riding at all!

Trail Riding

Most people get into horses for recreation. They envision an invigorating ride through the woods with some camping along the way. Trail riding can also be competitive. Serious trail riders seek out competitive events, such as the Cross State Trail Ride (a longtime long-distance ride that originates in Vermont) or the Tevis Cup endurance ride. Both involve serious planning, conditioning, and preparation before you and your horse can undertake them safely.

FACT

The Tevis Cup is to trail riding what the Iditarod is to dog sledding. Its slogan is "100 miles in one day," and the terrain is rough. It is said to have 19,000 feet of uphill riding and 22,000 feet of downhill riding. The trophy is awarded to the first rider to finish "whose mount is fit to continue."

Recreational Riding

Land use for recreational horseback riding, whether public or private, has become increasingly restricted with urban sprawl and development. Even if you live in a rural area, you should obtain permission to ride on someone else's land before you do so. Otherwise, you will be trespassing on private property. If a landowner is neighborly enough to allow you to ride on his property, stay in his good graces by shutting all gates behind you, not littering, and respecting the environment in general.

Avoid riding alone whenever possible, especially if you are an inexperienced rider or if your horse is new to the trails. If you must ride alone, let someone else know where you're going and when to expect you back. Always wear proper riding gear, including a safety helmet, and carry a cell phone (preferably with global positioning capability) with you in case you get lost or need to call for help.

Competitive Trail Riding

Competitive trail rides are typically sponsored by a riding club or organization. They average around twenty-five miles in length (which is about five to six hours of riding) and are judged. You wear a number and have a time frame in which you can complete the ride, although these rides are typically not won or lost on time. Judges are situated at key locations along the trail and rate your performance over a given obstacle—crossing a creek, a wooden bridge, a low jump, and so on. When you finish the ride, a judge usually examines your horse, checks his heart rate, looks for saddle sores, and determines how well your horse was ridden within the level of her fitness and ability for the ride. These rides can be a lot of fun and are often great for those who not only like to compete but also like to be somewhat solitary and don't enjoy performing in front of an audience.

Endurance Riding

Endurance riding takes competitive trail riding to the next level. Endurance trail rides usually average 100 miles in length, are spread over a longer period of time, and involve more challenging obstacles and terrain than the local competitive trail ride. Time is a huge factor in winning, as are the physical conditions of you and your horse. Terrain can include rocky slopes, mountain ridges, and large, deep rivers. Like competing in the national horse show circuit, you should be at the top of your game for this type of horsemanship.

If you're interested in endurance trail riding, check out the website *www. endurance.net*. It includes ride dates around the country, clinics, great links to other sites, articles and advice for newcomers to the sport, and classifieds selling and seeking horses, tack, and even property.

Saddle Seat Equitation

Saddle seat is a riding discipline identified with gaited and "park" horses, primarily the high-stepping, showy breeds such as American Saddlebreds, Morgans, Arabians, Tennessee Walkers, and National Show Horses. A uniquely American form of English riding that sprang from the Southern plantation walkers that could comfortably carry a rider for long distances over many hours, the competitive form has become highly stylized.

The English saddle used in the discipline is a called a cutback saddle because, unlike the jumping or dressage saddle, it has a cut-out notch in the front. It is also flatter and tends to position the rider slightly farther back on the horse than the other types of English saddles.

In addition to walking, trotting, and cantering, most gaited horses are ridden and shown in additional gaits, such as the slow gait or the rack. Many riders take up saddle seat equitation because they appreciate the style or are interested in learning about these additional gaits.

Jumping

Even if you have no real interest in jumping, every well-rounded rider should know how to jump a horse. For example, the trail rider may be faced with a fallen tree trunk he needs to jump. Jumping low-to-the-ground obstacles is generally within the capability of most horses or ponies and not overly difficult for the rider. Take some hunt seat lessons to acquire the proper position and balance for jumping so as not to jab your horse in the mouth as you sail over the obstacle.

Show Jumping

Also known as stadium jumping, this event involves jumps set up within the confines of a show arena. The event may be a class in a show, a show in itself, or one of the three legs of a three-day event. Riders are expected to follow a specific predetermined pattern around the jump course. Your ride around the course is timed, and faults are given for any rails knocked over. When riders tie scores for the finish, the rails are raised higher, and a jump-off is held to determine a winner.

QUESTION?

What are rails?
Rails are the individual horizontal bars that make up a jump. They can be easily removed or added to make the jump lower or higher.

Cross-Country Jumping

As with stadium jumping, cross-country jumping can be an event in itself or one of the three legs in a three-day event. The jump course is set up in a cross-country setting through woods and fields and on uneven terrain. You follow a specific course. Judges are stationed at each jump, and your run is timed. The jumps are often constructed to look natural to the setting and may include large brush jumps or wide water jumps. The horse must be trained to jump a variety of obstacles going uphill and downhill.

Fox Hunting

Fox hunting is an organized undertaking with a strictly followed protocol for beginners, who are expected to become familiar with the complex rules and etiquette of the hunt. Most fox hunts these days do not involve hunting and killing real foxes. Rather, they are drag hunts. They get their name from the practice of dragging a fox-scented cloth for the hounds to follow. This allows participants to go through the motions simply for the fun of "riding to hounds," as well as preserving the traditions of the English hunt.

Modern fox hunts still involve baying hounds, galloping horses, beautiful countryside, challenging jumps, and many riders. The hunt club designs a course that includes jumps. It is a great way to get your horse exposed and accustomed to a lot of excitement.

However, horses can be quite excitable around howling hounds and other horses running ahead of them. That's why you need to be an experienced rider capable of negotiating a variety of obstacles and controlling your horse to be invited to ride with a hunt. Usually there is ample opportunity for novice riders to follow the hunt without jumping or only jumping the smaller jumps. This gives the hunt master and other members of the club an opportunity to observe and evaluate your riding skills before allowing you to participate more.

If you're interested in fox hunting, here are some fun terms to become familiar with:

- Brush: The fox's tail
- Charlie: Another name for a fox
- Dog fox: A male fox
- Vixen: A female fox

- Cast: The hounds spread out searching for the scent of the fox
- Check: When hounds lose the scent and stop searching
- Nose: A hound's ability to follow the scent
- Working a line: When the hounds follow the scent of the fox
- Hilltoppers: Riders (usually novices) who ride along with the hunt but don't jump
- Huntsman: The person who is in charge of the hounds
- Juniors: Fairly inexperienced riders who are new to the hunt
- Master of the Hunt: The person or persons responsible for all the aspects of the hounds, maintaining cordial relationships with landowners, and scheduling meets and locations
- Tallyho!: What is yelled when the fox is spotted
- Whippers-In: Riders assisting the master in hunting the hounds, usually farther afield, to help keep the hounds on track with the hunt and from running out in roads

Dressage

In French, *dressage* means training. It is a systematic way of physically and gymnastically conditioning the horse to perform progressively more difficult movements. The conditioning and training progresses through a series of levels, starting at training level and culminating with the Grand Prix level. At each level, a series of tests are performed and judged in competition. In each, the rider measures how well the horse has mastered the requirements at that level of training.

Dressage Competition

Dressage is widely considered the most difficult and demanding of all riding disciplines, requiring years and years of study and practice to master. The discipline produces the most skilled riders and the best trained horses, and every horse and rider can benefit from some degree of dressage training, whether or not it is the equestrian activity that you ultimately want to pursue.

Dressage competitions are different from the typical horse show in that you perform in a test rather than a class. Also, although you compete against a group of other riders performing the same test, you enter the ring alone and execute your test in front of the judge. This can be quite unnerving to some riders. On the one hand, you don't need to worry about other riders zooming around you, which allows you to concentrate on your own performance. On the other hand, you are alone out there, and all eyes are on you and your horse.

Moving Up

Beginning dressage riders and their mounts may practice first at intro level in schooling shows or ride-a-tests and then enter at training level in recognized competitions. Few riders and even fewer horses reach the Olympic-caliber Grand Prix level. After you graduate beyond one level and begin working in the next, you and your trainer may decide that your horse is not the right horse in mind and/or body to take you to the next level of competition.

To reach the upper levels of dressage, a horse must have the right conformation to perform the required movements, and she must be even-tempered enough to accept the demands of the discipline. If you aspire to the higher levels of any equestrian sport, you will eventually need to consider trading up from your beginner mount to one more suited to your goals. The right choice depends on what you want going forward.

Three-Day Eventing

A three-day event is an English-riding competition that has three components: dressage, cross-country, and stadium jumping. Also known as combined training, the three-day event was added to the Olympic program in 1912. The intent is to show the physical and mental versatility of you and your horse—that you can go from being cleaned up and collected in the dressage ring one day to galloping cross-country and sailing over jumps the next. The winner is the team with the best combined score over the three days.

FACT

Olympic equestrians David and Karen O'Connor are a well-known three-day eventing couple. In 2000, David brought home a gold medal from the Sydney Olympics, the first equestrian gold medal for the United States since 1984. In an interview, the couple pointed out that the equestrian segment is the only Olympic event in which men and women compete as equals. Their website, *www.oconnoreventteam.com*, is well worth a visit.

Eventing is challenging and exhausting for both horse and rider. As with most disciplines, it's best to watch an event a few times to get a real sense of what goes on and whether it's for you. Like upper-level dressage, eventing goes way beyond pleasure riding and requires a certain kind of horse and a rider with complete discipline.

Western Events

Equestrian events such as reining, roping, and team penning started as a way for cowboys to show off the moves they and their horses could do when working cattle. All of the moves in Western events are derived from practical moves used to work cattle, but they've become more stylized for competition.

Reining

Reining has been called Western dressage because of the precise moves it requires. In reining, the horse needs to be taught the cues he needs to stop exactly when you ask him to, to spin in a circle moving only his front feet and stop before overshooting the number of spins required in a particular pattern, and to canter calmly in small and large circles without breaking stride. This is a discipline that can require many hours of drill work and is not in the realm of pleasure and recreational riding.

Roping

Horseback roping usually involves cows. If you want to become a skilled roper, you have to practice, practice, practice. You can practice with a fake cow—there are cow heads you can buy to stick into a bale of hay or attach to a sawhorse—and rope the cow while it's stationary. When you are ready to rope a moving cow, you can buy motorized fake cows on tracks that pivot and turn almost like the real thing.

Expert ropers are incredible to watch, and they make it look easy. The minute you pick up a sixty-foot lariat yourself and begin to build a loop, you truly appreciate how difficult and how fine an art it is. There are occasional classes in horse shows that involve roping, but classes involving this skill are more likely found at the rodeo.

Barrel Racing

Interestingly, barrel racing originally developed as something for the wives and girlfriends of bronc-busters and bull-riders to do while the men competed in rodeo events. Today the sport is open to both sexes. In barrel racing, a horse and rider go as fast as possible in a specific clover-leaf pattern around three fifty-five gallon barrels set up in a triangle pattern in an arena. In a rodeo event, the race is timed manually or by an electric eye device, tripped when the horse crosses a laser light beam. Points are taken off the time for hitting a barrel. The rider may be eliminated for knocking over barrels, going off course, or using unsanctioned equipment.

Team Penning

Team penning is an activity similar to the gaming events. It can be fun, but since it requires cattle, it probably isn't something you will set up in your backyard. You should scout out a local team-penning club that has events on a regular basis, offers some practice time, and is open to riders new to the event.

A team of three riders picks a number out of a hat. A herd of as many as thirty young cattle with numbers painted on them are waiting in the arena, and three of them are painted with the number the team picked. Two of the team members cut one of the cows with their number out of the herd and work the cow down to a small pen somewhere near the other end of the arena. When they get the cow into the pen—which is no small task, given a cow's desire to remain with the herd—the third rider stays behind to keep the cow there. Two riders head back to the herd, cut out the second cow, and herd the cow into the pen. They repeat the process for the third cow. When the pen door is shut, the team's time is recorded.

After all teams have competed, the team with the best time wins. Since this is a timed activity, horsemanship is not scored, but the better your riding skills and the more in tune you are with your horse, the less time you will waste in getting to the cattle and moving your horse where you need him or holding his position. Being involved with team penning will also expose your horse to cattle, yet another thing for you to support him through and help you gain further trust.

Rodeo

Cowboys invented the rodeo to have fun and to show off their ranch-work and cattle-driving skills. But riding in the rodeo circuit is now an intense activity in and of itself, and most people who pursue it seriously are professionals in the business. If you want to become a rodeo rider, you will probably need to be in the western part of the United States and Canada, where rodeos abound. For the armchair rodeo rider, you can often find a rodeo as Saturday night fare on the sports channels on television.

A typical rodeo includes events such as bull riding, bronc riding, and steer wrestling (where the rider leans off his horse to grab a steer by the horns and jumps off the horse to tie the steer). Obviously, these activities are extremely dangerous and sometimes result in serious injury.

Games on Horseback

Playing games on horseback can help you develop your riding skills. They teach your body to respond to and direct the horse's movements while you focus your mind and attention on the task at hand, whether you're trying to hit a ball with a stick, weave through poles, or balance a hard-boiled egg on a spoon.

Polo

Polo is a fast-paced game played on horseback in a field 160 yards wide and 300 yards long. It is played in six seven-minute chukkers over approximately ninety minutes. To compete, you need access to a string of polo ponies, which makes it expensive. Polo ponies are not a specific breed; any horse that is trained and well suited to the game can be a polo pony. They are compact, usually short in height, and have been exposed to the idea of having a mallet-wielding rider on their back. To play polo, you must be a confident and extremely well-balanced rider to make the quick turns and stops and to gallop for most of the game.

To find a club near you, learn all the rules of the game, and obtain lots more information about polo, visit the United States Polo Association website at *www.uspolo.org.*

Gymkhana and Omoksee

Gymkhana is a collective term for competitive games on horseback, organized mostly for youth participation by a 4-H or Pony Club. The events are usually won or lost solely on timing, but they typically require some riding skill, depending on the game. For example, pole bending, in which the horse and rider weave a serpentine path through a line of tall poles at a gallop, requires the rider to make alternating changes of hand and leads.

In the western United States, gymkhana-type horseback games are called omoksee, a Native American term meaning games on horseback. Other types of gymkhana and omoksee games include barrel racing, flag races, keg races, and relay races, all of which are excellent ways to hone your riding skills.

Vaulting

In vaulting competitions, riders perform acrobatic exercises to music on horseback. Most people have seen vaulting at the circus, where bareback riders perform stunning gymnastic feats such as mounts, dismounts, somersaults, handstands, and flips on horseback while the horse trots or canters in a circle. It is an extreme sport that dates back to the Roman games. The horse is carefully trained, usually works on a lunge line, and wears a bridle, side reins, and a surcingle around its girth instead of a saddle. The surcingle has handles, which the rider uses to execute certain moves. In competition, vaulters are judged on the difficulty of their moves, technique, balance, and form.

Jousting

An interest in the ancient activity of jousting, typically associated with knights in armor, has cropped up over the past several years. Although not widespread, jousting competitions can be found in pockets around the country and are enjoyed at popular Renaissance festivals. Today's rider aims a long lance at a ring instead of an opponent. With each round, the ring gets smaller, so accuracy at top speeds is the name of the game.

Drill Teams

Drill teams consist of lines of riders executing moves in formation. If you viewed them from above, you would see horses meeting at a point at the exact same time, moving together in the same gait and rhythm, and drifting apart at the same point. Every pairing in the drill team does the pattern in unison and in the same way as every other pairing, at the same point, in the same gait, and so forth.

Participation in a drill team teaches you great precision in your riding and requires lots of practice. They are organized mostly for youth participation by 4-H and Pony Clubs and by university riding programs. Drill teams are popular with spectators and are often invited to perform exhibitions at horse shows and other events with a sports or equestrian flavor.

Natural Horsemanship

In the past two decades or so, an approach to teaching and riding horses has been tagged as natural horsemanship. Educating humans about how to educate their horses through feel rather than force has become a popular hands-on clinic attraction. The basic premise of the natural approach involves educating horses using behavioral techniques and working with their natural instincts (such as herd dynamics) to mold those instincts into desirable behaviors. The result is a horse that responds out of respect to her handler (her herd leader) rather than fear.

It's Nothing New

Nicholas Evans's novel *The Horse Whisperer* and the subsequent movie directed by and starring Robert Redford thrust the natural horsemanship approach into the mainstream. It was heavily commercialized by national clinicians and pitched to the public as if it were some startling new breakthrough discovery about horse behavior.

Unfortunately, the original intent of natural horsemanship has become a bit convoluted by all the hype and marketing. Worst of all, it has misled some people to believe that they can accomplish miracles with their horses with little effort, education, or experience in horse training, which is simply not true. Natural horsemanship requires a great deal of study and accumulated knowledge, but it is a worthwhile pursuit for anyone who is interested in making life better for horses, as well as their personal relationship with them.

If you are willing to spend a lot of time at this rather difficult approach, it can result in a horse that works willingly in a relaxed frame of mind because he's not constantly fearful of punishment. Horses that respect and like their handlers learn to look to their people for support. They are much more apt to tuck some of their natural reactions aside and trust their people to help them through new or scary situations.

Racing

Nearly everyone has watched a horse race, either on television or in person. Racing on horseback—and the gambling that goes with it—has been around since ancient times, and with the number of racetracks in the United States that make it such a huge business, it is not going away any time soon.

FACT

Churchill Downs, the famous racetrack in Louisville, Kentucky, opened in 1875 and hosted the first Kentucky Derby that year. The grounds are spread across 147 acres with more than 1,400 stalls in forty-seven barns. The Churchill Downs website (*www.kentuckyderby.com*) includes a wealth of information about the sport's pre-eminent event.

Types of Races

Flat racing refers to the under-saddle kind of racing that most people are familiar with. Thoroughbreds comprise the majority of races and certainly the most glamorous ones, including the celebrated Triple Crown—the Kentucky Derby, the Preakness, and the Belmont Stakes.

American Quarter Horses also have an active and prestigious racing circuit, including the famed Ruidoso Downs in New Mexico. Arabians have a racing component in their registry, as do Appaloosas and some other breeds.

Steeplechase

Steeplechasing—which combines flat racing and jumping—is best known by the Grand National event in Liverpool, England, that has taken place since 1839. The event includes some thirty fences, and many horses and riders do not complete the race. The course is run twice for a total of 4.5 miles, sixteen jumps on the first round and fourteen on the second.

Driving competitions are increasingly popular, but there's much more to driving than just hitching a horse to a cart. If you'd like to try driving your horse, take some lessons and apprentice with someone for a while. One way to find someone who can teach you is to attend a nearby horse show that includes driving classes.

Harness Racing

Nonriding races involve mostly Standardbreds pulling an individual driver in a cart called a sulky. Unlike flat racing, harness races are run at the trot or pace, not the gallop. Typically, you see these races at county agricultural fairs throughout the country, as well as at local racetracks outside of the famed Kentucky Thoroughbred Bluegrass region.

CHAPTER 16

Tack, Apparel, and Accessories

As with any sport, activity, interest, or hobby, you can easily collect a lot of "stuff" when you are involved with horses. That's all part of the fun. There are zillions of items for you, the rider, as well as zillions of items for your horse. And if you keep your horse at home, there are zillions more items you can collect to enhance your stable.

Handling Equipment

First and foremost, you need a couple of halters and lead ropes. Even if you have only one horse, keep extras on hand in case your horse breaks a halter or lead.

Halters

Halters are generally made of leather or nylon. Leather halters are the most expensive, but if you are going to buy one, buy top quality. The fittings should be brass, and the leather should be soft and strong. Seams should be double stitched, not screwed or tacked together.

Halters made of nylon webbing are the most common and least expensive. They come in a variety of colors. They are stronger than leather halters, which is actually a strike against them. If a horse gets caught on a fence or hay feeder and struggles, a leather halter may eventually break free, but the web halter will not, and the horse could seriously injure himself or even break his neck. It's safer to remove any type of halter when the horse is loose in its stall or pasture. However, nylon halters do come in breakaway models, which have a leather crown piece that should break during a struggle.

Lead Ropes

You can never have too many lead ropes. Lead ropes are typically eight to twelve feet long and made of leather, cotton, flat webbing, or poly rope. They all last about the same length of time—which can be years, unless you leave them out in the rain consistently. You can purchase a halter and lead rope in matching colors. The important matter is how the lead rope feels in your hand.

Lead ropes with chain on the end are intended to wrap around an unruly horse's nose for better control. However, if you teach your horses to be respectful and behave while being lead, you will not need the chain, which just gets in the way in regular use.

Groundwork Equipment

Most of the groundwork you will do involves lunging, in which the horse moves through his gaits around you in a circle. Groundwork is essential for training and useful for letting a fresh horse blow off some steam before you mount him.

Lunge Line

You will need approximately thirty feet of lunge line and a long lunge whip. Lunge lines are strong and usually have a "donut" on the end for hanging onto without having to strap your hand into a loop, which you never ever want to do. If your horse happens to spook and bolt while she is on a lead rope or lunge line and you have it looped around your wrist, you could be dragged or break your arm from the force of the pull.

Lunge Whip

Lunge whips are standard tall whips with a long snapper. When on a lunge line, the horse circles around you, and the lunge whip helps you form a triangle (horse, line from his head to you, whip from you to his rear) to keep your horse moving forward on the circle. Lunge whips are not intended for actually whipping the horse.

Riding Equipment

Unless your horse is going to be strictly a lawn ornament, you'll definitely need a saddle and bridle to ride her. Whether you want an English or a Western saddle depends on what you're going to do with the horse. To ride recreationally, you can choose whatever saddle suits you.

Saddles

There are all-purpose English saddles that serve well for cross-country riding. For riding steep, rugged trails, a general purpose Western saddle might give you greater support and comfort. People who compete regularly at horse shows often invest in schooling tack for everyday use and reserve their fancier show equipment for competitions.

A tack shop can provide you with almost everything you need to get started. Some tack shops specialize in a certain riding discipline; for instance, if you're going to ride western, seek out a western tack store. At a good shop, the personnel are familiar with all the equipment they carry and can help you make sensible choices.

Saddle Cost

A saddle can cost you from several hundred to several thousand dollars, depending on the quality, brand, and other variables. The price will vary based on whether it's custom- or factory-made, leather or synthetic. Some shops sell used tack on consignment. A reputable shop will clean the tack and be honest about any required repairs. A good quality used saddle that has been well cared for will retain its value because they are made to wear well. If you're just starting out, buying a used saddle for everyday schooling is a good way to go, and the saddle will be better broken in.

Buy the best quality saddle you can afford. Higher-quality saddles are built to comfortably fit horses without any unusual traits, such as extra high or low withers or an extremely wide, narrow, short, or long back. They are also built to address such things as the best placement of straps and buckles for the horse's and the rider's comfort.

English Saddles

English or "flat" saddles basically come in three types: dressage, hunter/jumper (also called forward seat), or all-purpose. With English gear, the stirrup irons and leathers are often sold separately; with Western saddles, they are usually included as part of the saddle.

- **Dressage:** The design of this saddle is intended to keep the rider's legs fairly straight underneath him for the more upright position, deeper seat, and longer leg applied in dressage riding.
- **Hunter/jumper (forward seat):** As the name implies, the forward seat saddle is the one you should choose if you are interested in jumping activities (fox hunting, cross-country riding, stadium jumping). The

saddles are designed for a more forward seat and a more bent leg, and they have varying degrees of knee rolls for the bent knee to rest on.

- **All-purpose:** Intended for the general rider who rides for recreation, all-purpose English saddles often come with a slant toward hunter/ jumper position or dressage position.

English saddles come in 16-inch to 17.5-inch seats. Other specifics include the amount of padding in the seat, length and width of flaps, depth of seat, amount of twist (the angle of the slanted part of the saddletree), and height of the pommel. English saddles are designed to distribute the rider's weight evenly along the back of the horse's spine.

FIGURE 16.1:
English Saddle

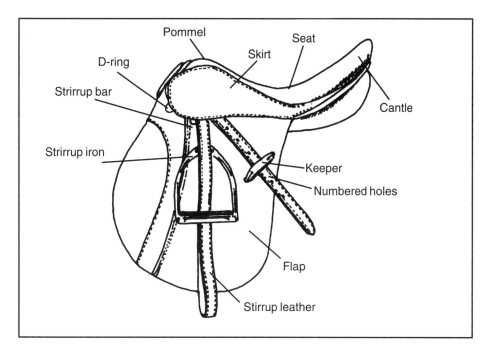

Here are some fine points to consider when shopping for a saddle:

- Fit the saddle to you, not you to the saddle.
- Try out the saddle either on a horse or on a saddle stand that is sturdy enough for you to take your feet off the floor and put them in the stirrups.

- Allow a little extra room in new saddles. Features such as knee rolls will roll back toward the rider when the saddle gets broken in.
- At the longest length of stirrup you would use, you should still have at least one or two inches of flap below the top of your boots.
- Flaps should be as short as possible but never so short that they catch on the top of a knee-high boot.

Western Saddles

Western or "stock" saddles are notoriously heavier and more accessorized than English-style saddles. The types of activities traditionally associated with the Western saddle include the heavy work of ranch life. Saddles used for doctoring cattle or long days on the trail need a horn for roping, strings for holding things such as rain gear and a bedroll, a rear cinch to keep the back of the saddle in place when the cow comes to the end of the rope that is dallied onto the horn, a pocket for a knife, and a breast collar to keep the saddle better in place over rough terrain.

FIGURE 16.2:
Western
Saddle

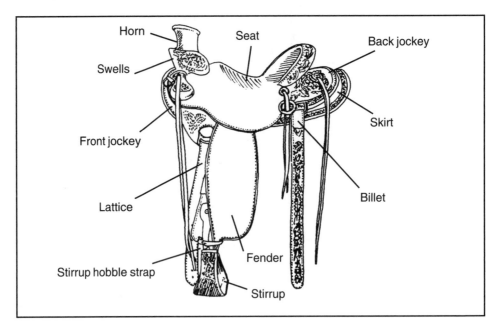

Western saddles are either working saddles or show saddles. Working saddles are more ruggedly built for heavy use, while show saddles are laden with silver or other decorations. Most people reserve their show saddle for the show itself and practice in it only enough to be comfortable at the show, keeping a less ornate saddle for everyday use.

Western-style endurance saddles are a hybrid of English and Western, but they look mostly like a regular Western saddle without the horn. They draw on the features of cavalry saddles and are well suited for long hours of riding. Mounted police units often use them.

Saddle Construction

All saddles, English or Western, are made around a basic structure called a saddletree, which can be made of wood or fiberglass and other synthetic (and often lighter-weight) materials. Saddletrees come in wide or narrow versions, making it possible to fit a variety of horses. The rider's major concern when it comes to the saddletree is the twist, which is the degree of slant in the sloped area in the front of the saddletree. The steeper the slant, the narrower the saddle will feel to the rider.

QUESTION?

How do you measure the horse for a saddle?
The best way is to try it on the horse. If that's not possible, one time-honored way to estimate the width of the horse's back is to bend a wire coat hanger over the withers and take it with you to the tack shop.

Saddle Fit

To decide whether you have saddle-fitting problems, in either English or Western, here are some things to look for:

- After a workout, look at the underside of the saddle pad. Is it unevenly dirty? Are there odd hair patterns, swirling or flattened areas that indicate uneven and misplaced pressure?
- When you groom your horse, does she drop her back away from your hand, as if her back were sore?

- Are there any sore spots, white hairs, or bumps where the saddle comes in contact with the horse's back?
- Does the horse exhibit agitated behavior when you tack up?
- Does the horse move in a constrained manner under saddle, rather than freely forward in a smooth, fluid motion?

These aren't all necessarily indications of poor saddle fit, but they definitely could be. You can use pads, inserts, and risers (collectively called shims) to adjust saddles that don't fit the horse quite right. Of course, it is always better to have the saddle fit well.

Girths and Cinches

English riders call them girths, while Western riders refer to them as cinches. Regardless of the name, their purpose is to hold the saddle on. Girths are typically made of leather, with buckles on both ends that fasten onto billet straps on both sides of the saddle. Some girths have a section of elastic on one side of the buckles, which makes it easier to tighten. You can also buy leather girths covered with fleece or foam, or you can buy all-cloth girths, which don't have the strength or give of leather.

Western cinches come in many materials, including foam-like neoprene, web material with felt or fleece lining, or wool-blend or mohair string girths, which consist of multiple strings gathered at rings with hooks on either end. Rings with buckles that fit into a hole in the latigo strap tend to be more secure than the empty ring the latigo ties into.

Saddle Pads

A saddle pad goes between the saddle and the horse's back to protect the horse from chafing. As with everything else horsy, there are many types of saddle pads to choose from. For Western riders, heavy wool-felt pads in varying thicknesses can be used alone or covered with a thinner wool blanket. Traditional Navajo-weave blankets in many beautiful colors and patterns are a perennial favorite in Western style.

Hunter/jumper-type saddle pads follow the shape of the saddle with very little pad exposed. They are often made of fleece. Square-quilted cotton pads are used more with dressage saddles. They come in many colors and fabrics and can be customized, like Western pads, with monograms and barn logos in the corners. They have nylon billets and girth straps to fit them to the saddle and keep them in place.

For the comfort and health of your horse, it's important to keep saddle pads clean. Wash them after each use to remove the sweat and dirt. One technique to clean heavy Western saddle pads is to take the pad to the hand car wash and hose the hair and dirt off with the power sprayer. English saddle pads are less bulky and can be run through the washing machine.

Bridles

The bridle's function is to keep the bit in the horse's mouth so that the rider can steer the horse with the reins. The bridle is comprised of a headstall, bit, chinstrap, noseband, and reins, although often the reins are sold separately.

FIGURE 16.3:
Bridle

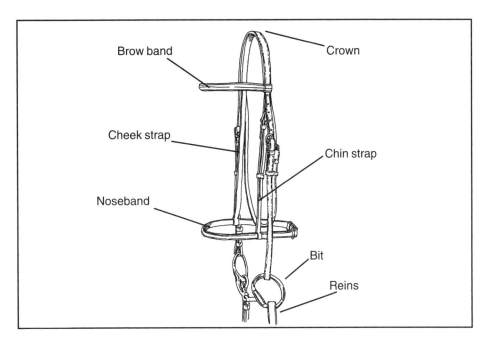

Western bridles come in split-ear, sliding-ear, or browband designs. Split-ear and sliding-ear bridles have a loop of leather that one ear goes through. A browband bridle simply fits over the head like a halter, with a band of leather across the horse's forehead. The headstall can range from plain harness leather to heavily tooled, silver-decorated, highly polished show bridles, and it will have a cheek strap that loops under the horse's jaw and buckles on the left side.

The most commonly seen English bridle is the snaffle bridle, fitted with a snaffle bit and a single pair of reins. More advanced riders sometimes use a double bridle, which consists of two bits—a bridoon (which is a light snaffle bit) and a curb bit—and two pairs of reins.

English bridles typically come with a noseband. The nosebands may be a regular cavesson, dropped, or flash noseband. Each type acts differently on the horse's mouth but all generally serve to keep the bit in the right place in the horse's mouth. Both the dropped and the flash nosebands fasten below the bit, serving to keep the horse's mouth shut, while the cavesson fastens above the bit.

Bits

The bit is a tool to let you and your horse communicate; therefore, choosing the right one is important. When you pick up the reins and the bit comes in contact with the corners of the horse's mouth, the horse should be taught to understand that this means something. Although what it means can vary with the type of horsemanship you learn and the education level of your horse, the most common message pressure from the bit communicates to a horse is to slow down or stop.

Snaffle Bit

A snaffle is basically a jointed piece of metal that goes in the horse's mouth and is attached to the reins with either O-shaped rings that can slide loosely around the ends of the bit or D-shaped rings that stay stationary. Snaffle bits are the best educational bit for the horse at any age and for the everyday rider, especially for beginners. They are the mildest bit (although any bit can be harsh in heavy hands). The snaffle bit exerts pressure on the horse's mouth, primarily on the tongue, lips, and bars of the mouth.

Curb Bit

The curb bit has long cheeks, called shanks, and a hump in the middle, called a port. It is a harsher device, exerting pressure on the bars of the mouth, chin, and poll. When used in conjunction with a snaffle bit in a double bridle, it enables the rider to gain greater collection. However, a great deal of sensitivity and experience is required on the rider's part to use this bit combination correctly, without harming the horse. The curb is not a bit for beginners.

The Truth about Bits

Although it would take a separate book to go into the other types of bits available and what they're designed to do, there is only one important truth you really need to know about any of them. Even the mildest snaffle bit can be abusive to the horse in the wrong hands. Some people think all their control comes from their hands on the reins. These are the uneducated riders who haul back on the reins to stop, causing the horse to throw his head up in the air to avoid the pain from the bit jabbing his mouth. Without realizing it, these riders are actually teaching their horse to get "above the bit" to avoid the harsh contact. When the horse starts to run away to escape the abuse, the rider thinks fitting him with a harsher bit will fix the problem.

ALERT!

The only bit you will probably ever need, English or Western, is a snaffle bit. If your horse is giving you problems and someone recommends that you get a harsher bit with more leverage (i.e., longer "shanks"), find someone else to get your riding advice from.

Real control comes not just from the hands, reins or bit, but from the combination of all of the rider's aids applied correctly. No bit—or any fancy piece of equipment—can give you better control or make you a better rider. Only knowledge can accomplish that. Rather than resorting to bigger bits to increase the leverage you use to put pressure on your horse's mouth, your money is better spent learning good horsemanship.

Accessories

Some items you need; others simply come in handy. If you are a novice, realize that you will develop preferences for materials and types of equipment over time. Sometimes it just takes trial and error, and no matter how frugally you go about collecting, you may end up with things you find you don't like or don't really need.

Sheets and Blankets

Blankets aren't just for keeping the horse warm in cold weather. For temperate climates, the horse's coat is designed to take care of that well enough on its own, and depending on where you live, blanketing during cold weather may not be necessary for your horse. However, you need to know that there are several types of blankets, also called rugs or sheets (especially the lightweight variety), designed for specific purposes. They include the following:

- **Fly sheet:** A thin mesh sheet that is cool in warm weather but protects the horse's body from biting flies.
- **Anti-sweat sheet:** A lightweight sheet used for cooling out a sweaty horse.
- **Cooler:** Traditionally wool, this lightweight blanket traps air while the horse cools off, helps wick away moisture, and provides some warmth once the horse has cooled. It usually fits the length of the horse, up to the ears.
- **Rain sheets:** Made of waterproof material, these sheets are also made big enough to cover a saddle while you're waiting for your class at the show.
- **Lightweight sheet:** This provides some warmth and protection from the wind.
- **Turnout rug:** These are traditionally wool-lined with a heavy canvas outer shell to provide protection from the weather. They are typically well built for turnout use, as opposed to the horse just wearing it in the stall.
- **Exercise rug:** Worn while riding, this rug fits under the saddle and covers the rump, keeping the loin area warm during warm-up and cool-down periods in cold temperatures.

Leg Protection

Boots and wraps on the horse are used for protection from external injury—usually the horse striking one leg with another foot or striking a rail when jumping. There are several kinds for different purposes:

- **Shipping boots:** These padded wraps help protect all four legs during trailering. You can purchase one-piece wraps made of Cordura nylon with fuzzy linings and Velcro closures. Or you can go the old-fashioned route of cotton sheets wrapped in place with stretchy wrapping that ties or shuts with Velcro at the end (also referred to as polo wraps).
- **Bell boots:** Bell boots are synthetic or rubber boots that look like the business end of a toilet plunger hung from the horse's fetlock joint. These boots protect the hoof while jumping. They are also used as corrective shoeing on horses whose foot construction leaves an edge of the shoe hanging over that's big enough that the horse might step on it with another foot and tear it off if it isn't protected.
- **Splint boots:** These protect the lower front leg area, both from striking it with the other foot and from the concussion of hard or deep, heavy footing.
- **Galloping boots:** Usually made of leather, these boots protect the back of the horse's front legs/feet from overreaching with the back legs at the gallop.
- **Open-front boots:** Another boot used in jumping, they are for the front legs and are open in the front.

Other Tack

As for most of the other gadgets you find in tack catalogs that claim to fix this or that problem, you probably won't find a need for most of them if you properly educate your horse and strive to perfect your own riding skills. Many mechanical gadgets force a horse into a physical frame when the rider isn't able to accomplish good carriage through her own skill.

For example, tiedowns prevent the horse from lifting his head above a certain point. It's basically a single piece of leather that runs from the breast collar to the bridle. Like many such gadgets, it's an unnecessary piece of equipment to the horseman who is more interested in improving her own riding and training skills, rather than forcing the horse to carry himself a certain way.

One item you might need is a breast collar, also referred to as a breastplate. Sometimes a horse's conformation makes a breast collar almost mandatory to keep the saddle from slipping back. Various other equipment, such as a martingale, attaches to the breast collar.

A martingale consists of leather straps attached to the breast collar that connect to each rein. Basically, it is designed to give you more leverage to, in the words of the tack catalogs, "use as an aid to develop a proper headset." They come as running style, in which the reins move up and down rings, or standing style, in which the martingale is affixed to the reins. In some situations, martingales may be useful. However, this is another one of those gadgets that is generally unnecessary if you invest in proper training for both horse and rider.

Cleaning Tack

If you ride a lot, your leather is going to get dirty. Sweat, mud from the trail, dust from the arena footing, and dirt from your hands all get rubbed onto tack. You should wipe it off with a damp rag after every ride and plan to do a thorough cleaning occasionally to keep things supple. Exactly how often you do this depends on how many hours a week you are in the saddle.

FACT

Cleaning your tack regularly gives you a chance to inspect it for wear. Immediately repair or replace anything that is about to break, and keep a close eye on anything that looks well worn. Good quality horse tack is made to hold up to the job it is made to do, but keeping it clean will help it hold up that much longer.

Cleaning Leather

Synthetic tack is easy to hose off with water and wipe down. It requires little maintenance other than regular inspection for wear and tear. To clean leather, you will need a good sponge, warm water, some saddle soap (or your favorite leather cleaning product), and a bottle of leather conditioner. Take apart the bridle and unbuckle any pieces that buckle on and off so that you can get to every little nook and cranny where dirt loves to hide and grind at the leather. Wash everything down with the warm water and the sponge, opening up the pores of the leather. Use some elbow grease to remove any surface dirt. Rinse off, get some clean warm water, dab some leather cleaner onto the sponge, and lather up your leather. Rinse it off and let it dry some. Before it is completely dry, work in some leather conditioner. Some leather conditioners may darken light leather, so test a hidden area first before doing the entire piece.

Keep your leather tack—saddles, bridles, and leather halters—in a cool, dry place. Dampness will cause mold to form on the leather, and too much heat and sun exposure will dry it out.

Safety Equipment for the Rider

Riding is an inherently dangerous sport. Falling off the horse accounts for most injuries, but there is also the potential to get kicked, trampled, or stepped on by a one-ton animal. Nearly all riding equipment or apparel is designed with some measure of protection in mind, from helmets that protect your head to chaps and tall boots that protect your legs.

Helmets

Your most essential piece of apparel is a safety helmet. Helmets are much more accepted in the English-riding world than the Western one. The deep bucket of a Western hat offers a limited amount of protection—and rarely stays on when you fall off your horse. Attempts to make a protective helmet that looks like a Western hat have not been widely accepted. Typically, riders in Western gear simply wear the basic helmets when they ride recreationally. However, when they ride in Western show classes, riders wear Western hats, not safety helmets.

Head injuries from kicks and falls account for the largest percentage of all serious injuries resulting from horseback riding accidents. Buy a helmet that fits well and always wear it when you ride, whether you ride English or Western.

The helmet you choose should fit snugly on your head. It should also meet or surpass American Society for Testing and Materials (ASTM) and Safety Equipment Institute standards for equestrian use. While they are better than nothing at all, bicycle helmets are not appropriate for riding because they are not certified to protect your head from a horse's kick.

Helmets come in all sorts of styles and even a few colors these days. There are different designs that are considered more appropriate than others for different types of riding. The velvet kind with the little button on the top is the style you'll see on the fox hunting grounds. Schooling helmets tend to have a lot of open ventilation, and helmets are even used in dressage competitions. You can accessorize your helmet with decorative helmet covers, rain covers, and even a cool pack to keep your helmeted head extra cool in hot temperatures.

Safety Vests

Not many recreational riders wear safety vests, but if you plan to do a lot of jumping or start a lot of young horses under saddle, a safety vest is a worthwhile investment. They can help pad your fall and protect your internal organs if you fall. Vests that meet ASTM safety standards are available.

Apparel for the Rider

What you wear in the show ring is dictated by tradition and horse show regulations. But what you choose to wear for everyday schooling should be dictated by safety and comfort.

Pants

Western riders tend to go for jeans. If you wear jeans for riding, look for brands that have the wide, double-stitched seam only on the outside of the leg and have a simple seam on the inside. A thick seam on the inside can cause you to chafe pretty quickly. Jeans that have a bit of stretch to them also work well and are very comfortable in the saddle.

English riders typically wear riding breeches, which are extremely comfortable and come in stretch fabrics intended to fit snugly. Almost all have suede patches inside the knees to protect your legs from friction and provide a little grip. You can also get full-seat breeches in which the suede runs from the knee of one leg all the way around the bottom, and back down to the knee of the other leg. Not only do they wear better, but the full-suede seat also helps you keep your seat in the saddle. Breeches come in many styles and colors, and as with many things, you will find your preference as you try out different kinds.

Riding gloves give you a better grip on the reins, especially in hot weather when your palms get sweaty and slippery. In cold weather, the lined or insulated varieties help keep your hands warm without compromising your feel on the reins.

Chaps

One way to save wear and tear on your jeans is to wear chaps. Chaps are very common in Western-style riding apparel and are often used by English riders as well. Western chaps can be leather or suede and may or may not have fringe. They are made to zip on the outside and fit quite snugly to your leg. Chaps are important when riding through sagebrush and backcountry areas where you might brush up against prickly plants.

Boots come in both English and Western styles that are traditional and popular. English riders in hunter/jumper or dressage competitions wear knee-high leather boots. Knee-high boots also come in rubber for everyday and schooling wear. Ankle-high riding boots, often called paddock boots, are also popular. Western-style boots are probably one of the most common icons of the cowboy tradition. They come in various styles as well.

Riding boots should have a significant heel to prevent your foot from slipping completely through the stirrup. Avoid rubber-soled boots, which can get slippery. Leather is best. Never wear sneakers when riding or working with horses. They are slippery in the stirrup, and they provide absolutely no protection if you are stepped on.

FACT

Boots for riding have a completely different purpose than boots for barn work. There's not much distinction between English and Western styles in this area—sturdy boots are a must, and you'll definitely want a waterproof pair around for rainy days. In winter, you'll also need a pair of warm boots. Manure and urine take a toll on leather and rubber, so expect to have to replace your boots at least every couple of years.

CHAPTER 17

Riding

Although horse owners take great pleasure in caring for their horses, riding is still typically the ultimate intent. It's fun, challenging, interesting, and physically demanding. But contrary to what many novices believe, you can't learn to ride well in a six-week crash course, nor can you learn to ride from reading books about it. While you can learn the basics of how to steer and stop in several weeks, it takes years of honing your skills to become a truly effective rider.

Learning How to Ride

If you've never ridden a horse before, the best place to take your first ride is at a reputable riding stable that teaches beginners the fundamentals. This is true for children and adults alike. A top-notch facility will have everything you need to get started: lesson horses, riding instructors, saddles, and safety helmets. However, you will need a pair of boots with at least a half-inch heel to prevent your foot from slipping through the stirrup in the event of a mishap.

How to Find a Good Lesson Barn

Your phone book is a starting place for collecting locations—look under riding academies or riding stables in the Yellow Pages. Another place to look is on the bulletin boards at local tack shops and feed stores for flyers from local stables offering lessons.

Do some investigating before signing up for lessons. Ask the staff at the tack and feed stores whether they know anything about the stable's reputation. You might also ask about any horse clubs in your area, attend a meeting or two, and talk to the experienced horse people there. You'll likely meet some barn managers or riding instructors or collect some names that way.

Once you've collected names, start with a phone call. Talk with the stable manager, who may be one of the instructors, about what is offered and how much different options cost. Ask if you can come for a visit and watch a lesson or two.

Types of Riding Lessons

Most barns concentrate in a particular riding discipline. If you just want to have a few lessons to get on a horse and start to develop your ability, it may not matter what the stable's focus is at first. After all, the riding basics can be applied in every discipline. But if you already have a certain goal in mind, such as learning dressage or learning to jump, seek out a barn that focuses on your interests. That way, if you decide to continue your rider training long term, you will already have established relationships with people who can help you reach your goals.

Group Versus Private Lessons

Usually, this is a cost consideration. Group lessons cost less than private lessons and are generally the best way to go if you're just trying out riding to see if you like it. However, some beginning riders want to start with private lessons until they develop their seat, and then after a few weeks, when they feel more secure and comfortable, they can join a group lesson to learn how to ride with other horses and riders around. Some people prefer just the opposite—to ride with a group for the moral support and camaraderie while learning the basics, then develop and refine their skills with private lessons later on.

The Lesson Horses

Good lesson horses are hard to come by. They are generally older horses with temperaments that are well suited to tolerating the bouncing bottoms, flopping legs, and flapping arms of beginner riders. They have been intensely schooled to change gait the absolute second they are asked, which helps when you are a beginner and don't have much of a feel for the horse.

FACT

Good lesson horses know how to do whatever they are expected to do so well that the rider can learn how something should feel—posting to the trot, for instance—without having yet fully mastered it. Beginning riders can learn to recognize how certain moves should feel and apply them to less experienced horses later.

Barns that accept novice riders generally have lesson horses on the premises, but don't take that for granted. Always ask if this is the case and find out about the horses' backgrounds. What the horses know will make a big difference in what you can learn from riding them. For example, if you want to learn dressage, you need to ride a schoolmaster, a horse that has been classically trained and already knows how to do the dressage movements.

The horses themselves will also tell you a lot about the overall quality of the barn and the experience you will have taking lessons there. Take note of how well cared for the horses appear. Lesson horses can work on a regular basis, which means they should be fit and trim, but not skinny. Are their coats tidy? Are their feet well cared for? Do you see lame horses being ridden for lessons?

The size of the horse doesn't matter much as far as learning to ride. However, if you are nervous atop a 16.2-hand horse, then certainly request a shorter horse and see whether that helps you feel more comfortable. The stable should be interested in getting you onto the horse most suitable for you.

Be Particular about Whom You Learn From

Pick your riding teachers carefully. As with almost anything else, not all teachers are equally qualified or gifted. In the United States today, anybody can hang a shingle out on the barn and claim to be a riding instructor, whether or not they know a lot. This is not the case in parts of Europe, where certification standards help ensure that instructors have at least a uniform base of knowledge.

Finding a Qualified Instructor

The lack of a credentialing process poses a real problem for people who don't know enough about horses to know what good riding is and what sound instruction should include. That's why it's important to do some homework and shop around. Otherwise, you can end up spending a lot of money on lessons that won't get you anywhere.

To learn a specific discipline, look for an instructor in that discipline. He will be able to teach you what kind of tack you will need, how to ride in the proper position, what to wear if you plan to compete, and the etiquette of competition for that discipline.

Some equestrian organizations have attempted to address the credentialing issue. One is the United States Dressage Federation (USDF), which has established education and certification programs for dressage instructors. The website, *www.usdf.org*, includes a list of instructors certified through these programs for each region of the country.

Another organization is the American Riding Instructors Association (ARIA), which has certification programs in several equestrian endeavors. To learn more, log onto the ARIA's website at *www.riding-instructor.com*. You'll find ARIA-certified instructors listed by state, along with the discipline they specialize in and their contact information.

Of course, do not overlook the many excellent instructors out there who have no formal qualifications, other than years of experience and, typically, a stellar show career. These folks may not advertise for (or even accept) new students because they don't have to. The local horse people know who they are, recognize and respect their abilities, and usually keep their schedules booked up. You'll find out about these instructors through word of mouth.

Teaching Styles

People teach and learn in different ways. If you lose confidence with an instructor who has a drill sergeant approach, barking out orders and screaming at you every time you do something wrong, this isn't the right teaching style for you. Someone else, however, may flourish the more they are yelled at and the more they feel they are challenged to perfect what they are doing.

You can learn something about how an instructor teaches by watching her give someone else a lesson. If that isn't an option, take one or two lessons to see if you feel comfortable with the instructor's style. Don't sign up for a series of lessons at the outset. Pay for them as you go until you decide whether you want to stay with it. If the first couple of lessons do not go well, try other instructors until you find your match.

Lessons on Your Own Horse

If you already own a horse, you may want to eventually use it for your lessons to improve your ability to handle your own horse. Ask up front if the facility permits this. Some will allow riders to truck in their own horses for lessons, while others may offer instruction only to their boarders.

Depending on your horse's temperament and level of education, the beginning rider may benefit more from taking lessons on the stable's horses to advance his skills on well-schooled mounts. After acquiring the basic skills, you can switch to your own horse with more confidence.

Getting the Most Out of Your Riding Sessions

Whether you ride a lesson horse or your own horse, there are some things you can do to get the most out of your sessions. First, be calm. Your calmness will help your horse to be calm. Horses can sense when their riders or handlers are nervous. Your tension and anxiety will convince your horse that there is cause for him to be nervous, too.

Remember to breathe. Holding your breath or taking shallow short breaths creates tension in you and your horse. Breathing normally will help you stay relaxed. Keep in mind that the horse can feel a fly land on any part of her body—so she can feel whatever you're doing up there, right through all that saddle leather.

Learn about how your horse perceives things and try to assess situations from his perspective. If you come upon a trouble spot with your horse, try to think like an animal of prey. Maybe that rustle in the tall grass means a predator is hiding there. That strange dog lurking on the other side of the fence may be a wolf scouting for dinner.

Develop your awareness of how the horse responds to what you do. The more aware you are of your body, your horse's body, and your surroundings, the better able you will be to adjust what you are doing to fit what the horse needs at the time. Sit on your horse like you intend to be there and do something. Don't slouch or sit stiffly and expect your horse to react positively. Move with the horse. Hold your position in a relaxed, inviting way and ride with purpose.

Do what you are ready for and work on preparing to get ready for more. To progress in riding, you have to challenge yourself and push past your comfort zone. But don't step up to the canter out on the trail if you don't think either of you are ready for it.

ALERT!

Always cool out your horse by walking her on a long rein for the last fifteen minutes of the session. Do not let her eat or drink while she's still hot and breathing hard. In warm weather, hose off the sweat and remove the excess water from her coat with a sweat scraper. In colder weather, sponge the sweaty areas with warm water and dry her off with towels.

Avoid gimmicks. If a piece of tack or a training device claims to work miracles, know it's just a marketing tactic. Effective riders don't need gimmicks because they've learned how to get their horses to respond without them. Nothing except hard work and good instruction can help you attain the proper skills.

Learning the Gaits

The horse has four natural gaits that the beginner will encounter and need to master over a period of time. A few unique breeds, such as the Tennessee Walker and the American Saddlebred, are labeled gaited horses. These horses will display more than the standard four gaits.

The Walk

The horse walks with three feet on the ground and one foot raised at any one time. Each hoof strikes the ground individually—one, two, three, four. Most people think the walk is an easy gait because they're not going fast. Actually, it is the hardest gait to perform correctly from a judge's standpoint, as many riders tend to let their horses drag along without being engaged.

At the walk, sit deeply in the saddle and let your hips move with the movement of the horse. Expect the horse to walk with energy and life, and don't let him stall to a dull, slow amble. You should both look like you are enjoying yourself and have somewhere to go.

The Trot

The trot is a two-beat gait. Two feet are on the ground and two feet are in the air at any one time. The legs operate on a diagonal pattern, with the left front and right hind either up or down at the same time, and the same with the right front and left hind, with a brief moment when all four feet are off the ground. In Western riding parlance, a slow trot is known as the jog. Most people can learn to sit the jog easily, but sitting a more vigorous trot is much harder to master. It takes a very skilled rider to sit a fully extended trot.

QUESTION?

What is the pace?
At the pace, the two legs on the same side of the horse move together, unlike the trot, in which diagonal pairs move together. Horses that pace do so naturally, particularly ones bred for harness racing. In certain easy-gaited breeds, the pace or a similar ambling gait completely replaces the trot.

In the beginning, it is easier to learn to post at the trot. Posting, also called rising trot, is a method of rising up and down to the rhythm of the horse's movement. You rise out of the saddle with the rise of the outside shoulder and foot (the one along the fence rail or arena wall), and you sit back into the saddle as that outside front foot falls to the ground. Posting is easier if the horse is going forward with some speed because the horse's trotting movement pushes you up out of the saddle.

When you're first learning, it will feel like you are being bounced high out of the saddle, but as you gain more control over the movement, you will be able to post lower and lower in the saddle until it feels fluid and almost effortless. Posting is easier on the horse's back and easier on the rider, too.

At some point, you will learn to sit the trot, using your lower back to absorb the shock of the up and down movement, and not flop around like a dying fish in the saddle. This is where riding good school horses helps because they know to keep up their trot speed, even though what you may be doing with your body may interfere with their ability to move forward. Although you won't see Western riders posting to the trot in a class at a show, you can easily post in a Western saddle if it makes you and the horse more comfortable.

The Canter

Sometimes called a slow gallop, the canter is a three-beat gait with a hind leg pushing off, then the other hind and the opposite front, then the other front leg, with a moment of complete suspension of all four legs. In the Western show world, the canter is called the lope, and is a slower gait than the working canter of the English riders.

Typically, most beginners are uncomfortable with—and even fearful of—trying the canter because the horse is going faster. A good instructor won't ask you to try this gait until she knows you have enough mastery over your body at a good working trot to be ready for it. If you're lucky enough to find a smooth, reliable horse to learn to canter on from the very beginning, you will save yourself a lot of canter angst and get this gait down very early in your riding career. Some horses truly have that proverbial rocking horse feel at the canter, while others can feel bouncy and rough.

The trick to cantering is to sit up straight (don't lean forward), keep your back relaxed and your weight balanced and in the stirrups, and scoop your seat along the saddle with the movement of the horse's back. Sometimes novice riders have trouble getting a horse to canter at all. Even if they apply the correct signals to ask for the gait, their anxiety causes their body to tense up and block the horse from moving out. As with anything involving horses, the more you canter in a controlled environment, the sooner you will be comfortable with this gait.

When cantering on a circle or around an arena, it is important to ask the horse to strike off on the correct canter lead. The horse generally leads with the inside legs on the circle reaching further forward. The more extended inside foreleg is matched by a slightly more extended hind leg on the same side. The hind leg comes further forward under the body to help the horse better balance the rider's weight on the turn. The horse is said to be cantering on the right lead if the right foreleg and hind leg extend further forward. For the left lead, it is the opposite.

What is the counter-canter?

The counter-canter is a special balancing movement in dressage in which the rider deliberately asks the horse to canter on the wrong lead for the direction he is going. Used to prepare the horse for higher-level movements, it is a difficult exercise that requires precisely coordinated aids from the rider.

When a horse switches from one lead to the other at the canter, this is called a flying change. Horses do flying changes naturally when cantering freely in the field and changing directions. Under saddle, flying changes on cue are harder to master, as the rider must learn to signal the horse at a precise moment during the canter sequence.

The Gallop

The gallop is a faster and more ground-covering variation of the canter. It is also a four-beat gait, instead of a three-beat gait. Racehorses gallop all out to reach the finish line, but in most other equestrian pursuits, riders gallop in hand, which is a slower, well-controlled version of this gait. To free the horse's back in the hand gallop, the rider assumes a two-point position in the saddle (similar to that in jumping), leaning forward slightly, with bottom out of the saddle and with weight firmly down in the heels for balance.

The Rider's Aids

After reading about the various gaits, you may be wondering how the rider gets the horse to do these things on command. The silent body signals used to communicate with the horse while riding are called the aids. Western and English riders use basically the same aids with some slight variation from one discipline to another. A good instructor will teach you how to use your natural aids—your hands, legs, seat, weight, and voice—and, when necessary, reinforce them with the artificial aids—whip and spurs—to achieve the desired response.

The Hands

Of all the aids, the hands can be the most abusive. Unschooled riders typically hang onto the reins for balance, which is exactly the wrong thing to do. This bad habit is damaging to the horse's mouth and will eventually create a problem horse that seeks to escape her rider's abusive treatment by rearing, bucking, bolting, or any other means possible. *Contact* is the term used for the connection between the horse's mouth and the rider's hands. The connection should feel soft and elastic, but the reins should be neither slack nor taut.

The rider regulates the contact and talks to the horse through his hands by gently squeezing and releasing the fingers, or by slightly turning the wrist to signal a change in direction. It takes good coaching and a lot of practice to develop good hands and to ride without yanking the horse's mouth.

The Seat

The rider does not use her hands on the reins alone to steer and stop the horse. She uses all of the natural aids together to influence the horse. The seat is the way the rider sits in the saddle and uses her weight, balance, lower back, and abdominal muscles to drive the horse forward. Developing a good seat is paramount to the rider's balance and stability in the saddle.

To help you develop a good seat, your riding instructor may give you some lessons on the lunge line, without reins and stirrups. This teaches you to maintain balance on a moving horse at each gait and develop what's called an independent seat. You learn not balancing off the reins or stirrups to stay in the saddle. You can never be a truly effective rider without developing an independent seat.

The Rider's Weight

After the rider develops a good seat, he can simply shift his weight more to one seat bone (buttock) or the other to communicate with the horse. This doesn't mean that the rider leans to one side or the other. Instead, he presses down through the leg and heel on the required side. This shifts slightly more weight to the seat bone on that side, which the horse feels and responds to by stepping in that direction.

When the weight rests equally on both seat bones, the horse knows to go straight. It sounds simple, but a lot of horses move crookedly because their riders don't realize that they are weighting one side more than the other and not balancing all their aids correctly.

The Leg Aids

Beginners try to stay on the horse by gripping with their legs, but again, this is the wrong thing to do and can become a bad habit to break. The legs should stay lightly in contact with the horse's sides. The thighs need to be open and relaxed at the hips but with no daylight showing between the knees and the saddle. Depending on the aid required, the rider may use her whole leg or the lower and upper parts of the leg independently. The leg aids may also be applied at the girth or behind the girth with varying amounts of pressure, depending on the horse and on the desired result.

When the rider presses her right leg against the horse's right side, the horse's natural response is to step away from the pressure to the left, and vice versa. When the rider presses both legs evenly against the horse's sides, the horse moves away from the pressure by stepping forward. The harder you squeeze with the legs, the faster the horse goes. This is why gripping with the legs is counterproductive for the frightened beginner—it urges the horse on.

The hands control the front end of the horse, while the legs steer the rear and keep the horse going. An educated rider applies the leg and seat aids first to engage or drive the hind end toward the front, then uses her hands to steer the front end and regulate the pace.

The Voice

Horses can tell by the tone and intensity of your voice whether you are pleased or angry with them. If you yell or growl at them when they do something you don't like, they will get the point. Likewise, if you croon softly to them when they do what you want, they will understand that you are pleased. Horses can also grasp the meaning of certain key words when used repeatedly and consistently, and the ideal time to teach the verbal commands you want them to know is during ground-work. They will come in handy later on when you are training under saddle.

For example, on the lunge line when you encourage your horse to move out from the walk with the whip and go faster, say "Trot" aloud every time. When you encourage him to move out from the trot and go faster, say "Canter." Be consistent and ask for the desired forward response the same way every time. In time, all you will need to do is say the appropriate word, and the horse will respond.

When you begin training under saddle, the horse will not understand the silent cues for the various gaits right away. But if she understands the word "trot," you can combine the verbal command with your silent aids and make the horse understand what you want. If you do this consistently, she will pick up the silent cues quickly, and then you can drop the verbal cues.

FACT

Voice commands are appropriate and useful schooling aids; however, you should not have to rely on them in a judged performance. The rules in dressage tests and some other types of horse show classes forbid you to cluck or speak to your horse. You are testing your horse's training and your ability to communicate and move in harmony on an unspoken level.

The Artificial Aids

Artificial aids support the natural aids but should not replace them.

Whips

Dressage whips and crops (a shorter type of whip, usually with a flat piece of leather on the end) are intended to be used as a training aid or incentive for getting or keeping a horse moving, not for punishment purposes. Riding with a whip helps the rider reinforce his leg aids if the horse tends to be sluggish or doesn't yet understand the forward driving commands. The rider generally carries the whip in his inside hand, changing it as he changes direction. He administers the reinforcement as a light tap or a flick on the hindquarters, but not with stinging force.

If the rider's legs are ineffective, sometimes it is better to use a crop or whip to get the horse moving forward than to dull her sides to the legs by constantly bumping on the horse with the legs without getting the desired effect. The horse will learn to ignore this constant bumping and won't respond at all. Of course, you can also dull your horse to the whip (or make her cranky) if you don't get any more results than you did with your legs.

The correct way to deal with a sluggish horse is to ask him to go forward with your leg aids first. If he hesitates the least bit, follow up with a light tap of the whip on his hindquarters to let him know you mean business. The next time, he should respond more willingly to your leg aids because he will anticipate the whip.

Spurs

Spurs also reinforce the leg aids and are used only as incentive, never as punishment. Both English and Western riders may wear spurs attached to their boots, and certain styles are traditional for each. Spurs should only be worn by accomplished riders with quiet legs. Worn by unskilled riders, they can be quite detrimental to the horse.

Large spinning rowels are what commonly comes to mind when you imagine a cowboy with spurs on, but the most common spurs worn by most riders have very short shanks. In certain horse show classes, such as advanced level dressage, riders are required to wear short-shank spurs as part of their traditional attire.

Physical Fitness

Riding horses is a strenuous physical activity that requires some fitness and flexibility on the part of both horse and rider. Anyone who thinks the horse does all the work and doesn't understand how riding can be good exercise has either never been on a horse or has merely been a passenger on a horse instead of a true rider.

Fitness of the Horse

Prepare and condition your horse for the level of riding you plan to use her for. If you take her out just on weekends for trail rides a mile or two long, being a little overweight and out of shape probably won't hurt her.

Don't expect a horse you normally take on two-mile trails to go out on a twenty-five-mile trail ride without coming home sore or lame. It just isn't fair to the animal. If you want to do that twenty-five-mile ride, plan months ahead for it, and condition your horse gradually by riding her consistently on longer and longer rides.

If you live in the northern states where winter is mostly down time, gradually build your horse up for the riding season. Take him to an indoor arena a couple of times a week if you can and keep him in some level of shape over the winter. Increase your conditioning as warmer weather approaches.

Fitness of the Rider

Keeping horses provides you some strength training just by doing day-to-day chores such as lifting water buckets, hay bales, grain bags, bags of shavings, and so on. But there are some things to add to your overall fitness regimen that can be helpful, specifically for riding.

As with any physical activity, you should do some warm-up stretches before you get on your horse. Yoga is especially beneficial to riders because of the increased stretching and flexibility it gives you. When your body is more supple, you can move with the horse better and liven up the energy level that needs to transfer from you to the horse.

Your lower back absorbs a lot of the shock of the motion of riding. A strong back and corresponding strong abdominal muscles will help keep this shock absorption from making your back hurt. Strong abdominal muscles will also help your posture in the saddle. Adding stomach crunches to your exercise program can help.

Falling Off

Everyone who takes up horseback riding will, at some point, fall off. It's not a matter of if but when. For safety's sake, it's best to never ride alone. Should you fall and get injured, someone will be nearby to help you.

If you're not injured after a fall, it is important to get right back on the horse, if possible. This lets the horse know that he can't escape work by getting you off. It's also important for your psyche because a fall can make a rider become very fearful. Getting back on helps you deal with it right then and there and keeps your confidence intact.

Think about why your horse spooked, bucked, reared, or whatever it did to send you flying. All horses spook occasionally, but if you've gained the appropriate skills, you should be able to ride through it and stay on in most cases. Regaining control and defusing the situation as quickly as possible is the key to avoiding bucks, bolts, and potential falls. Work on your seat and balance, as these provide your security and help you remain in the saddle.

Some people let their fear get the best of them and give up riding altogether. If you feel this happening to you, work with an instructor who can help you get past your mental blocks. Many instructors are sensitive to the issue because they've experienced it themselves. Getting over it may mean going back to square one and doing some remedial work to help you regain your confidence. If that's what it takes, then do it. With some good instruction and a horse that is suitable for your level of ability, you should be able to overcome your fears and continue enjoying your riding for years to come.

CHAPTER 18

Schooling and Training

A lot of people think that as long as the horse is well trained, they can learn a few basics and then just hop on and let the horse do the work. Well-trained horses can quickly become unruly when ridden by someone with poor form. This is why it's important to work with a trainer or riding coach at least periodically, so you can avoid common pitfalls and keep your relationship with your horse healthy and on track. Even Olympic-class riders work with coaches to keep their skills sharp.

Working with a Trainer

People often seek out a trainer because of a specific problem they are having with their horse. In some cases, the person has been injured working with the horse and has become frightened of the same thing happening again. The person sends the horse off to the trainer for some intensive work. And when the horse comes back, all seems to go well, at least for a while.

Trainer Versus Riding Coach

When you enroll your dog in obedience school, you don't just send your dog away to get trained. You attend obedience classes with your dog and learn how to give it the commands. The same should be true for your horse.

In some situations, it may be best to send the horse away for some specific training. But when the horse comes back and the rider continues to have problems with it, the rider needs to consider some training for herself, for therein lies the problem nine times out of ten.

Say, for example, the horse develops the problem of bolting. Horses do not always bolt and run away out of fear, although sometimes that is the case. Bolting is often a resistance to something the rider is doing that is making the horse feel uncomfortable or insecure. It is a symptom of a bigger problem. By working with a more experienced person, you may begin to find answers to what is going wrong in your relationship with your horse.

The terms *trainer, instructor,* and *riding coach* are often used interchangeably in the horse world. To be any of them, you have to know what's involved in teaching both horses and riders how to relate to each other. As your instructor watches you ride your horse, she can see how effectively you are using your aids and your body position to influence your horse. She can also observe how the horse is responding—whether he's annoyed, tense, distracted, paying attention, or simply tuning out the rider.

Returning to the example of the bolting horse, let's say the instructor notices that when the horse's paces get lively, you tend to tense up and grip with your inner thighs. This pushes your bottom out of the saddle, destroying the effectiveness and security of your seat. To steady yourself, you instinctively lean slightly forward and begin balancing off your reins, without even realizing that you're doing it. This jabs the horse in the mouth, and he gets fed up with this treatment and bolts to escape the abuse.

The Rider as Trainer

As a rider, you are also a trainer. Every time you ride or handle your horse, you are teaching it either good things or bad things. If you want your relationship with your horse to be a good one, it's your responsibility to make sure your skills are adequate enough to teach good things and avoid bad habits from creeping in and establishing themselves.

In the example of the bolting horse, it's clear that the rider's tension and poor riding habits resulted in the horse's misbehavior. The tension and gripping suggests that the rider doesn't trust her seat and lacks confidence in her ability to control this horse. The problem becomes a vicious circle—the more times the horse bolts, the more the rider's confidence gets chipped away.

Working with a good instructor can help heal this rider's relationship with her horse. The trainer may put the rider on a different horse to help restore her confidence in herself. Some lessons on the lunge line without reins and stirrups may be in order to improve the rider's seat and balance. Finally, the rider must get back on her own horse and apply her brushed-up skills to the problem. The horse has learned to bolt as a resistance to this rider, and the misbehavior has become an established habit. The trainer may ride the horse a few times to see if he tries to bolt. However, in the hands of a more skilled rider, the horse may behave differently and be completely obedient because he's not getting mixed signals that confuse and frustrate him. He has not forgotten his past training and good manners. His actions were simply a rebellion to the unfair and abusive (although unintentional) treatment of his rider. Once the rider gained the confidence to relax and employ her aids properly, without gripping or grabbing, her horse returned to his normal, well-trained demeanor.

Good riders make good horses. Bad riders turn good horses bad. A green or mediocre horse will improve in the hands of an effective rider because a skilled rider instills good habits in the horse every time he rides. An unskilled rider's poor habits will rub off on a good, well-trained horse, and that horse will eventually descend to that rider's level of bad habits.

This example illustrates why it is so important to learn to ride well and effectively. Horses do have an innate sense of fairness, some more so than others. Many horses that have been highly trained and consistently ridden by good riders often don't tolerate sloppy riders very easily. They will test your skill level as soon as you get on, and if they are of a mind to unload what they view as a nuisance on their back, you'll find yourself facedown in the dirt soon enough.

Avoiding Problems

Riding a horse is fraught with danger. To be safe riding, there are a few things you should expect of your horse, responses that make you feel safe when riding. If you have these things at your disposal, you will feel more in control and comfortable about being able to work through almost any situation. As a rider, you should constantly work, study, and practice to refine and exact the following things from your horse.

Responsiveness: The Key to Control

You want your horse to be responsive when you ask him to do something. When you pick up the reins, you want him to come to attention and do whatever you ask him to do. When you press your legs against his sides, you want him to move forward. If you don't expect your horse to be responsive, you teach him that you don't really mean business when you ask him to do something.

Of course, it is up to you to acquire the skills to communicate effectively with your horse and make him understand what you want. If the two of you aren't communicating well, then you need to go back and work with a riding coach until you can establish better communication. Sometimes when you ask for something, it is a matter of safety that your horse be responsive—such as stopping to avoid a kick from the horse up ahead or stepping one foot to the left to avoid falling off the edge of an embankment. Obedience is also a must for safety's sake. For example, when you are mounting, don't allow your horse to anticipate and move out before you give the signal. You must always be the one to say when.

Softness: The Key to Good Contact

When you pick up the reins, you want your horse to melt into your hands. Picking up those reins is a signal to your horse that you are about to get to work at something. Softness doesn't mean riding with a loose rein. It means that when you pick up the reins, the horse doesn't resist you, throwing his head up in the air to avoid contact. If an emergency should arise, you want softness, not resistance, to be your horse's first response to you; it is through this good contact that your horse receives your messages.

Much of the work you do with an instructor involves learning how to establish softness, which is so vital to good communication. Good contact comes not from pulling back on the reins but from driving the horse's hindquarters forward into your hands, where you simply hold him in a frame and direct him where you want him to go.

Say, for example, you are riding with others on the trail and something spooks the group, such as a grouse flying out of the bushes. More than likely, your horse will spook with the rest—it's only natural for him to follow the herd and react the way the other horses do. Ideally, what you want is for your horse to turn to you, his trusted master and leader, for a message about the situation. If you tense up, haul back on the reins, and yank his mouth, you'll convince him that he has something to fear. However, if you calmly reassure him that you're in control and your horse softens, the situation will go from potentially explosive to controlled. If the horse's first reaction is to resist your hands and throw his head up in the air, the situation is going to get more frightening.

Going Forward

You can avoid many problems simply by keeping your horse going forward correctly. Going forward isn't just going faster. It means using your legs and seat to drive the back end of the horse forward into your hands, where you regulate where he's going and how fast. If you keep the rear in gear this way, you have control over the whole horse, not just the front half. It's surprising how many people ride only the front half of the horse, steering with their hands but not really doing much with their legs or seat besides keeping themselves in the saddle.

When you consistently ride your horse from back to front, engaging the hindquarters and keeping both halves of the horse connected, he will feel more secure with you in charge. This is because you actually create a channel with your aids for him to move through, so he knows exactly where you want him to go. Your legs and seat tell his back end where to go, and your hands tell his front end where to go.

Let's say you're trotting around a schooling arena and a dog slips under the fence ahead and startles your horse. The horse's first instinct is to turn and flee from any perceived danger. What should you do to prevent this?

A rider controlling only the front half of the horse would pull back on the reins to try to prevent the horse from turning and bolting. Pulling back too hard on the reins might actually cause the horse to rear up. Rearing is one of the most dangerous things a horse can do because if he gets off balance, he may fall over backward on top of the rider. A rider controlling both halves of the horse would step on the accelerator, driving the horse forward with her legs and seat through that channel of aids so the horse has no chance to wheel around and run.

Clinics and Riding Camps

Attending clinics or riding camps offers a great way to spend an intensive amount of time working on issues or simply improving your skills.

Many clinics and camps give you the option of attending as a spectator or trucking in your horse for one-on-one lessons. You and your horse will develop a stronger relationship just by learning together under good instruction. Plus, the clinic environment provides instant camaraderie with other riders and instant access to a riding teacher.

Clinics give you a chance to broaden your horseback horizons and learn something new or dabble in a different discipline. Maybe you're a longtime dressage rider, but you've always wanted to try reining. Sign up for a clinic and try it out. You'll be surprised to discover what the sports of dressage and reining have in common.

Not all clinics involve riding instruction. They may cover specialized topics, such as types of bits and their uses, pasture management, parasite control, vaccinations, foaling, or numerous other subjects of interest to horse owners.

Clinics are typically a one-day or weekend affair, while riding camps are usually more intensely educational and last about a week. There are currently dozens of clinicians traveling the country giving clinics on horsemanship, colt starting, and handling. Some advertise in the local media, but you're more likely to learn about them through your contacts with the horse people in your community or through your horse club newsletters and websites.

Training Philosophies

Throughout the ages, many philosophies about training horses have come and gone, some of them good, some of them bad. In the days when people relied on horses for transportation, horses needed to be backed and broken quickly, often using barbaric methods, to supply the demand. While some people took great pride in their horses, others viewed them only as a means to get from point A to point B and took marginal care of them, similar to the way many people today treat their cars.

The Horsemanship Revolution

Today, we are in the midst of an unfolding revolution in horsemanship. At least in the United States, where owning a horse isn't out of reach for the middle class, many people no longer view horses as merely beasts of burden. Instead, horses have gained ground as companion animals, treasured and revered alongside our dogs and cats. Of course, horses are still exploited for many uses, racing for example. But more of them enjoy pampered lifestyles while they're working well and in the money.

Natural Horsemanship

The so-called natural horsemanship approach appeals to dedicated horse lovers who are truly interested in understanding their horses better and moving to higher levels of communication. The philosophy has increased awareness about good versus bad training methods and the use of humane, psychological methods versus forcing the horse into submission.

Classical Horsemanship

Of course, the knowledge that gentling the horse works better than brute force has existed for centuries in Europe among practitioners of classical horsemanship. Classical means old, but this style of horsemanship has become synonymous with modern-day dressage.

Dressage training takes years, even decades, for horse and rider to master the higher-level movements, if they even reach the upper levels at all. But the end result is a beautiful ballet on horseback executed with precision and lightness.

Becoming a Trainer

As a rider, you are already a trainer. It is up to you to make sure that you are teaching your horse good things. The results will be self-evident. You have many resources at your disposal to become a good trainer to your horse. Take advantage of them. Read, watch videos, and learn as much as you can.

When you have learned to ride effectively, you may wish to try taking on the training of a young horse yourself someday. It's not a task for everybody. But for the serious-minded horseman, the experience and knowledge gained from turning a green youngster into a fine, safe riding mount is like earning a doctorate degree in horsemanship.

Maybe your old schoolmaster is getting a bit long in the tooth by now, and you want to start bringing up a younger mount to take his place when the time comes. The first time you undertake the training of a young horse, work under the guidance of an experienced trainer, someone who has already done it more than once. Backing a young horse that has never been ridden is a dangerous endeavor. Do not attempt anything alone.

Realize that your horses will never be perfect, nor will you ever be a perfect rider. But what you put into it is what you get out of it. Learning to communicate with horses is a long and winding journey, joyous for some, jolting for others. Visualize what you want to become, set goals, and seek out the people who can help you reach them.

CHAPTER 19

Youth and Horses

City kids and country kids alike have long been captivated by horses. Little girls and boys dream of having their own pony to ride. Caring for a horse offers important lessons in responsibility and drives home the reality that even pleasurable things include a lot of hard work. If you're a parent just getting introduced to horses through your horse-crazy youngster, read on and learn how to make kids and horses a winning combination.

Good Responsibility Lesson

Although kids usually don't need to be pushed into the barn to be around horses, horse care is a big responsibility. Obviously, being around horses poses inherent dangers for children, especially for the very young ones. That's why all children need to be well supervised around horses, when they're riding and when they're caring for the horse. If a child is a member of a horsy family that has a barn full of horses and makes a living or a hobby of some equine activity, caring for horses and knowing how to act around them probably comes naturally from observing their parents.

ALERT!

The important thing to keep in mind is that a horse in the backyard is a living, breathing domesticated animal with daily needs that can only be met by its human caretakers. Make sure both you and your children are ready for this immense responsibility.

Getting Started

For the kid who has never been around horses, the best option may be to board the horse, at least for a while. In this situation, the parent needs to become as educated about horses as the child. By boarding, the child and the parents are automatically surrounded by more knowledgeable, experienced people who can help them learn the basics.

Often, owning a horse is only financially feasible when the horse can be kept in the backyard. If the parents are not horse savvy, then the responsibility is on them to find out what they need to know and to get their child in contact with people who have experience with horses. Perhaps someone in the neighborhood who has horses can spend time with the child and parents, preferably before the horse comes home. If keeping the horse at home frees up a little extra money to let the child take riding lessons, get well acquainted with the riding instructor. The instructor can steer you toward horse clubs and people who can help you gain the knowledge you need. If there is a barn in the vicinity that will let your child clean stalls or groom horses in exchange for riding lessons, that's the best of both worlds—learning about riding and general horse care at the same time! Programs such as 4-H and Pony Club can also provide the novice child with lots of help and educational materials.

A Word of Warning

An all-too-common scenario is for a horse to end up at a rescue shelter when undesirable behaviors, left unchecked by well-meaning but inexperienced owners, end up making her dangerous. If you see behavior in your child's horse that concerns you—such as aggressiveness during feeding time, turning her rear end to you when you enter the stall, kicking when her feet are handled, or misbehaving under saddle—don't let these things continue to the point of becoming dangerous. Get help from an experienced trainer or horse person whom you can trust. Find out what to do to turn these behaviors around before your child or someone else gets hurt. In the hands of an inexperienced owner, it's easy for bad habits to develop before you realize what's happening. This is rarely ever the horse's fault, as the horse is merely acting on natural instinct. Horses are also smart enough to take advantage of poorly trained riders and get out of doing work when they would rather be grazing.

Enroll in Riding Lessons

One of the best ways to learn about handling horses is to enroll in riding lessons with a qualified instructor and learn to ride properly. If you're considering buying a horse or pony for your child, you should enroll him in riding lessons at least six months to a year prior to purchasing the horse.

Learn the Basics First

By taking riding lessons, the child will learn a few basics before the horse arrives, such as:

- How to approach and walk around a horse safely
- How to lead a horse

- How to groom the horse
- How to tack up a horse for riding
- What gear to wear for safer riding
- How to cool out a horse after riding
- How to make the horse start and stop
- How to make the horse walk, trot, and canter under saddle

Another advantage of building a good rapport with a riding instructor is that many of them do double duty as horse trainers and brokers. If this is the case in your situation, you can ask the instructor to help you find a suitable horse for your youngster. You can expect to pay a fee for this service, but in return you'll have a knowledgeable person evaluating the horse for you. Some people end up buying the lesson horse and continue taking lessons on it.

Breed Association Youth Groups

Joining a horse club is a good way to meet other horse people and learn from them. Through the connections you make as a club member, you'll have access to firsthand accounts of local instructors and boarding facilities. Most horse breeds have a breed association that promotes them, and it's easy to locate these on the Internet simply by entering the breed name in a search engine. Breed associations realize that young riders comprise future adult members of their organization, and they encourage youths to be interested in their breed and take part in youth activities.

The Welsh Pony Club Youth Program

The Welsh Pony and Cob Society of America has a special youth program directed toward the many young people who ride Welsh Mountain ponies. As the name implies, this popular breed hails from Wales. The Welsh Cob is a larger version of the Welsh pony. In the United States, the breed can be found competing in nearly every riding discipline—English and Western pleasure, hunter/jumper, driving, dressage, and combined training. The club's website, *www.welshpony.org*, features a youth segment with online articles about pony care and offers tips as well as games, stories, and puzzles.

FACT

There are more than 600 Pony Clubs in the United States, with more than 12,000 members. The pony in the name actually refers to the young rider, not the mount. Pony Club members can ride either ponies or horses. Parental involvement is encouraged and expected. There is a membership fee. To find a group near you, look on the Pony Club website at *www.ponyclub.org*.

The American Quarter Horse Youth Association (AQHYA)

The AQHYA is for youths eighteen years old and under. The group has 30,000 members and offers scholarships, youth-specific shows, classes in general shows, a leadership conference, and other focused activities, such as the Youth Racing Experience. Visit the AQHA website at *www.aqha.com* and click on "Youth" for complete information about joining and participating in the AQHYA.

The International Arabian Horse Youth Association (IAHYA)

Like other breed-specific groups, this association exists for youths involved with Arabian horses. The IAHYA has more than 5,000 members, and its magazine and website (*www.arabianhorses.org*) have a special youth section called Generation Equus. The website tells about special events especially for youths, such as Youth of the Year and the Youth Nationals Arabian and Half-Arabian Championship Horse Show. Clubs are divided into geographic regions, so you can probably find one near you.

The U.S. Dressage Federation (USDF)

Dressage is one of the fast-growing equine sports in the United States. The USDF promotes dressage interest and education and offers activities for riders of all ages. The organization accepts individual members as well as those who join through a dressage club, called a GMO or group-member organization. You can find out about clubs in your area by visiting the website at *www.usdf.org*.

Over-Mounted Youths

One of the biggest mistakes most beginning riders make is getting on a horse whose level of training does not match their riding ability. An untrained rider needs a well-trained horse to learn on, and vice versa. Beginning riders need to be mounted on calm, quiet, obedient school horses that are tolerant of flapping reins and bouncing butts. And only the most skilled, experienced riders should attempt to mount a green, barely broke three-year-old.

Consider leasing tack or buying good quality used tack for growing children. There are also youth-specific tack items such as adjustable child stirrups, which come as an attachment to a full-sized Western saddle. Most riding apparel and footwear comes in youth sizes. Most importantly, buy a good-fitting safety helmet, and never let your child ride without wearing it!

Avoiding Common Pitfalls

Parents should be careful not to set their child up to become fearful of horses by putting them on an animal that is too big for them and not suited to their ability. A child should ride a well-trained mount of proportional size until she is a very experienced rider. A 14.2-hand horse is a fine size for many eight- to ten-year-old kids. Unless a child is exceptionally tall or has ridden since she was two, a seventeen-hand horse is unnecessarily tall for a young rider. Let the child develop some confidence a little closer to the ground. This means that when she falls off, she will have less distance to fall. It also means that when she looks down, things don't look so far away. The child's legs should reach a good distance down the horse's sides.

The horse's age is important, too, because older horses generally have had more training. It takes several years to train a horse to become a safe, reliable mount. They're not born knowing what's expected of them. Some horses' temperaments make them unsuitable as mounts for anyone except the most advanced riders. A rule of thumb is that horses under five years old are too young and green for novice riders, whether youths or adults.

Many young riders are just awesome to watch ride—their youth often lends balance and flexibility combined with a general lack of fear that allows them to float with the horse. Once they take the natural ability and create a refined, skilled ability as a rider, the size of the horse doesn't matter.

FACT

Horse care and horseback riding have long been topics for 4-H groups. This is an excellent way for kids to learn about horse care. Many 4-H groups focus on a different horse activity, such as showing or trail riding. Contact your county extension agency to find out if there is a 4-H horse group in your area.

Model Horse Shows

Collecting and showing model horses is an enjoyable and educational hobby for kids and adults alike. Those plastic Breyer horses you see in stores aren't merely toys. They are collectibles, and some of them hold high dollar value. Many people customize their models and compete for prizes in organized model horse shows. The hobby is educational and creative because all of the miniature tack and other appointments must be correct, just like in a real horse show.

Breyer, a well-known model horse manufacturer, hosts an annual Breyer-Fest at the Kentucky Horse Park in Lexington, Kentucky, that attracts hordes of model horse collectors from around the world. The three-day event includes a model horse show, a trade fair, a swap meet, workshops on model horse collecting and showing, and exhibitions by some of the guest horses that inspired Breyer models. To learn more about model horse shows and collecting, visit *http://breyerhorses.com*, or subscribe to Breyer's magazine, *Just About Horses*, which is geared to youth and covers all aspects of the model horse hobby.

Equine Careers

Don't be surprised if your horse-crazy youngster decides to pursue a career in horses. With the current explosion of the horse industry, more and more young people are finding job opportunities doing what they love most.

You can help by educating yourself about the opportunities available and encouraging your youngster to explore them.

Veterinarian

As in human medicine, extensive time in school is required to become a veterinarian. While in school, some people begin to hone in on a specialty that attracts them most—surgery, therapeutics, or research, for example.

Pets, including horses, are a vital part of the economy in the United States and developed nations around the world. Most horse veterinarians are on the road a lot doing farm calls, so you need to like to drive, find your way through country towns and roads, and improvise with whatever kind of facility you find at the end of the road. Time spent traveling on the job means you have less time to spend with your own horses at home, so that's something to consider when investigating this career path.

Veterinary Technician

The veterinary technician is a vital asset at an animal hospital of any kind. Vet techs in equine practices may find themselves doing anything from cleaning stalls to taking temperatures to regularly checking in-house patients for vital signs. Some vet techs go on the road with vets and help prepare vaccines, restrain horses while care is being administered, and so forth. The academic requirements for a veterinary technician typically involve a two-year vocational program.

Equine Dentist

The equine dentist is becoming a more common member of the horse care team. In choosing this career path, you will spend a lot of time with your hands in horses' mouths, working with power tools. Unless you can get yourself a few customers who have large facilities with lots of horses, you will need to travel around the countryside to visit your clients.

Farrier

The horse's foot is fascinating, and its well-being is vital to the overall health and serviceability of the horse. The tools needed for farrier work are fairly simple, the work is varied, and you get to be your own boss. Like the country vet, you have to travel around the countryside and deal with whatever barn setups you encounter. The farrier also often works in conjunction with the veterinarian on foot issues that involve disease and injury. The area of foot care is changing drastically, with new techniques and shoes made of new materials, and the need for people in this area of equine specialty is increasing.

QUESTION?

What's the difference between a farrier and a blacksmith?
A farrier is a blacksmith who does horseshoeing for a living but doesn't necessarily do other types of iron work. While a blacksmith make may horseshoes, he is also skilled at making other things with iron.

The constant bending over in farrier work can be hard on the body. If all horses were easy to handle, stood perfectly still, and held their own weight up while the farrier worked on a foot, it might be less of a backbreaking job. But those kinds of horses are more the rarity than the norm. As with any horse-related activity, the possibility of injury from kicks is quite real, perhaps even more so for a farrier dealing with an uncooperative or frightened horse.

Riding Instructor

If you become an expert in a particular discipline, a career as a riding instructor may be just right. Good riders are always trying to improve their skills. You don't have to have competed in the Olympics to help people be better riders.

FACT

Many people figure out how much time per week they can spend teaching riding and fill in the slots as customers come along. Most people who take lessons, especially beginners, expect to ride school horses. Therefore, if you give group lessons, you need to have enough horses to go around. That certainly adds to the expense of this kind of business.

Horse Trainer

If you become an excellent rider and you like working with young horses, perhaps you would like to make a living at starting horses under saddle. This is one of the hardest and most dangerous ways to make a living with horses—but it's also one of the most rewarding. If you become very good at it, your services will be in great demand.

Today, more owners want to be involved in their horse's training. They are not as willing to just send their horse away for three months and not care what you are doing with it. They want to observe and understand the process of educating a horse to riding. This is a good thing. In watching the process, the owner can become a better-educated rider and ultimately be able to handle her horse more effectively.

Breeder

Involvement in horse breeding can be approached in two ways: You can be a veterinarian who specializes in reproduction, or you can learn a lot about genetics and breed, raise, and sell your own horses.

QUESTION?

What does LFG stand for?
LFG means live foal guaranteed and is what you should expect to have to offer if you offer stallion services. Mares are receptive to a stallion for limited periods of time. If the mare aborts the foal, the mare owner will expect to rebreed at no additional stud fee.

Breeding and selling horses can be a complex undertaking, and because of the considerable expenses involved, most people don't make a lot of money from it. Typically, you choose a breed, maybe two, to specialize in. You need to learn a lot about equine genetics to be able to choose the best pairings of stallions and mares. Color tends to sell in the horse world, and there are specific genetic patterns that make it more likely that you will get palominos, buckskins, or Paints. However, luck of the draw always figures prominently.

To have a breeding program, you will probably keep a stallion on the premises. Handling a stallion requires considerable skill and knowledge and is not something a novice can undertake safely. You can, however, carry out a breeding program without a stallion and simply own mares that are artificially inseminated.

Having horses for sale is almost like retail sales—the more you have for people to look at, the more likely they will find one they want. When breeding, you should know how to market young horses. Otherwise, if they have to be broke to ride before they are sold, plan to feed them and have them around for a while—as long as three to four years.

Professional Rider

Making a living wage from a career riding horses is a bit of a pipe dream for most. A few people manage to do it, but it is not for the faint of heart. The bills are big—you need high-quality horses, tack, a trailer, and so forth. Travel expenses are extensive, and entry fees to events can add up fast. Purses in the horse world are smaller than in other sports, such as golf and tennis. But if you are extremely competitive and successful, the effort can bring you a good living later on, when you translate your fame and reputation into a career in instruction or training.

CHAPTER 20

Entering Your First Show

Horse showing is probably the most common horse activity. It has something for everyone—beginner and advanced, Western and English, in-hand or under saddle, high-speed games or relaxed circuits around the show ring. However, you must understand that the horse show world is competitive and expensive, even at the local levels. If you are interested, be sure you are fully prepared to commit the time and money that is required to place or win ribbons.

Different Levels of Shows

Horse shows are run by local riding clubs, statewide horse associations, and national associations. Each tends to have the same basic setup: Horse and rider accumulate points throughout the year, and at the end of the season awards are handed out at a special banquet.

Local Shows

The local riding clubs are lots of fun, and they are a great way to accumulate some horse friends if you keep your horse at home and don't have the advantage of the built-in peer group, as you do when you board your horse at a stable. Local shows are also good places for beginners to overcome their show jitters (for both rider and horse!) before venturing into the more competitive arenas. These shows are smaller, which means there are fewer horses and smaller classes and, therefore, you might be able to build your confidence and win some ribbons early on.

Local shows and clubs also offer the opportunity to widen your circle of horse friends by volunteering in any number of capacities, from club treasurer to ring steward, or simply to tidy up the ring and grounds after a show. Volunteering at horse shows is a great way to learn the ropes and see how things work before you begin participating as a competitor.

Regional Shows

Regional shows are often sponsored by state components of national organizations. Almost every breed has them—the American Quarter Horse Association has an affiliated club in almost every state, with some more active than others. Morgans, Arabians, and many other breeds also have similar state groups. They often put on statewide shows, where the competition gets a little tougher—in numbers and in skill level. These types of shows might be a good next step after spending some time showing locally.

National Shows

The national shows, which are often also affiliated with breed associations, are highly competitive and mostly well attended. It is really not worth the time and money to attend one of these with your horse unless you have spent the energy in thorough preparation and training, probably gaining experience in the local and regional shows first. It's a good opportunity to talk to some other competitors about their experiences showing at the national shows. And if it all sounds exciting, then by all means go for it!

Attend one or two national shows as a spectator before you decide to compete in one. That way, you can get a feel for the atmosphere and whether you can ever be comfortable competing at that level. It's not for everybody, and many riders find it more fun and fulfilling, and less stressful, to stick with the smaller-scale shows.

Types of Classes

The average-size regional horse shows are made up of several classes that might last for fifteen to twenty minutes and have about twenty-five riders. Classes are divided up into three general categories.

Pleasure Classes

Pleasure classes are subjectively judged and are based on the performance of the horse. Both English and Western riding styles have pleasure classes. Typically, there is a separate class for each and also an open class where both styles and all ages and levels compete together. Pleasure classes are judged on how pleasurable to ride the horse appears to be. To win, your horse needs to be well behaved and to change gaits immediately and only on command. The gaits should be smooth and in keeping with the style of riding you are presenting with your attire and tack.

QUESTION?

What is a recognized or rated show?
They are typically organized by a local or state horse or breed club chapter and sanctioned by the United States Equestrian Federation, Inc. (USEF), the regulatory organization for most U.S. horse sports. Unlike schooling or "practice" shows, recognized shows offer riders an opportunity to compete for year-end points and awards. Visit the website at *www. usef.org* for more information.

Equitation Classes

In equitation classes, the riders are judged for their riding skills. Also, they need to know the current style of riding. For example, Western riders who use one hand to hold the reins have to know what the current acceptable position is for the other hand. The rider also needs to be able to give commands smoothly and effectively.

Timed Classes

These classes are, as the name says, based on time. They often consist of games, such as barrel racing or pole bending. Other classes have a specific objective. For instance, there is the fun class called Egg and Spoon, in which the last rider still carrying both the egg and the spoon wins. Jumping classes combine the two types of classes—they often have time limitations and you lose points for knocking down rails.

Halter Classes

In halter classes, horses (usually young ones) are shown in-hand, which means they are led before the judge on a lead rope. Horses typically compete against each other by age group and are judged on conformation. For example, are the horse's legs and feet of a sufficient size compared to the body? Is the neck nicely built without an overall structural flaw such as getting very narrow toward the head? In breed-specific shows, horses compete against their own breed. In larger nonbreed shows, there will often be different classes for different horses of the predominating breeds.

For showing at halter, your horse must be impeccably groomed, and you should follow the rules of the class or the style of the moment, whichever applies. (Consult the USEF Rule Book.)

Showmanship Classes

Although it is not a riding class, showmanship is considered a performance class. Unlike halter classes, where your horse stands still and is looked over, in showmanship you are required to move your horse through a pattern. That pattern is usually posted at least an hour before the class, so be sure to study it. Types of things you will need your horse to be able to do include leading, backing, and turning around (with either the forehand or the hindquarters staying in one place).

The Competition Horse

Generally speaking, you don't need a specific kind of horse to become part of the show world unless you are interested in breed-specific shows. Almost all the breeds have their own breed shows. If you are buying a horse with the intention of showing it, you should pay particular attention to conformation. Conformation flaws won't eliminate you, but it is an advantage to have a mount that is put together well. If you are showing in a particular discipline, you want a horse that is well suited in its conformation and training to that discipline, such as jumping or dressage.

Training the Competition Horse

How does your horse need to be trained to compete? Whether you agree with the style or not, your horse needs to move the way everyone else is moving. For instance, for several years the appropriate style for Western pleasure riding for stock-type horses has been to ride with the horse's head and neck tilting toward the ground and at speeds in every gait that are very slow and don't bounce the rider around (i.e., the horse is "pleasurable to ride").

Chances are you want to win some competitions, so teaching your horse the correct style for the class you are in and type of horse you have is crucial. Spend as much time as needed in the practice ring to teach your horse what it must know. If you don't know how to train your horse to do what she needs to do to win, then work with a trainer who does.

FACT

Horses often behave unpredictably in strange surroundings. If your horse has never been to a show, it will be good training for him to experience new sights and sounds. Expect the worst but hope for the best. It's a good idea to have your instructor go with you the first time in case your horse gets out of hand.

Beyond Backyard Training

If you plan to participate in shows that are more competitive than your local riding club fun shows—either regional or national—you will certainly need to work with a trainer to succeed. The trainer for your discipline will know all the rules, all the current accepted styles, and where all the shows are—and many trainers are well known by the judges. Many riders who get serious about horse showing board their show horse at a trainer's barn, pay the trainer to continue to work with their horse, take regular lessons from the trainer or the barn's instructor, and travel with the trainer and the trainer's other students to the shows. You can also do all this with a horse that is owned by your trainer or instructor. Whatever you decide, make sure your bank account for your horse activities is well padded. It may all be well within your price range, but you need to know that there will be constant, and sometimes unexpected, costs.

There are also many administrative things to keep track of, such as registering for the show, picking classes, paying for classes, asking for tack change breaks between classes if they are allowed, and bringing health certifications as needed for your horse.

The Competitive Rider

To be competitive in the show ring, you need to constantly upgrade and refine your riding skills, both on your own and with an instructor. You will run up against very good riders in the show ring, and you need to match and better their skills, even for the classes that are judged solely on the horse's performance.

Skills

A highly trained horse can take a rider through a fifteen-minute horse show class without the rider having to know more than the basic cues. These are good horses for novices to ride in a show to learn the ropes. Trainers who focus on showing often keep a couple of these show veterans in their barns to lease out to new students for a couple of shows or even a whole showing season.

When you and your horse are learning the show ropes together, you will want to take your riding skills to a higher level than is required to hack through the woods—if for no other reason than to know how to deal with a show ring full of other riders.

ALERT!

Dogs generally are not welcome at horse shows. Some horses aren't accustomed to dogs and may spook easily at the sight or bark of one, potentially causing injury to the rider or nearby onlookers. Check the rules first to see if dogs are allowed. Keep the dog confined or restrained at all times, and stay away from the arenas where riders are warming up or competing.

Some horses are not suited for the pressures of showing—which include long hours in the trailer traveling to an event, constant changes in environment, long periods of time confined to a stall or tied to the side of the trailer, and going around and around a show ring. This can stress out some horses and cause ulcers, so be mindful of your horse's comfort level and well-being.

Retired show horses in their teenage years can make great horses for beginner riders, young or older. However, some have not seen much of the world outside the show ring and need some exposure to trail riding and other activities, with a supportive and experienced rider, before being retired to such an activity.

Tack and Clothing Styles

The required riding apparel and accessories (called "appointments") will differ for every type of show and riding discipline. For example, if you plan to ride in "over fences" classes, you need a hunt seat saddle, riding breeches, a coat, tall boots, and a helmet. If you plan to take your horse in the Western pleasure class, you will need a complete change of clothes and tack. Even within the English riding disciplines the tack and clothing requirements are vastly different.

Read the USEF Rule Book

The USEF Rule Book is an annual publication that lists in detail all the rules governing every type of horse sport and class it oversees, including conduct, clothing, appointments, participation and class requirements, and much more. Before entering a show, read and familiarize yourself with the rules and information that pertain to your division. The show world has an appropriate etiquette for every discipline—how and when to pass a horse that is slower, for example—and your instructor/trainer can help you learn the specifics. The rules can be different for each kind of show and type of riding. If you've switched riding disciplines, for example, and are showing in the new style for the first time, make sure you know what rules apply to the type of show and classes you're entering.

A rule violation could get you eliminated from the class or the show, and ignorance of the rules is never an excuse. The rules change periodically, so get your hands on the most recent version. As a USEF member, you're entitled to receive a print copy on request, or you can easily view it online at *www.usef.org*.

Preparing for a Show

Showing isn't for everyone. It can be a nerve-wracking, stressful experience, which can rob it of all its fun. Just the sheer effort and the hours of planning and preparation can be too much for some people. To others, the thrill of competition is exhilarating. To enjoy the experience as much as possible, it's important to arrive fully prepared, relaxed and ready to show.

Things You Need

The following are some items you won't want to be without at a show.

For the Horse

You must anticipate what you will need for your horse and for the competition. Plan on bringing the following supplies:

- First aid kit
- Saddle(s), girth(s), pad(s), and stirrup leathers (extras are handy in case of breakage)
- Portable saddle rack
- Tack trunk and cleaning supplies
- Protective leg wraps and shipping boots
- Bridle(s), reins, halter(s), lead ropes (again, extras are handy in case of breakage)
- Grooming equipment and products
- Bathing supplies, sweat scraper, wash buckets
- Mane braiding kit (if mane braiding is required for your classes)
- Hay and grain
- Feed and water buckets
- Blanket(s), cooler
- Fly spray
- Stall and/or trailer bedding, as needed
- Muck bucket, muck rake or shovel
- Lunge line and lunge whip

For the Rider

The following supplies are important for you:

- Clean riding apparel and accessories required for every different class you entered
- Smock or apron to keep your riding clothes clean between classes
- Spot cleaners and mini-sewing kit for soiled or torn riding clothes
- Helmet or riding hat, as required for each class

- Hairpins, bands, and barrettes, as needed
- Appropriate riding boots, boot pulls, and boot jack
- Boot polish and cleaner
- Whip or riding crop, as needed for your class
- Street clothes and comfortable shoes for before and after the show
- Rain gear
- Personal items
- Folding chair, snacks, cooler, drinks, and other comfort items
- Band-Aids, antibacterial spray, ointments, aspirin, and other medical supplies
- Any required paperwork and identification, such as a current negative Coggins test

Signing Up for a Class

If you work with an instructor, she will know what classes you are best suited to enter, based on your riding experience. When the two of you decide, the next step is to contact the show secretary and request the necessary forms. The Prize List describes all the classes, names of the judges, and details about fees, stabling, motel accommodations, and any other requirements. The entry form is what you need to fill out completely and return to the show secretary with the entry fee and a photocopy of your horse's current negative Coggins certificate. If the entry form lists an opening date for the show, you should not mail your entry prior to this date, as it will not be accepted if it is postmarked any earlier than the opening date.

QUESTION?

What is the closing date?
The closing date is the deadline for entering a class. If a closing date is given on the entry form, honor it and send in your entry on time or you may be out of luck. Some types of competitions allow you to show up on the day of the show and enter a class, while others do not.

Get Ready in Advance

Your horse and tack need to be spotlessly clean for a show, so start ahead of time and get everything ready. If you have show tack that is separate from your schooling tack, your job will be easier. Just get out your show gear, dust it off, and inspect it for anything that needs to be touched up or repaired.

Know in advance how your horse needs to be turned out for the class. For example, will her mane need to be braided? Will her shoes need to be reset? If so, plan ahead for how much time you'll need to get her mane in shape for braiding and her feet reshod.

The day before the show, have your horse groomed, bathed (weather permitting), and show clipped. Pack everything you need for your horse and yourself. That way, you won't feel rushed.

The night before, do whatever you do to help yourself relax. It's important to calm your mind in preparation for any competition. Get a good night's sleep and eat a healthy breakfast with some protein for energy. You'll need it, because the day ahead will be busy and challenging!

Show Time!

Plan to arrive at the show early so you can get your horse settled in. He needs some time to adjust and relax in his new surroundings, too. Walk him around to let him see the sights and stretch his legs after his trailer ride. If you groomed him well the day before, you should only have touch-ups to worry about before your class.

Before you tack up your horse and start warming him up, warm yourself up with some gentle stretching exercises to loosen your calf and thigh muscles. Most show grounds have designated areas for warm-up on the lunge line and under saddle. Find out where they are and what times you can use them. Don't pass over the warm-up session; it is essential to preparing yourself and your horse physically and mentally to enter the ring.

Check the rules to see what you and your horse are allowed to wear in warm-up before you go in. Some shows have specific regulations regarding what schooling equipment can be used on the grounds. In the warm-up area, try to keep as much distance between yourself and the other riders as possible. Some horses kick, so never ride up close on the rear end of one.

The bumper-to-bumper traffic going in all directions in warm-up arenas scares many first-timers, but there is some order to the chaos. For example, in most situations, it is customary to pass riders going in the opposite direction with your left shoulder to their left shoulder. It is also best to ride with the flow of the majority of other riders, and reverse when they reverse. Pass to the inside of riders going in your direction. If you are schooling over fences, always give the right-of-way to another rider who is on the jumping line.

In the Ring

Listen to the announcer call the class entries into the ring. Enter the ring promptly, stay sharp, and be mindful that the judge may be watching you even though the class isn't officially underway yet. The ringmaster or announcer will call the class to order when the judging begins.

In a large class, it can be difficult to get the judge to see you enough at each gait with so many other riders whizzing by. But it's your job to present yourself at your best in front of the judge as often as possible. Keep enough distance between yourself and the other horses. Circle away from them if you need to, but look around you before you turn to avoiding turning into someone else's path.

When the ringmaster calls for lineup, ride toward the center of the ring and form a line alongside the other riders. Make sure your horse is standing square and that you are sitting straight. Smile, look happy, and don't chitchat with other competitors while the judge is making her inspection.

If you receive a ribbon, women should nod their heads in thanks to the ringmaster and judge, and men should tip or remove their hats. On your way out of the ring, thank the gatekeeper for holding the gate for you. Outside the ring, you may congratulate the winners and the other competitors.

If you are showing over fences or in dressage, you and your horse will enter the ring alone. In hunt seat classes, it is customary to make a courtesy circle in front of the first fence and after the final fence, so the judge can evaluate your position. In dressage classes, it is customary to ride past the judge first with the entry number on your horse's bridle showing, so the judge can match the number to her score sheet.

If something goes wrong, try to remain calm. Do not punish the horse, and do not leave the ring without permission from the judge first. Some people have nightmares about falling off in the ring in front of all those spectators. It does happen, but not often, and the thought of it shouldn't prevent you from experiencing the fun of showing. If it happens to you and you're not hurt, catch your horse and remount, or ask to be excused from the ring and lead the horse out quietly.

These are the little nuances about showing that your instructor can help you learn. Above all, focus on having fun. After all, riding is supposed to be fun, so enjoy every minute of it. Showing can help you grow into a well-rounded horseman, even if you don't participate in a big-time, big-money way. After you have honed your horsemanship skills, you can share them with others and help them get started, just like others helped you along the way. When the day when you can share your skill and expertise with others comes, you'll experience familiar challenges through fresh eyes, and find a new sense of fulfillment in your lifelong passion for horses.

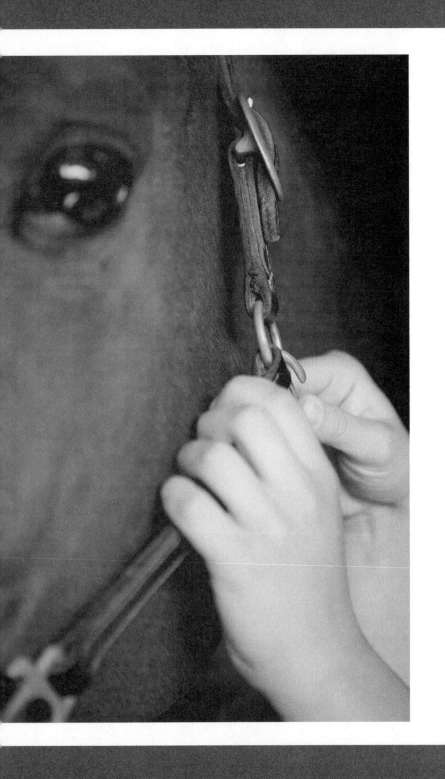

Resources and Reference Materials

Books

Benedik, Linda, and Veronica Wirth. *Yoga for Equestrians*. North Pomfret, VT: Trafalgar Square, 2000.

Blake, R. L. V. *Dressage for Beginners: U. S. Edition*. Boston: Houghton Mifflin, 1976.

Brennan, Mary, and Norma Eckroate. *Complete Holistic Care and Healing for Horses: The Owner's Veterinary Guide to Alternative Methods and Remedies*. North Pomfret, VT: Trafalgar Square, 2004.

Budiansky, Stephen. *The Nature of Horses: Exploring Equine Evolution, Intelligence and Behavior*. New York: The Free Press, 1997.

Burkhardt, Barbara. *Dressage from A to X: The Definitive Guide to Riding and Competing*. North Pomfret, VT: Trafalgar Square, 2004.

Crabtree, Helen K. *Saddle Seat Equitation*. New York: Doubleday, 1970.

Davis, Karen Leigh. *Deciphering Dressage*. Hoboken, NJ: Howell Book House, 2005.

de Ruffieu, Francois Lemaire. *The Handbook of Riding Essentials*. New York: Harper & Row, Publishers, 1986.

Evans, J. Warren, Anthony Borton, Harold Hintz, and L. Dale Van Vleck. *The Horse*. New York: W.H. Freeman & Company, 1990.

Ganton, Doris. *Breaking and Training the Driving Horse*. Chatsworth, CA: Wilshire, 1984.

Green, Ben K. *Horse Conformation as to Soundness and Performance*. Flagstaff, AZ: Northland, 1969.

Griffin, James M., MD, and Tom Gore, DVM. *Horse Owner's Veterinary Handbook*. Hoboken, NJ: Howell Book House, 1998.

Guay, Mary, and Donna Schlinkert. *Buying Your First Horse: A Comprehensive Guide to Preparing for, Finding and Purchasing a Great Horse*. Marietta, GA, White Papers Press, 1997.

Haas, Jessie. *Safe Horse, Safe Rider: A Young Rider's Guide to Responsible Horsekeeping*. North Adams, MA: Storey, 1994.

Harris, Moira C. *Dressage by the Letter: A Guide for the Novice*. Hoboken, NJ: Howell Book House, 1997.

Harris, Susan E. *The United States Pony Club Manual of Horsemanship* (editions for Basic, Intermediate, and Advanced Horsemanship). Hoboken, NJ: Howell Book House, 1994–1996.

Hawcroft, Tim. *A-Z of Horse Diseases and Health Problems*. Dorking, UK: Ringpress, 1990.

Hourdebaigt, Jean-Pierre. *Equine Massage*. Hoboken, NJ: Howell Book House, 2007.

Jackson, Jamie. *The Natural Horse*, 2nd ed. Fayetteville, AR: Star Ridge Books, 1997.

Kamen, Daniel. *The Well Adjusted Horse*. Cambridge, MA: Brookline Books, 1999.

Kellon, Eleanor. *Dr. Kellon's Guide to First Aid for Horses.* Emmaus, PA: Breakthrough Publications, 1989.

Kidd, Jane. *Dressage Essentials: Takes the Mystery Out of the Fastest Growing Equestrian Discipline.* Hoboken NJ: Howell Book House, 1998.

Lang, Amanda. *Rider's Handbook.* New York: Sterling Publishing Co., 2003.

Loch, Sylvia. *The Classical Rider: Being at One with Your Horse.* North Pomfret, VT: Trafalgar Square Publishing, 1997.

Lyons, John, with Sinclair Browning. *Lyons on Horses.* New York: Bantam, 1991.

Mariani, Gael, and Martin Scott. *Bach Flower Remedies for Horses and Riders.* Addington, UK: Kenilworth Press, 2000.

McCall, Jim. *Influencing Horse Behavior.* Mount Holly, AR: Jimani Publications, 1988.

Mettler, John J., DVM. *Horse Sense.* North Adams, MA: Storey, 1989.

Miller, Robert. *Imprint Training of the Newborn Foal.* Augusta, GA: Western Horseman, 1991.

Mills, Daniel, and Kathryn Nankervis. *Equine Behaviour: Principles and Practice.* Oxford, UK: Blackwell Science, 1999.

Morris, George H. *Hunter Seat Equitation.* New York: Doubleday, 1990.

Müseler, Wilhelm. *Riding Logic: Transform Riding Skills to "Art on Horseback" with Classical Lessons in Flatwork and Jumping.* North Pomfret, VT: Trafalgar Square, 2007.

Norback, Craig, and Peter Norback. *The Horseman's Catalog.* New York: McGraw Hill, 1979.

O'Connor, Sally. *Common Sense Dressage: An Illustrated Guide.* Boonsboro, MD: Half Halt Press, 1990.

Oliveira, Nuno. *Reflections on Equestrian Art.* London: J.A. Allen, 1988.

Pavord, Marcy, and Tony Pavord. *Complete Equine Veterinary Manual.* Newton Abbot, UK: David and Charles Publishers, 2004.

Podhajsky, Alois. *My Horses, My Teachers.* North Pomfret, VT: Trafalgar Square, 1997.

Podhajsky, Alois. *The Complete Training of Horse and Rider in the Principles of Classical Horsemanship.* New York: Doubleday, 1979.

Rees, Lucy. *The Fundamentals of Riding.* New York: Roxby Paintbox Co., 1991.

Roberts, Peter, ed. *The Complete Book of the Horse.* New York: Gallery, 1985.

Savoie, Jane. *It's Not Just about the Ribbons: It's about Enriching Riding and Life with Innovative Tools and Winning Strategies.* North Pomfret, VT: Trafalgar Square Publishing, 2003.

Self, Hilary Page. *A Modern Horse Herbal.* Boonsboro, MD: Half Halt Press, 2004.

Siegal, Mordecai, editor. *UC Davis School of Veterinary Medicine Book of Horses: A Complete Medical Reference Guide for Horses and Foals.* New York: Harper Collins Publishers, 1996.

Sivewright, Molly. *Thinking Riding Book 1: Training Student Instructors.* London: J.A. Allen, 1979.

Sivewright, Molly. *Thinking Riding Book 2: In Good Form.* London: J.A. Allen, 1983.

Swift, Sally. *Centered Riding.* North Pomfret, VT: Trafalgar Square, 1985.

Tellington-Jones, Linda. *Improve Your Horse's Well-Being: A Step-by-Step Guide to TTouch and TTeam Training.* North Pomfret, VT: Trafalgar Square, 1999.

Twelveponies, Mary. *Everyday Training.* Emmaus, PA: Breakthrough Publications, 1980.

United States Dressage Federation. *Classical Training of the Horse.* Lexington, KY: United States Dressage Federation, 2006.

Wilde, Clare. *Hands-On Energy Therapy for Horses and Riders.* North Pomfret, VT: Trafalgar Square, 1999.

Wilde, Clare. *Endurance Riding: From First Steps to 100 Miles.* Boonsboro, MD: Half Halt Press, 1996.

Zidonis, Nancy A., Amy Snow, and Marie Soderberg. *Equine Acupressure: A Working Manual.* Larkspur, CO: Tallgrass Publishers, 1999.

Zieler, R. Lee. *Easy Gaited Horses.* North Adams, MA: Storey, 2005.

Magazines

Horse Illustrated
www.horsechannel.om/horse-magazines/horse-illustrated

America's Horse
www.aqha.com/magazines/americashorse/index.html

Dressage Today
www.equisearch.com/dressagetoday

Equus
www.equisearch.com/equus

The Gaited Horse
www.thegaitedhorse.com

Horse & Rider
www.equisearch.com/horseandrider

The Horse
www.thehorse.com

Horse Journal
www.horse-journal.com

Practical Horseman
www.equisearch.com/practicalhorseman

Western Horseman
www.westernhorseman.com

Equine Organizations

American Association of Equine Practitioners
www.aaep.org

American Farrier's Association
www.americanfarriers.org

American Horse Council
www.horsecouncil.org

American Riding Instructors Association (ARIA)
www.riding-instructor.com

Federation Equestre Internationale (FEI), the International Federation of Equestrian Sport
www.fei.org

U.S. Equestrian Team (USET)
www.uset.com
United States Polo Association
www.us-polo.org
United States Dressage Federation (USDF)
www.usdf.org
United States Equestrian Federation (USEF)
www.usef.org
United States Pony Clubs, Inc.
www.ponyclub.org

Other Useful Websites

Tallgrass Publishers LLC
Acupressure and natural health resource
www.animalacupressure.com

Bach Flowers
Bach's flower remedies
www.bachcentre.com

Half Halt Press
Books about horses
www.halfhaltpress.com

Trafalgar Square Publishing
Books about horses
www.horseandriderbooks.com

International Alliance for Animal Therapy and Healing
Alternative healing for horses
www.iaath.com

Tellington TTouch Training
Resources on TTouch
www.tellingtontouch.com

Natural Horse Vet
Alternative health for horses
www.thenaturalhorsevet.net

Back in the Saddle
Horse equipment catalog
www.backinthesaddle.com

State Line Tack
Horse equipment
www.statelinetack.com

Movies

Black Beauty (1971)
Black Beauty (1994)
The Horse in the Gray Flannel Suit (1968)
The Horse Whisperer (1998)
Into the West (2005)
Lucky Luke (1991)
National Velvet (1944)
The Red Pony (1949)
Speedy (1928)
White Mane (1953)
Wild Hearts Can't Be Broken (1991)

Glossary

Above the bit

A horse that raises his head high and sticks his muzzle straight out is said to be above the bit because he is attempting to evade the rider's contact through the reins.

Aids

The signals the rider uses to tell the horse what to do, using his hands, legs, weight, seat, and voice, and sometimes reinforced by whip and spurs.

Airs above the ground

Haute école (high school) maneuvers comprised of controlled rears (levade) and leaps (capriole), performed primarily by the classically trained Lipizzan stallions at the Spanish Riding School in Austria. The airs are not part of any dressage test for competition.

Azoturia

Also known as tying up or Monday morning disease, azoturia refers to the cramping of a horse's large muscles. It is caused by a lack of electrolytes.

Blind staggers

Moldy corn poisoning, caused by certain fungi growing on corn. The condition affects the horse's brain and liver.

Breeding stock

Mares and stallions that meet the eligibility requirements (e.g., through lineage) to be registered in the stud books of a given breed association.

Broken wind

Damage to the respiratory system, usually causing permanent unsoundness.

Broodmare

A mare used for breeding purposes.

Bute

The abbreviated term for phenylbutazone, an anti-inflammatory drug commonly used in horses.

Cast

The term used when a horse lies down and gets himself caught against a wall or fence in such a way that he cannot roll and rise to his feet without assistance.

Collection

The gathering of the horse's hind legs and driving them toward the forelegs, so that the rider rides both ends of the horse together in a nice frame.

Colt

A young male horse, under four years old.

Conformation

The overall structure and body build of the horse is known as its conformation. Few horses, if any, have perfect conformation. What is considered good conformation depends a great deal on what you plan to do with the horse.

Contact

The connection between the rider's hands and the horse's mouth through the reins that establishes and maintains communication.

Dam

The proper term for a horse's mother.

DMSO

Abbreviation for dimethyl sulfoxide, a topical agent used to reduce swelling and inflammation caused by trauma.

Esophagal choke

A condition that is often caused when horses gulp down pelleted feeds too rapidly. To deter this, place a couple of large stones or half a salt block in the feed bucket—having to eat around them makes the horse slow down.

Farrier

A farrier is a blacksmith who does horseshoeing but doesn't necessarily do other types of iron work.

Filly

A young female horse, under four years of age.

Flake

The term used to describe a measurement of hay for feeding purposes. A bale of hay contains ten flakes that easily pull apart.

Flehman response

This term refers to the curling of the upper lip a male horse makes in response to the scent of a female.

Foal

A baby horse, male or female, under one year old.

Gelding

A castrated male horse.

Green horse

A horse, usually a youngster, with little training or experience at carrying a rider.

Groundwork

Training starts with you working with the horse from the ground, not in the saddle. Groundwork might include teaching the horse to stand quietly while tied or while his feet are being picked up and cleaned. The obedience and good manners you teach him in groundwork generally transfer to your work under saddle.

Half-halt

A slight checking of the pace, using coordinated hand, leg, and seat aids, used to prepare the horse for a transition, to rebalance his movement, or to get his attention.

Hand

The unit used to measure a horse's height. One hand equals four inches.

Herbivore

An animal, such as a horse, that subsists totally on plant life. This distinction makes the horse a prey animal (with those that hunt them considered predators), a category that contributes greatly to the overall behavior of the species.

Impulsion

Forward-moving energy developed by driving the horse on from the hindquarters, rather than allowing him to move off the forehand and drag along the hind end.

In season

The term used to describe a mare's sexual status when she is in heat (in estrus).

Leg-yield

A lateral exercise in which the horse moves sideways off the rider's leg and carries his head flexed away from the direction of travel.

Lunging

This is a groundwork exercise, often used in training, in which you circle the horse around you at the various gaits at the end of a long rope, called a lunge line. It is useful for teaching voice commands, for warming up a horse prior to riding, and for allowing a fresh horse to expend some pent-up energy before you mount.

Mare

A mature female horse, four years of age or older.

Moonblindness

Common term for recurrent uveitis, an inflammation of the horse's eyes.

On the forehand

A horse is said to be moving "on the forehand" when he carries most of his weight on the front end, rather than the hind end. Such a horse lacks collection and generally appears to be moving downhill.

Passage

An upper-level dressage movement that is a slow, cadenced trot having a slight moment of suspension between each step.

Piaffe

An upper-level dressage movement that is a highly collected trot in place.

Poll

The top of the horse's head, just behind the ears.

Proud flesh

Scar tissue that protrudes from the wound area, creating an unsightly scar.

Put down

Euthanize or humanely destroy a horse.

Rein-back

The proper term for backing up a horse.

Saddletree

The basic underlying structure, usually made of wood or fiberglass, that English and Western saddles are built upon. A saddletree can be narrow or wide, depending on the horse's back and the comfort of the rider.

Sound

If a horse is perfectly healthy and not lame, it is said to be sound.

Stallion

A mature, intact male horse, usually used for breeding.

Sire

A horse's father.

Turnout

The period when your horse is out of the confinement of his stall and loose in a larger area—either outside in a corral or pasture, or in an indoor arena if the weather is bad.

Unsound

If the horse is temporarily lame, it is considered unsound until it recovers completely. Anything that adversely affects a horse's health, including a temporary eating problem, is considered an unsoundness. If the condition is chronic and ongoing, the horse is permanently unsound.

Weanling

A young horse under one year of age that is no longer suckling its dam.

Withers

The raised area on the horse's back where the shoulder meets the base of the neck, usually the highest point of the back, and the point to which we measure the horse's height from the ground.

Yearling

A young horse that is one year old.

INDEX

The EVERYTHING Series!

BUSINESS & PERSONAL FINANCE

Everything® Accounting Book
Everything® Budgeting Book, 2nd Ed.
Everything® Business Planning Book
Everything® Coaching and Mentoring Book, 2nd Ed.
Everything® Fundraising Book
Everything® Get Out of Debt Book
Everything® Grant Writing Book, 2nd Ed.
Everything® Guide to Buying Foreclosures
Everything® Guide to Fundraising, $15.95
Everything® Guide to Mortgages
Everything® Guide to Personal Finance for Single Mothers
Everything® Home-Based Business Book, 2nd Ed.
Everything® Homebuying Book, 3rd Ed., $15.95
Everything® Homeselling Book, 2nd Ed.
Everything® Human Resource Management Book
Everything® Improve Your Credit Book
Everything® Investing Book, 2nd Ed.
Everything® Landlording Book
Everything® Leadership Book, 2nd Ed.
Everything® Managing People Book, 2nd Ed.
Everything® Negotiating Book
Everything® Online Auctions Book
Everything® Online Business Book
Everything® Personal Finance Book
Everything® Personal Finance in Your 20s & 30s Book, 2nd Ed.
Everything® Personal Finance in Your 40s & 50s Book, $15.95
Everything® Project Management Book, 2nd Ed.
Everything® Real Estate Investing Book
Everything® Retirement Planning Book
Everything® Robert's Rules Book, $7.95
Everything® Selling Book
Everything® Start Your Own Business Book, 2nd Ed.
Everything® Wills & Estate Planning Book

COOKING

Everything® Barbecue Cookbook
Everything® Bartender's Book, 2nd Ed., $9.95
Everything® Calorie Counting Cookbook
Everything® Cheese Book
Everything® Chinese Cookbook
Everything® Classic Recipes Book
Everything® Cocktail Parties & Drinks Book
Everything® College Cookbook
Everything® Cooking for Baby and Toddler Book
Everything® Diabetes Cookbook
Everything® Easy Gourmet Cookbook
Everything® Fondue Cookbook
Everything® Food Allergy Cookbook, $15.95
Everything® Fondue Party Book
Everything® Gluten-Free Cookbook
Everything® Glycemic Index Cookbook
Everything® Grilling Cookbook
Everything® Healthy Cooking for Parties Book, $15.95
Everything® Holiday Cookbook
Everything® Indian Cookbook
Everything® Lactose-Free Cookbook
Everything® Low-Cholesterol Cookbook

Everything® Low-Fat High-Flavor Cookbook, 2nd Ed., $15.95
Everything® Low-Salt Cookbook
Everything® Meals for a Month Cookbook
Everything® Meals on a Budget Cookbook
Everything® Mediterranean Cookbook
Everything® Mexican Cookbook
Everything® No Trans Fat Cookbook
Everything® One-Pot Cookbook, 2nd Ed., $15.95
Everything® Organic Cooking for Baby & Toddler Book, $15.95
Everything® Pizza Cookbook
Everything® Quick Meals Cookbook, 2nd Ed., $15.95
Everything® Slow Cooker Cookbook
Everything® Slow Cooking for a Crowd Cookbook
Everything® Soup Cookbook
Everything® Stir-Fry Cookbook
Everything® Sugar-Free Cookbook
Everything® Tapas and Small Plates Cookbook
Everything® Tex-Mex Cookbook
Everything® Thai Cookbook
Everything® Vegetarian Cookbook
Everything® Whole-Grain, High-Fiber Cookbook
Everything® Wild Game Cookbook
Everything® Wine Book, 2nd Ed.

GAMES

Everything® 15-Minute Sudoku Book, $9.95
Everything® 30-Minute Sudoku Book, $9.95
Everything® Bible Crosswords Book, $9.95
Everything® Blackjack Strategy Book
Everything® Brain Strain Book, $9.95
Everything® Bridge Book
Everything® Card Games Book
Everything® Card Tricks Book, $9.95
Everything® Casino Gambling Book, 2nd Ed.
Everything® Chess Basics Book
Everything® Christmas Crosswords Book, $9.95
Everything® Craps Strategy Book
Everything® Crossword and Puzzle Book
Everything® Crosswords and Puzzles for Quote Lovers Book, $9.95
Everything® Crossword Challenge Book
Everything® Crosswords for the Beach Book, $9.95
Everything® Cryptic Crosswords Book, $9.95
Everything® Cryptograms Book, $9.95
Everything® Easy Crosswords Book
Everything® Easy Kakuro Book, $9.95
Everything® Easy Large-Print Crosswords Book
Everything® Games Book, 2nd Ed.
Everything® Giant Book of Crosswords
Everything® Giant Sudoku Book, $9.95
Everything® Giant Word Search Book
Everything® Kakuro Challenge Book, $9.95
Everything® Large-Print Crossword Challenge Book
Everything® Large-Print Crosswords Book
Everything® Large-Print Travel Crosswords Book
Everything® Lateral Thinking Puzzles Book, $9.95
Everything® Literary Crosswords Book, $9.95
Everything® Mazes Book
Everything® Memory Booster Puzzles Book, $9.95

Everything® Movie Crosswords Book, $9.95
Everything® Music Crosswords Book, $9.95
Everything® Online Poker Book
Everything® Pencil Puzzles Book, $9.95
Everything® Poker Strategy Book
Everything® Pool & Billiards Book
Everything® Puzzles for Commuters Book, $9.95
Everything® Puzzles for Dog Lovers Book, $9.95
Everything® Sports Crosswords Book, $9.95
Everything® Test Your IQ Book, $9.95
Everything® Texas Hold 'Em Book, $9.95
Everything® Travel Crosswords Book, $9.95
Everything® Travel Mazes Book, $9.95
Everything® Travel Word Search Book, $9.95
Everything® TV Crosswords Book, $9.95
Everything® Word Games Challenge Book
Everything® Word Scramble Book
Everything® Word Search Book

HEALTH

Everything® Alzheimer's Book
Everything® Diabetes Book
Everything® First Aid Book, $9.95
Everything® Green Living Book
Everything® Health Guide to Addiction and Recovery
Everything® Health Guide to Adult Bipolar Disorder
Everything® Health Guide to Arthritis
Everything® Health Guide to Controlling Anxiety
Everything® Health Guide to Depression
Everything® Health Guide to Diabetes, 2nd Ed.
Everything® Health Guide to Fibromyalgia
Everything® Health Guide to Menopause, 2nd Ed.
Everything® Health Guide to Migraines
Everything® Health Guide to Multiple Sclerosis
Everything® Health Guide to OCD
Everything® Health Guide to PMS
Everything® Health Guide to Postpartum Care
Everything® Health Guide to Thyroid Disease
Everything® Hypnosis Book
Everything® Low Cholesterol Book
Everything® Menopause Book
Everything® Nutrition Book
Everything® Reflexology Book
Everything® Stress Management Book
Everything® Superfoods Book, $15.95

HISTORY

Everything® American Government Book
Everything® American History Book, 2nd Ed.
Everything® American Revolution Book, $15.95
Everything® Civil War Book
Everything® Freemasons Book
Everything® Irish History & Heritage Book
Everything® World War II Book, 2nd Ed.

HOBBIES

Everything® Candlemaking Book
Everything® Cartooning Book
Everything® Coin Collecting Book
Everything® Digital Photography Book, 2nd Ed.

Everything® Drawing Book
Everything® Family Tree Book, 2nd Ed.
Everything® Guide to Online Genealogy, $15.95
Everything® Knitting Book
Everything® Knots Book
Everything® Photography Book
Everything® Quilting Book
Everything® Sewing Book
Everything® Soapmaking Book, 2nd Ed.
Everything® Woodworking Book

HOME IMPROVEMENT

Everything® Feng Shui Book
Everything® Feng Shui Decluttering Book, $9.95
Everything® Fix-It Book
Everything® Green Living Book
Everything® Home Decorating Book
Everything® Home Storage Solutions Book
Everything® Homebuilding Book
Everything® Organize Your Home Book, 2nd Ed.

KIDS' BOOKS

All titles are $7.95
Everything® Fairy Tales Book, $14.95
Everything® Kids' Animal Puzzle & Activity Book
Everything® Kids' Astronomy Book
Everything® Kids' Baseball Book, 5th Ed.
Everything® Kids' Bible Trivia Book
Everything® Kids' Bugs Book
Everything® Kids' Cars and Trucks Puzzle and Activity Book
Everything® Kids' Christmas Puzzle & Activity Book
Everything® Kids' Connect the Dots
  Puzzle and Activity Book
Everything® Kids' Cookbook, 2nd Ed.
Everything® Kids' Crazy Puzzles Book
Everything® Kids' Dinosaurs Book
Everything® Kids' Dragons Puzzle and Activity Book
Everything® Kids' Environment Book $7.95
Everything® Kids' Fairies Puzzle and Activity Book
Everything® Kids' First Spanish Puzzle and Activity Book
Everything® Kids' Football Book
Everything® Kids' Geography Book
Everything® Kids' Gross Cookbook
Everything® Kids' Gross Hidden Pictures Book
Everything® Kids' Gross Jokes Book
Everything® Kids' Gross Mazes Book
Everything® Kids' Gross Puzzle & Activity Book
Everything® Kids' Halloween Puzzle & Activity Book
Everything® Kids' Hanukkah Puzzle and Activity Book
Everything® Kids' Hidden Pictures Book
Everything® Kids' Horses Book
Everything® Kids' Joke Book
Everything® Kids' Knock Knock Book
Everything® Kids' Learning French Book
Everything® Kids' Learning Spanish Book
Everything® Kids' Magical Science Experiments Book
Everything® Kids' Math Puzzles Book
Everything® Kids' Mazes Book
Everything® Kids' Money Book, 2nd Ed.
**Everything® Kids' Mummies, Pharaoh's, and Pyramids
  Puzzle and Activity Book**
Everything® Kids' Nature Book
Everything® Kids' Pirates Puzzle and Activity Book
Everything® Kids' Presidents Book
Everything® Kids' Princess Puzzle and Activity Book
Everything® Kids' Puzzle Book

Everything® Kids' Racecars Puzzle and Activity Book
Everything® Kids' Riddles & Brain Teasers Book
Everything® Kids' Science Experiments Book
Everything® Kids' Sharks Book
Everything® Kids' Soccer Book
Everything® Kids' Spelling Book
Everything® Kids' Spies Puzzle and Activity Book
Everything® Kids' States Book
Everything® Kids' Travel Activity Book
Everything® Kids' Word Search Puzzle and Activity Book

LANGUAGE

Everything® Conversational Japanese Book with CD, $19.95
Everything® French Grammar Book
Everything® French Phrase Book, $9.95
Everything® French Verb Book, $9.95
Everything® German Phrase Book, $9.95
Everything® German Practice Book with CD, $19.95
Everything® Inglés Book
Everything® Intermediate Spanish Book with CD, $19.95
Everything® Italian Phrase Book, $9.95
Everything® Italian Practice Book with CD, $19.95
Everything® Learning Brazilian Portuguese Book with CD, $19.95
Everything® Learning French Book with CD, 2nd Ed., $19.95
Everything® Learning German Book
Everything® Learning Italian Book
Everything® Learning Latin Book
Everything® Learning Russian Book with CD, $19.95
Everything® Learning Spanish Book
Everything® Learning Spanish Book with CD, 2nd Ed., $19.95
Everything® Russian Practice Book with CD, $19.95
Everything® Sign Language Book, $15.95
Everything® Spanish Grammar Book
Everything® Spanish Phrase Book, $9.95
Everything® Spanish Practice Book with CD, $19.95
Everything® Spanish Verb Book, $9.95
Everything® Speaking Mandarin Chinese Book with CD, $19.95

MUSIC

Everything® Bass Guitar Book with CD, $19.95
Everything® Drums Book with CD, $19.95
Everything® Guitar Book with CD, 2nd Ed., $19.95
Everything® Guitar Chords Book with CD, $19.95
Everything® Guitar Scales Book with CD, $19.95
Everything® Harmonica Book with CD, $15.95
Everything® Home Recording Book
Everything® Music Theory Book with CD, $19.95
Everything® Reading Music Book with CD, $19.95
Everything® Rock & Blues Guitar Book with CD, $19.95
Everything® Rock & Blues Piano Book with CD, $19.95
Everything® Rock Drums Book with CD, $19.95
Everything® Singing Book with CD, $19.95
Everything® Songwriting Book

NEW AGE

Everything® Astrology Book, 2nd Ed.
Everything® Birthday Personology Book
Everything® Celtic Wisdom Book, $15.95
Everything® Dreams Book, 2nd Ed.
Everything® Law of Attraction Book, $15.95
Everything® Love Signs Book, $9.95
Everything® Love Spells Book, $9.95
Everything® Palmistry Book
Everything® Psychic Book
Everything® Reiki Book

Everything® Sex Signs Book, $9.95
Everything® Spells & Charms Book, 2nd Ed.
Everything® Tarot Book, 2nd Ed.
Everything® Toltec Wisdom Book
Everything® Wicca & Witchcraft Book, 2nd Ed.

PARENTING

Everything® Baby Names Book, 2nd Ed.
Everything® Baby Shower Book, 2nd Ed.
Everything® Baby Sign Language Book with DVD
Everything® Baby's First Year Book
Everything® Birthing Book
Everything® Breastfeeding Book
Everything® Father-to-Be Book
Everything® Father's First Year Book
Everything® Get Ready for Baby Book, 2nd Ed.
Everything® Get Your Baby to Sleep Book, $9.95
Everything® Getting Pregnant Book
Everything® Guide to Pregnancy Over 35
Everything® Guide to Raising a One-Year-Old
Everything® Guide to Raising a Two-Year-Old
Everything® Guide to Raising Adolescent Boys
Everything® Guide to Raising Adolescent Girls
Everything® Mother's First Year Book
Everything® Parent's Guide to Childhood Illnesses
Everything® Parent's Guide to Children and Divorce
Everything® Parent's Guide to Children with ADD/ADHD
Everything® Parent's Guide to Children with Asperger's
  Syndrome
Everything® Parent's Guide to Children with Anxiety
Everything® Parent's Guide to Children with Asthma
Everything® Parent's Guide to Children with Autism
Everything® Parent's Guide to Children with Bipolar Disorder
Everything® Parent's Guide to Children with Depression
Everything® Parent's Guide to Children with Dyslexia
Everything® Parent's Guide to Children with Juvenile Diabetes
Everything® Parent's Guide to Children with OCD
Everything® Parent's Guide to Positive Discipline
Everything® Parent's Guide to Raising Boys
Everything® Parent's Guide to Raising Girls
Everything® Parent's Guide to Raising Siblings
**Everything® Parent's Guide to Raising Your
  Adopted Child**
Everything® Parent's Guide to Sensory Integration Disorder
Everything® Parent's Guide to Tantrums
Everything® Parent's Guide to the Strong-Willed Child
Everything® Parenting a Teenager Book
Everything® Potty Training Book, $9.95
Everything® Pregnancy Book, 3rd Ed.
Everything® Pregnancy Fitness Book
Everything® Pregnancy Nutrition Book
Everything® Pregnancy Organizer, 2nd Ed., $16.95
Everything® Toddler Activities Book
Everything® Toddler Book
Everything® Tween Book
Everything® Twins, Triplets, and More Book

PETS

Everything® Aquarium Book
Everything® Boxer Book
Everything® Cat Book, 2nd Ed.
Everything® Chihuahua Book
Everything® Cooking for Dogs Book
Everything® Dachshund Book
Everything® Dog Book, 2nd Ed.
Everything® Dog Grooming Book

...nizer, $16.95
...Tricks Book
...rd Book
...ver Book
...ook, 2nd Ed., $15.95
...e Book
...ck Riding Book
...or Retriever Book
...e Book
...d Book
...ppy Book
...Small Dogs Book
...Tropical Fish Book
... g® Yorkshire Terrier Book

REFERENCE

...ything® American Presidents Book
...erything® Blogging Book
...erything® Build Your Vocabulary Book, $9.95
...ything® Car Care Book
Everything® Classical Mythology Book
Everything® Da Vinci Book
Everything® Einstein Book
Everything® Enneagram Book
Everything® Etiquette Book, 2nd Ed.
Everything® Family Christmas Book, $15.95
Everything® Guide to C. S. Lewis & Narnia
Everything® Guide to Divorce, 2nd Ed., $15.95
Everything® Guide to Edgar Allan Poe
Everything® Guide to Understanding Philosophy
Everything® Inventions and Patents Book
Everything® Jacqueline Kennedy Onassis Book
Everything® John F. Kennedy Book
Everything® Mafia Book
Everything® Martin Luther King Jr. Book
Everything® Pirates Book
Everything® Private Investigation Book
Everything® Psychology Book
Everything® Public Speaking Book, $9.95
Everything® Shakespeare Book, 2nd Ed.

RELIGION

Everything® Angels Book
Everything® Bible Book
Everything® Bible Study Book with CD, $19.95
Everything® Buddhism Book
Everything® Catholicism Book
Everything® Christianity Book
Everything® Gnostic Gospels Book
Everything® Hinduism Book, $15.95
Everything® History of the Bible Book
Everything® Jesus Book
Everything® Jewish History & Heritage Book
Everything® Judaism Book
Everything® Kabbalah Book
Everything® Koran Book
Everything® Mary Book
Everything® Mary Magdalene Book
Everything® Prayer Book

Everything® Saints Book, 2nd Ed.
Everything® Torah Book
Everything® Understanding Islam Book
Everything® Women of the Bible Book
Everything® World's Religions Book

SCHOOL & CAREERS

Everything® Career Tests Book
Everything® College Major Test Book
Everything® College Survival Book, 2nd Ed.
Everything® Cover Letter Book, 2nd Ed.
Everything® Filmmaking Book
Everything® Get-a-Job Book, 2nd Ed.
Everything® Guide to Being a Paralegal
Everything® Guide to Being a Personal Trainer
Everything® Guide to Being a Real Estate Agent
Everything® Guide to Being a Sales Rep
Everything® Guide to Being an Event Planner
Everything® Guide to Careers in Health Care
Everything® Guide to Careers in Law Enforcement
Everything® Guide to Government Jobs
Everything® Guide to Starting and Running a Catering Business
Everything® Guide to Starting and Running a Restaurant
Everything® Guide to Starting and Running a Retail Store
Everything® Job Interview Book, 2nd Ed.
Everything® New Nurse Book
Everything® New Teacher Book
Everything® Paying for College Book
Everything® Practice Interview Book
Everything® Resume Book, 3rd Ed.
Everything® Study Book

SELF-HELP

Everything® Body Language Book
Everything® Dating Book, 2nd Ed.
Everything® Great Sex Book
Everything® Guide to Caring for Aging Parents, $15.95
Everything® Self-Esteem Book
Everything® Self-Hypnosis Book, $9.95
Everything® Tantric Sex Book

SPORTS & FITNESS

Everything® Easy Fitness Book
Everything® Fishing Book
Everything® Guide to Weight Training, $15.95
Everything® Krav Maga for Fitness Book
Everything® Running Book, 2nd Ed.
Everything® Triathlon Training Book, $15.95

TRAVEL

Everything® Family Guide to Coastal Florida
Everything® Family Guide to Cruise Vacations
Everything® Family Guide to Hawaii
Everything® Family Guide to Las Vegas, 2nd Ed.
Everything® Family Guide to Mexico
Everything® Family Guide to New England, 2nd Ed.

Everything® Family Guide to New York City, 3rd Ed.
Everything® Family Guide to Northern California and Lake Tahoe
Everything® Family Guide to RV Travel & Campgrounds
Everything® Family Guide to the Caribbean
Everything® Family Guide to the Disneyland® Resort, California Adventure®, Universal Studios®, and the Anaheim Area, 2nd Ed.
Everything® Family Guide to the Walt Disney World Resort®, Universal Studios®, and Greater Orlando, 5th Ed.
Everything® Family Guide to Timeshares
Everything® Family Guide to Washington D.C., 2nd Ed.

WEDDINGS

Everything® Bachelorette Party Book, $9.95
Everything® Bridesmaid Book, $9.95
Everything® Destination Wedding Book
Everything® Father of the Bride Book, $9.95
Everything® Green Wedding Book, $15.95
Everything® Groom Book, $9.95
Everything® Jewish Wedding Book, 2nd Ed., $15.95
Everything® Mother of the Bride Book, $9.95
Everything® Outdoor Wedding Book
Everything® Wedding Book, 3rd Ed.
Everything® Wedding Checklist, $9.95
Everything® Wedding Etiquette Book, $9.95
Everything® Wedding Organizer, 2nd Ed., $16.95
Everything® Wedding Shower Book, $9.95
Everything® Wedding Vows Book, 3rd Ed., $9.95
Everything® Wedding Workout Book
Everything® Weddings on a Budget Book, 2nd Ed., $9.95

WRITING

Everything® Creative Writing Book
Everything® Get Published Book, 2nd Ed.
Everything® Grammar and Style Book, 2nd Ed.
Everything® Guide to Magazine Writing
Everything® Guide to Writing a Book Proposal
Everything® Guide to Writing a Novel
Everything® Guide to Writing Children's Books
Everything® Guide to Writing Copy
Everything® Guide to Writing Graphic Novels
Everything® Guide to Writing Research Papers
Everything® Guide to Writing a Romance Novel, $15.95
Everything® Improve Your Writing Book, 2nd Ed.
Everything® Writing Poetry Book